Access
in
Paris

Access
in
Paris

A GUIDE FOR THOSE WHO HAVE PROBLEMS GETTING AROUND

Research and survey work carried out by Pauline Hephaistos Survey Projects

and written by Gordon Couch and Ben Roberts

Quiller Press
London

Dedication

We have dedicated this project and guidebook to Tim Burke who was a much loved member of the group for some ten years. We remember particularly his inspiration, determination and patience, and hope that he will be happy to be associated for ever with a project that aims to help people break down barriers and overcome difficulties.

The guide is based on survey work carried out in 1992 and early 1993 by members of the Pauline Hephaistos Survey Projects Group. The group of surveyors included a variety of people, some able-bodied, some wheelchair users and some disabled walkers. We come from several universities and colleges, from St Paul's School in London, and from Lord Mayor Treloar College in Alton in Hampshire. A few of the group are of 'post-student' age, and are working in a variety of jobs.

Over the years the group has produced over fifteen access guides, and this is the third edition of the Paris one. The name sounds a bit of a mouthful, but Pauline arises from St Paul, and some of us come from a Christian group attached to St Paul's School. The Hephaistos part of the name arises from the Greek god who was the smithy and the equivalent of Vulcan in Roman mythology. He was a son of Zeus, who was foolish enough to defend his mother, Hera, during some major row. Zeus kicked Hephaistos off Mount Olympus and, after a long fall, he landed at the bottom and broke his leg. In frescoes he is shown with one leg facing one way and the other turned through 90°. Hence, he has been adopted by some as the Greek god for disabled people and gave his name to a school near Reading which a number of the group attended before its recent closure.

First published 1993 by Quiller Press Ltd
46 Lillie Road, London SW6 1TN

Copyright 1993 © **Pauline Hephaistos Survey Projects**

Line drawings: Emma M^cleod-Johnstone
Cover illustration: Peter Frost

Production in association with Book Production Consultants, Cambridge

Design Criteria diagram reproduced from *Designing for the Disabled* by Selwyn Goldsmith with the kind permission of the publishers RIBA Publications Ltd

ISBN 1 870948 62 9

Contents

List of useful addresses:

Access Project (PHSP), 39 Bradley Gdns, West Ealing, London W13 8HE.

Association des Paralysés de France (APF), 17 bd Auguste Blanqui, 75013. *Tel:* (1) 45.80.82.40.

Comité National Français de Liaison pour la Réadaptation des Handicapés (CNFLRH), 38 bd Raspail 75007. *Tel:* (1) 45.48.90.13.

Disabled Drivers Association, Ashwellthorpe, Norwich NR16 1EX. *Tel:* (050) 841449.

Disabled Drivers Motor Club, Cottingham Way, Thrapston, North-amptonshire NN14 4PL, *Tel:* (0832) 734724 *Fax:* (0832) 733816.

French Government Tourist Office (FGTO), 178 Piccadilly, London W1V 0AL. *Tel:* (071) 491 7622.

Holiday Care Service, 2 Old Bank Chambers, Station Rd, Horley, Surrey. *Tel:* (0293) 774535.

John Grooms Freeway, 10 Gloucester Drive, London N4 2LP. *Tel:* (081) 802 7272 *Fax:* (081) 809 1754.

Moss Rehabilitation Hospital, Travel information service, 1200 West Tabor Rd, Philadelphia, PA 19141-3099, USA. *Tel:* (215) 456 9600.

Office de Tourisme de Paris, 127 av des Champs Elysées, 75008. *Tel:* (1) 47.23.61.72.

RADAR (Royal Association for Disability and Rehabilitation), 25 Mortimer St, London W1N 8AB. *Tel:* (071) 637 5400.

Tripscope, The Courtyard, Evelyn Rd, London W4 1JE. *Tel:* (081) 994 9294.

Acknowledgements
·····································

This project has involved a large number of people, without whom the guide would never have been researched or written. The various activities have included:

- Ensuring that the necessary financial basis was secure, for which we are particularly grateful to the trustees of the charitable trust, to past members and friends of the group who have contributed by covenant and to various charitable trusts and companies who have sponsored or supported us.
- Careful preparation and planning of what was to be visited and ensuring that the surveyors were well briefed about what to look for.
- Undertaking the practical research, by visit, mainly during the summer of 1992.
- Writing, proof reading, editing, preparing diagrams and symbols and the host of meticulous and time-consuming activities that are necessary in putting together the text of such a guide.
- Publishing, distribution and publicity.

We would like to express our thanks to all of the following, in their different roles:

The surveyors who did the foot and wheel work in Paris and who contributed to various phases of the project:

Sue Acton, Francis Adie, Liz Ayres, John Bhoyroo, Clem Boden, Ali Bool, Catherine Burke, Donna Cobb, Gordon Couch, Mark Crouch, Giles Disney, Robert Droy, Polly Ferguson, Robert Gibbs, Dickie Hamilton, Ben Hayward, Mark Lascelles, Anna Lawrence, Rebecca Leete, Iain MacLeod, Mayo Marriott, Sara McDouall, Rory Mee, Craig Newport, Chris Pietroni, Adrian Rates, James Rhys, Ben Roberts, Clare Roberts, Emerson Roberts, Zinnie Shaw, Rob Stanier, Ted Stewart, Ben Stimson, Eleanor Vale, David Wallace and Matthew Woodeson.

Other members of the group who made substantial contributions including:

Roger Ayers, James Droop, Tony Eastmond, James Ferguson, Ian Gwalter, Emma St Giles, Martin Skinner, James Trapp and Mark Worledge.

Past members and friends of the group who are contributing with covenants and who gave us the confidence to commit ourselves to the project:

Bill Hollins, Dave Allport, Dave Aubrey, Peter Aubrey, Duncan and Debbie MacConnol, Geoff Matthews, Gordon Couch, Raymond Couch,

Ian and Rachel Copeland, James Clay, Marcus Sen, Matthew Boulton, Mayo and Thalia Marriott, Paul Haines, Robert Gibbs, Roger Stone.

The trustees of the charitable trust which finances the activities:

Dave Aubrey, Isabel Baggott, Gordon Couch and Mukesh Patel and their honorary auditor Peter Stevenson.

Our sponsors, who provided essential supplementary finance to the charitable trust:

Abbey National CT
Alchemy Foundation
Courage CT
Esmée Fairbairn CT
Express Newspapers
Ferguson Benevolent Fund
Godinton CT
Hoover Foundation
John Ellerman Foundation
KPMG Peat Marwick
Mercers Company
Mr and Mrs JA Pye's Charitable
   Settlement
North London Polytechnic
Peter Minet Trust
Platinum Trust
Rayne Foundation
RTZ Group
St John's College, Cambridge
Tim Burke Memorial Fund

We would also like to thank:

The Arcade hotel in Paris for putting up with our permanent residence in the conference room and some rearrangement of their car park approach.

Ian, from Crystal Holidays, for organising the ferry crossings.

Ealing Community Transport for the use of accessible minibuses which made our summer visit much simpler.

The CNFLRH in Paris for help and advice.

Finally Quiller Press for agreeing to publish the guide, which will ensure that it is widely available through conventional bookshops as well as through disability organisations and the 'disability' network.

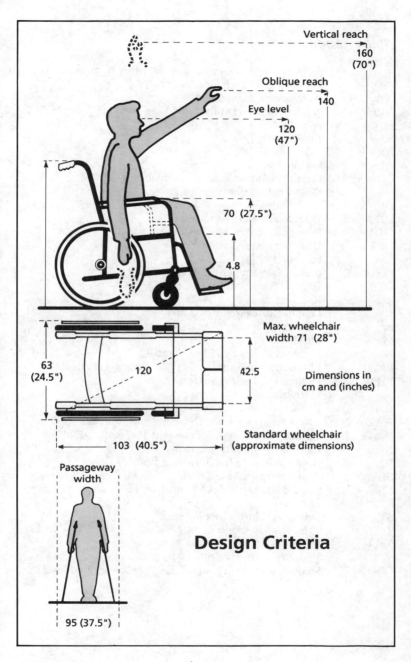

Vertical reach
160 (70")

Oblique reach
140

Eye level
120 (47")

70 (27.5")

4.8

Max. wheelchair width 71 (28")

63 (24.5")

120

42.5

103 (40.5")

Dimensions in cm and (inches)

Standard wheelchair (approximate dimensions)

Passageway width

95 (37.5")

Design Criteria

Abbreviations

+	Steps up (after a number it means over or more than)
A	Autoroute (French motorway)
AA	Automobile Association
APF	Association des Paralysés de France
av	Avenue
bd	Boulevard
BR	British Rail
cm	Centimetre/s
CNFLRH	Comité National Français de Liaison pour la Réadaptation des Handicapés
D	Door width
DDA	Disabled Drivers Association
DDMC	Disabled Drivers Motor Club
DLF	Disabled Living Foundation
Fax	Fax number
FGTO	French Government Tourist Office
GFB	Ground floor bedroom
km	Kilometre/s
L	Length (for example of a lift)
m	Metre/s
M	Motorway
N	Nationale (minor road in France)
PHAB	Physically handicapped and able-bodied (youth clubs)
PHSP	Pauline Hephaistos Survey Projects
pl	Place/square
RAC	Royal Automobile Club
RADAR	Royal Association for Disability and Rehabilitation
RATP	Réseau Autonome du Transport Parisien
RER	Réseau Express Régional
RN	Route nationale (main road in France)
SIA	Spinal Injuries Association
SNCF	Société Nationale des Chemins de Fer Français (French railways)
ST	Sideways transfer to a loo seat
Tel	Telephone number
VAT	Value added tax
W	Width (for example of a lift)
−	Steps down (or, in context, floors below ground level)

Introduction

This guide sets out to give detailed information about travel, accommodation and the tourist attractions for people with mobility problems. Mostly this will be because walking any distance or climbing stairs is difficult. Some readers will be wheelchair users. Where possible we have included information for those who are partially sighted or hard of hearing. The guide can be useful to families with young children and/or elderly relatives, since they have mobility problems and will be interested in the easiest way of doing things. It deals with distances, ease of access, steps, the provision of lifts, details about toilets and the like.

We assume that people will use it in conjunction with other guides, particularly the Michelin Green Guides (the English editions to both Paris and the Ile-de-France). There are frequent cross-references to the Michelin guides, because we think that they include the clearest maps and diagrams as part of the write-ups. This is particularly useful for clarifying the shortest and easiest routes to places and we think that some of the Michelin pictures are even better than an ordinary map.

A large print version of *Access in Paris* can be obtained from: **Access Project**, 39 Bradley Gardens, West Ealing, London W13 8HE.

It is surprising what you can get to see if you use the easiest methods of transport and know the best way to get into buildings. We hope that this book will encourage people to get about, either alone or with friends, and that they will feel more confident about making adventurous holidays and trips. We also hope that it will encourage able-bodied people to go with disabled friends to places like Paris, because the majority of obstacles that are there can be surmounted with a minimum of effort.

Overall Paris offers far more accessible accommodation at a reasonable price than London. There are some wheelchair loos, although they're somewhat scattered. Getting around by car or public transport can be something of a problem, but it's not too bad if you know what you are doing. It is easier than it would be in London, particularly as some limited sections of the underground railway in central Paris are accessible. During the past five or ten years considerable progress has been made in making sites in Paris more accessible. As in many places there are still hassles. In particular signposting is poor and other reliable information about access is almost non-existent. Too many provisions depend on using some special route or equipment such as wheelchair stair lifts, making the disabled visitor dependent on help from staff. Being a foreigner has certain advantages and we have generally found that people are helpful in enabling us to overcome difficulties. *Much depends on who you meet and also on your own approach and attitude.*

We have tried to ensure that the entries have been visited, walked into and wheeled over by one of our survey teams. Inevitably a few mistakes will have crept in and, with time, changes will take place. We have included a very small amount of information which we have either acquired by letter or which has been supplied by the French organisations for disabled people, the APF or CNFLRH. **The APF is the Association des Paralysés de France, and the CNFLRH is the Comité National Français de Liaison pour la Réadaptation des Handicapés.** It should be clear from the text when we have used information we have been given by others and it should be pointed out that we can't be quite as sure of its accuracy because we haven't visited the places ourselves.

Please note that a listing does not imply accessibility. We have described the barriers in our write-ups and you must make your own decision about what is possible for you. We include some places that are inaccessible by most people's standards, simply so that you know what the problems are and don't waste time and effort.

Most of the information should be valid for at least five years, and much of it for longer than that.

We have covered the main aspects of travel, hotels and the sights, but we have deliberately not included eating places, since many Paris restaurants and cafés are easily accessible and people can eat outside if they wish. The problem is that the loos are commonly in the basement down narrow twisting steps. Hopefully the '*good loo guide*' chapter will help.

Wherever possible we would suggest that you make enquiries and arrangements well in advance. If you need particular information, forms or services etc, and you write in for them, don't wait too long before you follow up with another letter or a phone call saying politely, '*What are you doing about my query?*' The chances are that your letter is sitting in someone's 'in' tray and they have gone off sick or on holiday – or they are just waiting for someone to remind them! Prospective tourists are advised to read the section on insurance, and particularly on health insurance. Fortunately this is something that has become considerably easier over recent years.

Travelling to Paris is comparatively easy and, with the Channel Tunnel due to open in 1994, should get even easier.

For getting around, it may be sensible to hire a car for all or part of the time, if you have not got your own transport. It is not desperately expensive particularly for four or five people sharing. However, you may not be keen on driving in the rather wild traffic in Paris. It's not everyone's cup of tea.

We have included hotels which are just outside Paris, some of which are near accessible RER railway stations, and using these could make your sightseeing relatively easy to organise. **The RER is the Réseau Express Régional**, providing a new network of railway lines which are underground in the centre of Paris and on the surface in the suburbs. Quite a number of the stations are fully accessible to the wheelchair user and details are given later on.

Alternatively it may often be advisable to use a taxi rather than public transport and again, if done selectively, this shouldn't be too expensive. We list some wheelchair accessible taxi/minibus services.

There is plenty to see and do. It is undoubtedly best to plan what you want to see and perhaps even to stay near the places of greatest interest to you. There are enough sights with relatively easy access to fill any holiday itinerary. If you visit even a handful of the places with reasonable access mentioned in this guide, you will be in Paris for quite some time and will have seen quite enough to make your trip memorable and worthwhile.

In terms of accessibility all the views expressed are those of the survey teams and they relate to the place at the time of the visit. Readers must appreciate that accessibility will vary according to the time of day, the time of year and which officials are on duty. Some people will be prepared to break or bend rules, while others will be more rigid. If particular features of access are especially important to you it may be possible to check before setting off. We have included telephone numbers wherever possible, but these will probably not be of much use unless your French is adequate.

Why travel and why Paris ?

The cliché says that travel broadens the mind and there's a lot of truth in that. All these PHSP (Pauline Hephaistos Survey Projects is the name of our group) access guides started back in the 1970s when some of us wanted to travel. The group consisted of disabled and able-bodied young people and over the years we have been to various parts of France, to Jersey, Norway, Germany and Israel.

We had an enormous amount of fun. We met all kinds of problems and it was a challenge sorting them out, although perhaps it didn't always seem to be fun at the time. We learned a lot. We encountered new cultures and people. We have met many people who have been helpful, friendly and interesting, as well as a few who were downright awkward and unhelpful. Overall we have a lot of things to look back on and to talk about.

You will have your own reasons for wanting to travel. We hope that you'll find it as interesting and rewarding as we have! If you haven't travelled much and feel a bit hesitant about it, we recommend that you look at *Nothing ventured* edited by Allison Walsh (a Rough Guide special, published by Harrap Columbus, London). This includes the stories of disabled people going to all kinds of exotic places, as well as to destinations in Britain and in northern Europe. If you haven't got the travel bug already, some of the tales will probably give it to you.

Paris is unquestionably a lovely city; many would argue it is the most beautiful in the world. It is far closer than you might think and travelling will get easier when the Tunnel opens. For a capital city, Paris is relatively small, and has a layout which has been controlled and developed for centuries. This gives it a certain grace and cohesion. The authorities have been careful to restrict the construction of high buildings and you will find the skyscrapers are all outside the main ring road, the boulevard Périphérique.

Paris is a historic city with monuments that include Notre Dame, the Louvre and the Eiffel Tower. There are many many others. French history over the past three hundred years has been pretty dramatic with the rule of the aristocrats, the Revolution, the successes of Napoleon, the threat of invasion during the first world war and the reality of occupation in the second.

For a capital city there is a lot of reasonably inexpensive (and accessible) accommodation. Paris has a first class public transport system, although only small parts of it are accessible to wheelchair users. Wouldn't sitting outside a café in a Paris square on a wonderfully sunny day, watching the world go by, be a welcome change? You can make your own pace and see a lot or a little. You may enjoy going to French restaurants and cafés much more than the culturally correct churches and art galleries. Either, or both, will give you new experiences.

If you have a problem in getting around, then one reason for going to Paris is that it is one of the few places with a well researched and up-to-date access guide!

How the Guide is arranged

We have tried to identify particularly accessible sights and also some small areas where there is plenty to see without too much walking or wheeling. The sights are listed in alphabetical order and we have tried to include the main variations on place names, including both French and British versions where appropriate. In this respect we have initially listed most sights by their French names, since this is what you may see signed or listed in Paris. In the text we have frequently reverted to using the more familiar British version for convenience.

The small areas are identified in the *Recommended itineraries* chapter. If you are limited in the distances you can cover, then have a look at these. They have been put together with the aim of maximising the amount you can see while expending a minimum of energy. They include a wide range of interests.

There are two chapters on travelling: one covering the various ways of getting to Paris and the other with advice and information on how to get around once you are there. General information is given early on in the guide and the various sections are listed on the Contents page. As already mentioned, *it has been assumed that you will use this book in conjunction with a good map and a conventional guide book and we have made extensive reference to the Michelin Green Guides to Paris and the Ile-de-France.*

A variety of entertainment venues is included under appropriate headings and there is a good loo guide and map.

In other publications you will see more reference made to the arrondissement in which various places are. The arrondissement is the local government area and numbers go from 1 to 20. In the Paris address there is a post code which starts with 750, and then gives the number of the arrondissement. Hence 75018 is in the 18th and 75005 in the 5th arrondissement. In quoting addresses we have normally included this post code, and you can thus work out where things are more easily.

We have avoided using abbreviations in the guide as far as possible. We have, however, shortened the title of a few organisations which are mentioned several times like the Royal Association for Disability and Rehabilitation (RADAR) and the French Government Tourist Office (FGTO). We have used some 'shorthand' when referring to important facilities and not worried too much about the precise use of language, which can sometimes be rather tortuous. For example we have talked about 'wheelchair loos' when we mean a toilet which is accessible to a wheelchair user and we trust that no-one is going to get upset over this kind of shortening of the text.

We have used abbreviations when giving both lift, doorway and loo (toilet) measurements. The numbers are in centimetres and D refers to door width, W to the width and L to the length of a lift. ST is the space for sideways transfer on to a loo seat. Steps are normally abbreviated as numbers, with a plus (+) sign for up and minus (−) sign for down. Watch out for confusions when the levels in a building are also listed as numbers. If a dimension is over 70cm, we mark it as 70+, and in this context, the + sign means 'greater than'. We have abbreviated ground floor bedrooms to GFBs. There is a full list of abbreviations.

French roads are designated as A for autoroute and RN for route nationale or main roads. Smaller roads simply have the prefix N. These are abbreviations that may appear in the text from time to time.

Units

We have given measurements in centimetres (cm), metres (m) and kilometres (km). Although these are the units increasingly being used internationally, many English people and Americans still think in imperial measures. To convert metric measurements to the older imperial units use the following guidelines:

> 10 centimetres is about 4 inches (2.5cm = 1 inch)
> 1 metre is about a yard
> 3 kilometres is about 2 miles (1.6km = 1 mile)

Also,

> 1 gallon is about 4.5 litres (US gallon, about 3.8 litres)
> 1 kilo is about 2 pounds (weight)

We include a diagram earlier on page ix which shows the approximate dimensions of a standard wheechair but as chairs vary considerably in size you should check the exact dimensions of yours against the measurements of lifts and loos given in the guide.

There is reference to the use of abbreviated dimensions in the previous section.

Symbols

Some years ago the use of a symbol to denote facilities for disabled people was agreed internationally and everyone is now familiar with the 'wheel-chair' sign. In theory the sign is used in accordance with certain criteria, such as flat or ramped access, doors wider than a known amount and so on. Unfortunately, in practice the symbol has been misused so widely that it has become virtually meaningless, particularly when used in general guide books and listings. The problem is that assessment of accessibility is made by so many different people with different perceptions of disability. Some places listed as being accessible have steps at the entrance as well as other barriers. The French Government Tourist Office hotel listings are a case in point and their use of the symbol in this and other information can be very misleading. Its use does, however, give you a bit of a lever when a place is listed with the symbol and you want to get in! Meanwhile, we advise making further enquiries before you trust the use of the wheelchair symbol in other peoples' listings.

Symbols have been used in this guide to highlight certain data. The key has been translated into French, German, Italian and Spanish, to enable the information to be used by a wide variety of visitors. We hope that a system like this will soon be used to summarise important access data in conventional guidebooks, encouraging writers to provide more precise information. While it is not perfect, the system does at least form a basis for giving accurate information without, we hope, being over-elaborate.

General Information

Car hire

For some visitors there is great advantage in being able to fly to Paris and pick up a hire car at the airport. For a group of three or four people car hire can be a reasonably priced option, but remember all the extras not mentioned on the basic tariff, such as passenger insurance, collision damage waiver and VAT. The big companies such as Hertz, Avis, Budget, Europcar etc, all offer this service. They tend to charge what one might call 'business' prices and only Hertz has cars that are adapted for hand controls. They have the advantage of airport check-in desks and can be booked quite easily by a British travel agent. It's definitely worth shopping around and getting a quote from all of them as the rates vary a lot. The FGTO can supply a list of firms in Paris offering hire at more competitive rates, but probably with a less comprehensive service. One company, Inter Touring Service, are mentioned below, because they also have cars adapted for hand controls.

The minimum age for hiring a car is usually 21, but with some companies it is 25. Some also have an upper age limit. You're recommended to take out CDW (collision damage waiver) insurance, even though it may cost £7-8 per day. This means that if you are unlucky enough to damage the car, it is all paid for under the insurance whether it was your fault or not. You have no open-ended financial commitment related to the car.

Hire cars with hand controls are available in Paris from:

— **Inter Touring Service**, 117 bd Auguste-Blanqui, 75013, *Tel:* (1) 45.88.52.37 *Fax:* (1) 45.80.89.30 and they currently offer a Renaut Clio or a Peugeot 309.
— **ARP (Amitié Rencontre Partage)**, 48 rue de Paris, Franconville, 95130, *Tel:* (1) 34.13.72.90 have a Renault 5 and a Renault 20 available with hand controls. Franconville is in the Paris suburbs north of la Défense, and across the Seine.
— **Hertz** both in the city centre and at the airports. Hertz have six Pegueot 309s which can be fitted with hand controls, given a few days notice. Hertz can be contacted on *Tel:* (1) 45.74.97.39. The cars are hired at the same rate as other cars.

In Britain **Kenning Car Hire**, 477 Green Lane, Palmers Green, London N13 4BS, *Tel:* (081) 882 3576, offer a selection of hatchback and saloon cars with hand controls. Details of hire conditions, insurance and the notice required need to be considered carefully.

An idea which might appeal to some is to hire a Dormobile or motor caravan with bunk beds, cooker, sink etc and maybe even a loo. This can make you both mobile and independent, but you will need to make your booking well in advance as there are relatively few such vehicles available. A firm offering such motor homes is **Leisure Hire**, Brook Cottage, Stainsby, near Heath, Chesterfield, *Tel*: (0246) 851454.

Climate

This is not dissimilar to that in the south of England. Average autumn, winter and spring temperatures in Paris are much the same as those in London. Temperatures rise in July and August making it fairly hot and sticky, an excuse many Parisians use for getting out of town. When packing, allow for variability, particularly in the winter and spring. In general the weather poses relatively few problems for the disabled visitor. In the winter it can be both cold and damp. Average temperatures can be misleading, since Paris is more influenced by continental extremes than London. It can easily be −5 or even −10°C for short periods and much colder than you may be used to in Britain. Either the spring or autumn are probably the best times for a visit if you are concerned about the weather.

Coach and minibus hire

There are an increasing number of organisations, both commercial and voluntary, which have adapted coaches available for hire to groups. Some local Community Transport organisations can provide wheelchair-accessible minibuses and small coaches. There is a list of several companies in RADAR's *Holidays and travel abroad* by John Stanford which is updated regularly. There is also a list of escort and private ambulance services in this useful publication.

Minibus hire sources include the **Rod Surrage Appeal Fund** (Trevor Pollitt), 1 Johnston Green, Guildford, Surrey, *Tel:* (0483) 233640. In early 1993 they have one car and seven minibuses adapted to carry wheelchair users. These can be used in France, subject to the insurance requirements for covering the able-bodied driver concerned. Also there is **Mobility Ambulance Services**, VIC Industrial Park, West Street, Erith, Kent DA8 1AA, *Tel:* (0322) 441155 *Fax:* (0322) 441011. They have some seventeen vehicles ranging from front line ambulances and adapted minibuses to a 53-seater coach. Their vehicles are let out on contract hire, but some are available from time to time for groups and/or individuals. They organise occasional trips to EuroDisney and Paris, and one of these trips in a wheelchair-accessible vehicle for three days cost less than £200 in 1993.

Some companies and organisations such as Mobility Ambulance Services, will supply a driver. Others, such as Rod Surrage and most Community Transport groups, allow you to provide your own if you wish. They will brief you on the various requirements and you should remember that you will need to use the tachograph speed recording system in France in any vehicle for over nine people. *You will find that French regulations are generally stricter about what you can and can't do with a minibus.*

Currency

It is pretty simple to get foreign currency these days, but you will get it most cheaply if you follow a few basic principles. You can order currency from your bank, building society or travel agent before you leave. Alternatively you can get it en route at the port or airport if you exchange cash or have an appropriate cheque guarantee card.

Credit cards such as Access (Mastercard) and Visa (Carte Bleu) are increasingly accepted. These can provide a cheap and convenient way of paying for hotel bills, meals and for larger purchases in shops. Generally you get a very fair exchange rate, though we wouldn't recommend using cards for small bills of under £10. They have the advantage that you don't have to pay for several weeks and, provided you pay up when the bill comes in rather than using them for longer-term credit, they are a cheap way of getting francs. Credit cards can also be used to obtain cash, which can be useful in an emergency, but this attracts immediate interest and a handling charge.

You may prefer to get a Eurocheque card which is a separate cheque guarantee card from the bank which currently have a limit of £75 per cheque. All the major high street banks offer Eurocheque cards typically costing about £8/10 per year for the card and an additional £1 or £1.50 for each Eurocheque used. It saves you carrying cash but is relatively expensive.

Travellers cheques can be in sterling or francs and cost £1 per £100 purchased. If you are worried about the possibility of the pound falling substantially, then get travellers cheques in francs and get them early. Alternatively you could use the numerous Bureaux de Change, which are found in most tourist locations, or change money at your hotel, but if you do this watch out for the charges and/or the exchange rate used. A bureau de change will change sterling cash as well as travellers cheques. Remember that changing travellers cheques or using your Eurocheque card in a bank will probably be disproportionately time-consuming, and you'll have to find somewhere accessible.

One thing to watch out for is security. Don't keep everything together (cards, cash, cheques etc). There are pickpockets and thieves in a large city such as Paris just like everywhere else. Make sure you have a record of your card details and cheque numbers and find out what your insurance policy covers. If you want to claim you will almost certainly have to produce a note proving that you reported it to the local police, even if there is little chance of anything being recovered.

Documents required

British nationals should still carry a valid passport which can either be a visitor's passport obtainable at post offices and valid for a year, or a full British Passport valid for ten years obtainable from the Passport Office, Petty France, London SW1. Visitors from other EEC countries need either a passport or an identity card. No visa is required for American or Canadian visitors, as a passport is sufficient.

If you are coming by car, or intending to hire one, then remember that all the drivers must have their driving licences with them. If you are bringing a car you also need the logbook, and an insurance certificate proving that you have third party insurance.

Equipment repair and hire

If one of your wheels drops off in the Champs Elysées or if you need to hire special equipment for any reason, the following contact addresses should be useful. **It is always a good idea to carry a repair kit, including some simple tools. Taking a few vital spares can pay too**, especially if your chair isn't standard, and carrying one of the instant tyre-repair kits available from shops like Halfords may well be a sensible precaution.

We have listed shops and showrooms where you may be able to get repairs to equipment such as wheelchairs or where you may be able to hire things, although several are a little way outside the centre:

— **AMMA**, 170 rue Henri Barbusse, 95100 Argentueil, *Tel:* (1) 39.61.11.35 or 105 bd Ney, 75018, *Tel:* (1) 42.54.02.02, offer a range of equipment and do repairs on the spot.

— **Moreau Medicale**, 35 bd Pasteur, 93120 La Courneuve, *Tel:* (1) 48.34 66.90, are agents for Vessa, Everest & Jennings, Carter, Poirier, Dupont and others. They offer a repair service for any of these makes and have Poirier or Vessa chairs for hire.

— **Hygiène-Service**, 92 rue du Mont Cenis, 75018, *Tel:* (1) 42.64.23.62, can offer chairs or equipment for sale or hire. Agents for Vessa, Carter and Invacar Poirier. They can also offer the possibility of repairs. The shop is in the Montmartre area and is small.

— **Tout le Confort de Malade**, 193 rue Lecourbe, 75015, *Tel:* (1) 48.42.54.95 are agents for all types of chair, including Vessa, Carter and Everest & Jennings. They offer facilities for the hire and repair of wheelchairs and other equipment.

— The **Centre d'Information et d'Orientation pour les Handicapés**, Hôpital Ste Anne, 1 rue Cabanis, 75674, *Tel:* (1) 45.65.80.00 is mainly for resident disabled people and is concerned with equipment, practical help and disability benefits. Nonetheless it is a possible source of information or advice.

If the shops can't help then you could try the APF or the CNFLRH. Other potentially good contacts for running repairs would be specialist schools or institutions where there are disabled residents and someone on the administrative staff who is used to doing running repairs. An example of such a school is the Ecole Nationale pour Handicapés Moteurs, bd Raymond Poincaré, in Garches just outside Paris.

A further suggestion is to try a small garage or motor-bike shop. Alternatively you might even ring the British Hertford Hospital for possible assistance and/or the temporary loan of equipment. France has, of course, branches of the Red Cross (Croix Rouge) and their main Paris address is Le Brasset, 14 rue Louis Braille, 77103 Meaux, *Tel:* (1) 64.34.52.48.

Escalators

Elderly people and some disabled walkers find escalators difficult and they are obviously a problem for wheelchair users. There are dozens of escalators in new shopping developments, on the metro and in shops. Some are 'user-friendly' in that they are stationary until approached and only start going when you walk over a pressure pad a couple of metres away. A few are too narrow for wheelchairs.

In the guide we have highlighted the provision of lifts, since these can be used by nearly all disabled people. However, our experience with escalators is that they *can* be a safe and easy way of changing levels for chair users who have the help of one or two experienced or well-trained able-bodied friends. Most of our survey teams have learned how to cope with them. It is essential that everyone concerned is confident of their strength and control.

Once on an escalator the trick is simply to balance the wheelchair on the back wheels at the point of balance. The person behind pulls or pushes the chair on to the escalator, placing the wheels in the middle of a step as it opens up. The person in front simply pushes gently and horizontally against the chair and is only there to steady the chair if necessary.

The procedure is essentially the same whether you are going up or down. When you are going down the person in front walks on to the escalator, turns round and walks back upwards. The person behind has the chair at its point of balance and wheels it on to the escalator finding a suitable slot as the steps open up. The person in front takes charge of the front of the chair, pushing gently backwards when the chair is secure on a step. As the escalator flattens out at the bottom the person in front walks off out of the way, and the chair rolls off. Going up, the person behind the chair again finds the point of balance and walks on to the escalator backwards with the chair. As the steps open he finds a secure slot and the person in front, who has followed on, simply steadies the chair. It is much easier than it sounds, though don't try it unless your able-bodied friends are adequately strong, and don't try it if you consider yourself to be too heavy.

French organisations for disabled people

Rather like the situation in Britain there are numerous organisations set up to meet the needs of disabled people and to work for changes in attitude. Organisations cover different disabilities and encompass umbrella set-ups as well as those with particular objectives such as providing holidays, improving access, talking to government departments, coordinating information, action and research. It means, again rather like things in Britain, there is duplication and overlapping of function resulting in a fragmentation of effort. It is also quite difficult to know who to go to for information or help. We mention here two of the principal umbrella organisations and one other information source. You should be able to get contacts, address lists and information through one or more of these.

The two main groups we have come across are the **Association des Paralysés de France (APF)**, 17 bd Auguste Blanqui, 75013, *Tel:* (1) 45.80.82.40 and the **Comité National Français de Liaison pour la Réadaptation des Handicapés (CNFLRH)**, 38 bd Raspail 75007, *Tel:* (1) 45.48.90.13.

The **APF** publish an accommodation list of hotels throughout France which is potentially useful to disabled visitors although only limited information is given. It is called *Où Ferons-nous Étape?* (Where Shall We Stay?). They also have a network of local associations who can provide help and advice in every Département (county) throughout the country.

The **CNFLRH** publish *Touristes Quand-même* (Travel anyway) and *Touristes Quand-même Paris* in conjunction with various government departments. *Touristes Quand-même* covers the whole of France and contains information on places with induction loops, a listing of places with special facilities for people who are blind or partially sighted and a range of places accessible to wheelchair users. However, in terms of usefulness, a book of 160 pages trying to cover the whole country, largely excluding Paris, must inevitably be somewhat scrappy in its information on any one place. *Touristes Quand-même Paris* is a guide dedicated to Paris and contains information on facilities for disabled people at tourist attractions and other places of entertainment. It also contains information on wheelchair hire, but nothing on accommodation. These guides were produced during the mid 1980s, and we were told that there are no plans to update them, so, regrettably, they are getting increasingly out of date.

Centre d'Information et de Documentation Jeunesse (Information Centre for Young People), 101 quai Branly, 75015, *Tel:* (1) 45.66.40.20 publish *Vacances pour Personnes Handicapées* (Holidays for Disabled People) and leaflets on activity holidays for young disabled people. They also publish a comprehensive list of all the organisations with a brief description of what they do. This is regularly updated. It can be extremely useful and includes organisations for people with learning difficulties, elderly people, those who are deaf or hard of hearing and people who are blind or partially sighted.

Information services and organisations

The main sources of information about France are the French Government Tourist Office (FGTO), your local travel agent and the standard guidebooks. In addition, organisations in Britain like the Royal Association for Disability and Rehabilitation (RADAR), physically handicapped and able-bodied youth clubs (PHAB), Mobility International and others will have experience of organising groups of visitors or will know of people who have gone there.

RADAR, 25 Mortimer Street, London W1N 8AB, publish *Holidays and travel abroad – a guide for disabled people* each year. Written by John Stanford it is full of useful information and includes a section on France. There are lists of voluntary organisations involved with making holiday provisions for people with disabilities and of commercial companies offering facilities for disabled travellers. There is also updated information about hotel chains in France which have adapted rooms for disabled people throughout the country, including some in Paris.

The French Government Tourist Office (FGTO) is at 178 Piccadilly, London, W1V 0AL, *Tel:* (071) 491 7622. If you write in they will try to be helpful. If you want hotel lists etc they ask that you send 75p in stamps to cover postage. Their telephone line is often extremely busy and you usually have to be patient to get through at all. They publish accommodation lists (hotels, logis and gîtes), a holiday reference guide with useful information and addresses, *The Traveller in France*, a glossy brochure, and lists of major events in Paris and elsewhere. Their listing of 'Hotels, Paris Ile-de-France' will give you up-to-date prices. The amount of information they have for the disabled traveller/visitor is extremely limited and, like that supplied by most other agencies, it is suspect unless the person supplying it happens to have experience and knows what she or he is talking about.

The Office de Tourisme de Paris, 127 av des Champs Elysées, 75008, *Tel:* (1) 47.23.61.72 is the main FGTO office in Paris and, as well as offering general assistance, there is a desk from which you can book accommodation. They are good on standard 'tourist' information like which times things are open, but their specialist knowledge for disabled visitors is very limited. Our experience has been that they are over-busy and really not that interested if you don't fit into an easy category which can be dealt with quickly and painlessly. We tried to interest them in this guide, but, even though we spoke to four different people, they showed no interest whatsoever. There are also Bureaux d'Accueil (Welcome Offices) at the main railway stations and airports and a municipal (ie Paris) Tourist Information Office in the north vestibule of the Hôtel de Ville, 29 rue de Rivoli, 75004. We hope that you have rather more luck with these agencies than we had!

If you make your bookings through your local travel agent remember that they will have a lot of trouble getting accurate and reliable information about any access problems you may encounter either en route or at your hotel. It is precisely because of this that these Access Guides are necessary. If certain things are important to you (eg avoiding steps, using a wheelchair, having a large bathroom) then make sure you check with the airline, port or hotel owner yourself to ensure that the facilities are what you need.

Other information sources in Britain are:

— The *Directory for disabled people – a handbook of information and opportunities for disabled and handicapped people* by Ann Darnbrough and Derek Kinrade. This is a substantial volume covering a wide range of subjects, and you should find it in your local reference library if you can't afford to buy it.

— *The world wheelchair traveller* by Susan Abbott and Mary Ann Tyrrell is jointly published by the Spinal Injuries Association (SIA) and the Automobile Association (AA). It is available from AA offices and from the SIA, 76 St James La, London N10 3DF and is full of practical tips based on experience. It includes sections on medical matters and on travelling by air, rail, road and sea. You will also find it has some useful contact addresses.

— **The Disabled Living Foundation** (DLF), 380 Harrow Rd, London W9 2HU, *Tel:* (071) 289 6111 have an Incontinence Advisory Service and maintain a database on the suppliers of all kinds of equipment and adaptations for people with disabilities. They also offer a Clothing Advisory Service and are knowledgeable about a whole range of issues connected with disability.

— **Holiday Care Service**, 2 Old Bank Chambers, Station Rd, Horley, Surrey, *Tel:* (0293) 774535 is an organisation providing free information and advice on holidays for anyone who finds it difficult for whatever reason. Enquiries from individuals, from carers or from organisations are welcomed by letter or by phone. They do not get involved in making reservations and their main data base is on accommodation and opportunities in Britain. However, they will be able to give practical advice about many aspects of travelling and of finding accommodation.

— **John Grooms Hotel and Travel Service**, 10 Gloucester Dr, London

N4 2LP, *Tel:* (081) 802 7272 *Fax:* (081) 809 1754. *John Grooms Freeway* is a travel service which works in conjunction with disabled passengers. They offer holidays at Euro Disney and in Paris. They can give advice about accessible accommodation and about travel bookings and travelling. They have a fully accessible coach enabling them to provide holidays to a range of destinations in addition to Euro Disney.

— **Phab UK**, Phab Publications, Padholme Rd, East Peterborough PE1 5UL is part of the National Association of Youth Clubs. They can send you a list of the network of local Phab clubs throughout the country and may be able to put you in touch with someone, possibly local, with travelling experience.

— **Mobility International**, 228 Borough High St, London SE1 1JX, *Tel:* (071) 403 5688 is an independent organisation offering educational experiences to disabled people aged from 18 to 30. They also have extensive experience of travelling and might perhaps be able to put you in touch with someone with the right experience if you have a particular problem.

— **Tripscope**, 64 Esmond Rd, Chiswick, London W4 1JE, *Tel:* (081) 994 9294 provide an information service on all aspects of travelling and transport for people with disabilities. Again their main knowledge is about the UK, but they also have experience of advising people on travelling abroad.

In the USA three principal information sources about travel for people with disabilities are:

— **Moss Rehabilitation Hospital**, Travel information service, 1200 West Tabor Rd, Philadelphia, PA 19141-3099, USA, *Tel:* (215) 456 9600

— **Mobility International**, PO Box 3551, Eugene, Oregon, 07403, USA, *Tel:* (503) 343 1284 *Fax:* (503) 343 6812.

— **Society for the Advancement of Travel for the Handicapped (SATH)**, 347 Fifth Ave, Suite 610, New York, NY 10016, USA, *Tel:* (212) 447 7284 *Fax:* (212) 725 8253.

Insurance

People rarely go on holiday without some sort of insurance, largely because of a greater awareness of the risks involved in travelling abroad. You hear a lot about overbooked hotels, legionnaire's disease, insolvent airline companies and the work of pickpockets and general rip-off merchants, even though the risk to the individual traveller is very small indeed. Insurance is offered as part and parcel of most holiday package deals, but **for the disabled traveller special policies normally have to be used.**

Many policies will have a clause excluding those with a pre-existing medical condition or disability. *It is unfortunately necessary to look at the small print on any policy and remember that your travel agent may not understand the implication of an exclusion clause for you.*

When this guide was first published in 1974 the insurance world, with one or two notable exceptions, proved to be very uncooperative in providing cover for disabled travellers as they were generally considered to be a bad risk! It was not realised that very few people would want to travel abroad if they were likely to be ill. Thankfully since then much has changed and there are some policies which provide good cover for the disabled traveller. For up-to-date information contact RADAR and ask for the Holidays Officer. Alternatively look in RADAR's *Holidays and travel abroad* which has already been mentioned and is updated every year and includes a section on travel insurance. The information here was collected in 1992.

The following companies do not require medical certificates:

— **Campbell Irvine Ltd**, PO Box 53, Reigate, Surrey RH2 7YQ, *Tel:* (0737) 223687.
The cover: **medical expenses £1,000,000 (excluding UK treatment)**; hospital benefit at £10 per day up to £200 (not in UK); personal accident up to £50,000; personal liability up to £1,000,000; personal luggage up to £1250; money up to £200; delayed baggage up to £100 per person; cancellation and curtailment up to £3,000; travel delay up to £75; travel disruption up to £300; legal advice up to £15,000; failure of tour operator/transport provider £5,000.
Notes: **the policy does not exclude pre-existing medical conditions but confirmation is necessary**, by a handwritten note from the traveller, that the trip is not taken against medical advice. **Exclusions:** any fees arising from childbirth or pregnancy; for persons aged 70 years or over double the usual cost for insurance applies.

— **Commercial Union Assurance Travellers Insurance Association**, Bridge House, 102 George St, Croydon CR6 6HD.
The cover: **medical expenses £2,000,000 (excluding UK treatment)**; hospital benefit at £10 per day up to £500 (not in UK); personal accident up to £15,000; personal liability up to £1,000,000; personal luggage up to £1000; money up to £250; delayed baggage up to £100 per person; cancellation and curtailment up to £3,000; travel delay up to £60; repatriation service; travel disruption up to £300; legal advice up to £25,000; failure of tour operator/transport provider £5,000.

Notes: **exclusions:** "anyone who has received treatment as an in-patient in the six months before the holiday booking, or who is waiting for such treatment, must have taken medical advice and not be travelling against it"; any fees arising from childbirth or pregnancy. **No specific mention of wheelchairs**, but they might be included under personal effects etc.

— **Extrasure Policy**, Extrasure Holdings Limited, 6 Lloyd's Ave, London EC3N 3AX, *Tel:* (071) 488 9341.
The cover: **medical expenses £1,000,000 (excluding UK treatment)**; hospital benefit at £10 per day up to £500 (not in UK); personal accident up to £15,000; personal liability up to £500,000; baggage and personal effects up to £1,000; money up to £100; delayed baggage up to £50 per person; cancellation and curtailment up to £3,000; travel delay up to £60; repatriation service; travel disruption up to £300; with each insured person one child 11 years or under insured free.
Notes: no age limit (although health questionnaire for over 70s); **no exclusions for pre-existing medical physical conditions** (except childbirth, HIV/AIDS, psychiatric disorders); no specific mention of wheelchairs, but they would be included under personal effects, so the cover might be inadequate.

— **Holiday Care Service**, 2 Old Bank Chambers, Station Rd, Horley, Surrey RH6 9HW, *Tel:* (0293) 774535.
The cover: **unlimited medical expenses (excluding UK treatment)**; hospital benefit at £10 per day up to £500 (not in UK); personal accident up to £15,000; personal liability up to £1,000,000; personal property including money up to £1,000; delayed baggage up to £100 per person; cancellation and curtailment up to £2,000; travel delay up to £60; repatriation service; travel disruption up to £500.
Notes: **exclusions:** "if you are undergoing or awaiting medical treatment as an in-patient within 6 weeks of departure date you must obtain confirmation from your usual medical practitioner that you are fit to travel"; travel contrary to medical advice; pregnancy (within 2 months of expected delivery date). **Cover for wheelchairs and dialysis machines etc is available.**

Companies requiring medical certificates/questionnaires:

— **Europ Assistance**, 252 High St, Croydon, Surrey, *Tel:* (081) 680 1234.
The cover: **medical expenses £2,000,000**; hospital benefit at £25 per day up to £250 (not in UK); additional accommodation for someone required to stay with you on medical grounds £750; personal acci-

dent up to £15,000; personal liability up to £2,000,000; personal luggage up to £1,250; money up to £200; delayed baggage up to £100; cancellation and curtailment up to £3,000; travel delay up to £60; repatriation costs on medical or compassionate grounds; travel disruption £350; legal advice up to £25,000; children aged two to sixteen years benefit from 50% discount.

Notes: they have a very comprehensive set of policies and there is a disability clause, but "pre-existing medical conditions can be included if a current doctor's letter of fitness to travel is provided at time of application." **A medical certificate is required to be filled in by the person's usual doctor** stating the patient's medical conditions and approving that the patient is fit to travel.

— **Travelmarrs' Caretravel**, A M Marrs (PG) Ltd, Altay House, 869 High Rd, North Finchley, London, *Tel:* (081) 446 9620.

The cover: **medical expenses £2,000,000 (not in UK)**; personal accident up to £5,000 (not for persons over 75); personal liability up to £1,000,000; personal luggage up to £1,000; money up to £250; delayed baggage up to £50; cancellation and curtailment up to £1,000; travel delay up to £60; travel disruption £1,000; **wheelchair indemnity up to £1,250 with £50 per week hire of similar replacement.**

Notes: Caretravel is designed for both the disabled traveller and those able-bodied travellers that accompany them; **it is required that at least one able-bodied adult is insured under Caretravel insurance in addition to the disabled member of the party**. A supplementary medical questionnaire may be required and, although there is no age limit, visitors must not be travelling against medical advice.

Particular clauses in insurance forms that people should look out for are:

— "If you have received treatment as an in-patient in the 6 months preceding the holiday booking then you must have sought medical advice about taking the proposed journey or holiday."

— "You must not be travelling against medical advice or specifically to obtain medical treatment."

The exclusions above illustrate the possible pitfalls and problems. Another point people should watch out for is insurance covering a maximum of £200 on any one item of baggage lost – which is not much good for wheelchairs nor for other more costly items of equipment. The main thing is not simply to accept the 'standard' policy offered by your tour operator, ferry company or travel agent. You need to make sure that the health cover is large enough, there is no disability exclusion clause and that repatriation expenses are covered if you are unlucky enough to have an accident. Other risks should be adequately covered.

Some of the policies offer the facility of an air-ambulance to fly you home if necessary but don't run away with the idea that these are readily available. Simply because of the cost involved, the insurance company will only use an air-ambulance if in their view it is absolutely essential. Generally the insurance will pay for the cost of medical treatment abroad, the cost of someone to stay with you and of a normal flight home where necessary. Only when long-stay or complicated hospital treatment is involved will the insurance company consider an air-ambulance.

Maps and guides available

There are a large number of guidebooks to Paris. **We have made reference to the Michelin Green Guide in this one because it has excellent maps and diagrams and its descriptions are built around small geographical areas which is particularly useful for the disabled visitor.** Other guides containing more or different information include the *Footloose Guide*, a weighty book containing many practical tips and *Fodor's Paris* written particularly with visitors from America in mind. Which particular style you like depends very much on your personal choice – some will prefer an informal prose as in *Paris the Rough Guide*, whilst some will go for the compact *American*

Bookshop, Latin Quarter

Express Guide. There are guides available for younger visitors interested in the nightlife and entertainments including the *Time Out Paris Guide*, and for the visitor with a tight budget called *Pauper's Paris*. There are also pocket size guides like the *Collins 'Traveller' Paris City Guide* and the *Berlitz Pocket Guide*. Most of them are well researched but we did come across one published recently that listed our old address from ten years ago and several 'accessible' hotels that no longer exist quoted from the 1973 edition of *Access in Paris*! **Most make only passing reference to visitors with disabilities.**

There are also several street-plans and maps available. Some are very old-fashioned in style. We think the Michelin *Paris Plan* which includes one-way streets is the best and it can be obtained either in book form or as a large folded sheet. The book will last longer, but is not so easy to work out routes for driving.

For the suburban areas around the city there are two or three street-plan/ directories covering each named area, including a Michelin guide called *Ile-de-France*. Others are called *Paris Banlieue* or something similar. These publications are bulky and relatively expensive and you will really only need one if you are visiting friends and places outside the centre.

The Tourist Office publish various listings of events and will probably be available at your hotel along with others. They include *L'Officiel des Spectacles*, *Une Semaine de Paris, Pariscope* and *Allo Paris*. You can get other listings such as *Passion* and *Time Out* from the numerous corner newspaper kiosks.

Medicalert

The Medicalert Foundation, 21 Bridge Wharf, 156 Caledonian Rd, London N1 9UU, *Tel:* (071) 833 3034 **provides a useful service for those with medical problems that could be compounded by treatment after an accident** if the patient is unable to make known his or her particular condition. It is of special importance to those suffering from epilepsy, haemophilia, diabetes or allergies and to those who need regular dosage of a particular drug. Life membership is available to anyone for a nominal fee. **Members wear a metal emblem** engraved with the name 'Medicalert' on one side and the telephone number of the Medicalert Emergency Service on the other, along with the immediate medical problems of the wearer – for example, 'allergic to penicillin', 'taking anti-coagulants', 'wearing contact lenses', 'under steroid treatment', 'diabetic' etc. Additional medical information is filed at the Emergency Headquarters where the telephone is staffed 24 hours a day and can, of course, be readily accessed from France.

SOS Talisman Co Ltd, 21 Grays Corner, Ley St, Ilford, Essex, *Tel:* (081) 554 5579 operate a similar service which works on the basis of including information in a small locket which is worn permanently.

Medical advice

There should be no special problems when travelling anywhere in Western Europe. No jabs or inoculations are either required or advised for nearby continental countries. If you have any doubts check with your doctor as to whether there are any particular precautions you should take.

It is worth noting again that the best health insurance policies now have a clause which says you are covered *'providing you are not travelling against the advice of a doctor'*. This is a great improvement on the old 'pre-existing disability' exclusion, but it does mean that your doctor has to agree that travelling is a reasonable and sensible thing to do.

If you are taking important drugs or medicines, make sure that you know both the pharmacological name and dosage. We suggest you split your supply, carrying some in your pocket or handbag and some in your luggage. This minimises the possibility of loss. It is also no bad thing to take a doctor's note and a prescription with you with amounts and dosage clearly stated.

A **first-aid kit** is invaluable for dealing with travel sickness, stomach upsets, sore throat, cuts and bruises, headaches and stings. It is much better to take brands of drugs and medicines that you are used to, rather than having to experiment with the local ones.

Other sources of advice, apart from your GP or specialist are:

— The **National Asthma Campaign**, Providence House, Providence Pl, London N1 0NT, *Tel:* (071) 226 2260 produce a leaflet called *The asthmatic on holiday*.

— **British Diabetic Association**, 10 Queen Anne St, London W1M, 0BD, produce leaflets for travellers which give information about insulin dosage, local foods and contact addresses and have a translation of some useful phrases.

— **Northern Region Continence Advisory Service**, *Tel:* (091) 213 00500 (weekdays 14.00-19.00) operate a telephone helpline for those with incontinence problems.

— **Coloplast**, Peterborough Business Park, Peterborough PE2 0FX, *Tel:* (0800) 220662 offer travel hints for those who have a colostomy, ileostomy or urostomy in a booklet called *Your guide to trouble-free travel*.

Medical treatment and emergencies

British travellers are entitled to the same health service benefits in France as the French, provided they are armed with the appropriate piece of paper. Details are set out in the DHSS leaflet T2 *Health advice for travellers in the European community*. **This includes the form E111 which must be filled in and stamped before you leave the UK.** It is available from the DHSS Leaflets

Unit, PO Box 21, Stanmore, Middlesex, and from post offices. If you are a UK citizen you can reclaim some 70-80% of any medical costs incurred during a stay in France. Unlike the British National Health Service, French citizens pay for part of their medical costs. The procedure is bureaucratic, and you have to get and keep records and receipts for virtually everything. Consequently **the benefits of the Reciprocal Health Agreement are no substitute for proper health insurance cover** discussed and outlined in the paragraphs on Insurance.

Chemists

There is an **English Pharmacy**, 62 av des Champs Elysées, 75008 Paris, *Tel:* (1) 43.59.22.52 which is open 08.30-20.30 and also the **British-American Pharmacy**, 1 rue Auber, 75009, *Tel:* (1) 47.42.49.40 open 09.00-20.00. Both have English-speaking staff and stock a wide range of British and American proprietary medicines.

In case of emergency, **Pharmacie des Champs Elysées**, 84 av des Champs Elysées, 75008, *Tel:* (1) 45.62.02.41 is a small chemist open 24 hours a day and **Le Drugstore**, bd St-Germain (corner of rue de Rennes) *Tel:* (1) 45.48.04.55 is open until 02.00 seven days a week.

Useful telephone numbers:

SOS Handicap (medical help for disabled people), *Tel:* (1) 47.10.70.20. This is the number of the Hôpital Raymond Poincaré, Garches, 92380 just past St Cloud. It is a major centre for both treatment and rehabilitation and consequently might be able to help with advice or with broken equipment.
SOS Médecin (at night and on Sundays), *Tel:* (1) 43.77.77.77 or (1) 47.07.77.77
Ambulances (public services), *Tel:* (1) 45.13.65.89
Radio Ambulances, *Tel:* (1) 45.67.50.50
SOS Dentist for nights, Sundays, Saturdays & holidays, *Tel:* (1) 43.37.51.00

Emergencies

What would almost certainly happen in the event of a serious accident or illness is that someone around would arrange for an ambulance to take you to the nearest hospital. If you have an accident at your hotel or hostel then the management will organise things for you. **Ambulance** information is available on *Tel:* (1) 45.13.65.89, but what they will do is to give you the numbers of various private companies. In Paris, if you have an accident at the roadside, you would be dealt with by a public ambulance, but from private premises such as a hotel the ambulance would probably be a private one. We have referred above to the need to keep records of expenditures and to keep receipts for money paid. *It cannot be emphasised too strongly that things will be much easier if you have adequate insurance. An E111 certificate described in the section on the Reciprocal Health Agreement gives only partial cover.*

For information on national health hospitals (*Assistance publique*), *Tel:* (1) 40.27.30.00.

Unless your French is fluent you may be wise to ask to be taken or transferred to either the British or the American hospital:

—   The **British Hertford hospital**, Centre Hospitalier Franco-Britannique, 3 rue Barbès, 92300 Levallois-Perret, *Tel:* (1) 47.58.13.12 has some 90 beds and good facilities for dealing with most kinds of illness or injury. Although by law the doctors are French, all the nurses and some of the other staff are British and you won't have any major language problems. British residents and visitors have priority access to the hospital.

—   The **American hospital**, 63 bd Victor Hugo, Neuilly, *Tel:* (1) 47.47.53.00 is a little larger but offers similar facilities and can cope with dental as well as medical problems.

If you only need medical advice, these are probably the best places to go. They are normally open 24 hours a day, but you should be aware that due to their size sometimes all the beds are occupied.

Museums and monuments pass

If you are likely to visit several of the main and more expensive museums, houses and collections, you can buy a one-, three- or five-day pass. In 1992 it was just over £6 for one day, £12 for three and £18 for five days. The pass has advantages, more perhaps for disabled walkers than for chair users and their companions who may find concessionary discounts already. Principally it will help you to avoid the inevitable queues at the big venues. However, be careful; some of the places included in the pass will have access problems, so make sure that you will be visiting enough places to make it worth while. *One advantage of having a pass is that it gives you access to quite a number of wheelchair loos around Paris* and, even though it is quite time consuming to have to go through some museum or monument just to go to the loo, it could be useful, given the general shortage.

The passes can be bought at museums, tourist offices and métro stations.

Pedestrians

Apart from keeping a sharp look-out the only things we feel we should mention are that **zebra crossings don't give you priority as they do in Britain** and that at light controlled crossings you are expected to obey the lights. Also watch out for French drivers filtering, ie turning at right angles to the lights.

Postal and other services

The main post office is at 52 rue du Louvre, 75001, *Tel:* (1) 40.28.20.00. It has ramped access to the main entrance and most facilities are on the ground floor. Counter 12 is specially low to suit those who use chairs and the **poste restante** counter is to the right of the main area. Remember that you will need identification to collect your mail. If it is addressed to two people you should both go to claim it.

If your delivery involves dealing with French customs, a lift (D70 W115 L135) will take you to the second floor. The fax office is −14 steps with handrails on the third floor from a second lift at the other end of the main hall. If that causes you a problem the staff will be happy to send anything for you.

Telegrams can be sent from any post office, but the delivery service is now somewhat restricted in Britain. There is a special telephone number for telegrams in English, *Tel:* (1) 42.33.21.11.

Price concessions

A few places will offer price reductions for wheelchair users and/or a pusher. This applies mainly to entrance fees of one kind or another. Reductions are not often available for other disabled people except, occasionally, people who are blind or partially sighted. The problem is that the whole business is highly capricious and depends as much on who is on the door as it does on official policy. Thus **we have made virtually no reference to concessions** because the information might be misleading.

Nevertheless **the fare concession to disabled drivers offered by most of the ferry operators** is worth mentioning. The concession involves the vehicle travelling free of charge or at a discount. This concession has certain conditions different for each operator, such as whether the disabled person is driving or is a passenger etc. Most of the companies give the reduction to DDA and DDMC members (Disabled Drivers Association, Ashwellthorpe, Norwich NR16 1EX, *Tel:* (050) 841449; Disabled Drivers Motor Club, Cottingham Way, Thrapston, Northamptonshire NN14 4PL, *Tel:* (0832) 734724 *Fax:* (0832) 733816. They rely on the clubs validating the application. Details are available from each operator but the procedure is somewhat long-winded and bureaucratic so make sure you apply well in advance, especially during peak periods when a month's notice is requested.

Shopping and business hours

Shops are generally open later than is usual in Britain but a few of the smaller ones will shut for a siesta around lunch-time. **Banks** are normally open 09.00-12.00 and 14.00-16.00. There are **bureaux de change** near all the main tourist spots, open most of the day, which are much less bureaucratic than banks for currency exchange, but may give you a poorer rate of exchange. **Post offices** are normally open 08.00-19.00 on weekdays and from 08.00-12.00 on Saturdays.

Telephones

There are more low level telephones in Paris suitable for chair users than in London. There are even some street call boxes at the right height and with no door on one side. More generally there are telephones in post offices, hotels and railway stations and in cafés. An increasing number use a phone card.

To ring France dial 010 33, then the département (area) code, which for Paris is simply (1) followed by eight digits. Most département codes are two digits.

To ring the UK from France dial 19, wait for a continuous tone, then dial 44 followed by the STD code and number but leaving off the first 0. For example, for central London the 19 and 44 replace the 0 in the 071 code before the number, ie 194471 followed by seven digits.

What to take

You will be wise to travel with as little luggage as possible, but wheelchair users may like to consider the advantages of bringing or hiring a narrow chair if your normal one is wide.

A good phrase book and dictionary are useful for those who don't speak fluent French and we found the pocket dictionary to be of most practical value.

Travelling to Paris

There are several ways of getting there with varying degrees of accessibility. The ones which involve minimal problems to the disabled traveller are the various routes which enable you to take your own car with you and the direct flight air routes. *The Channel Tunnel is due to open shortly and this should provide the easiest potential route for people with disabilities*. This is because if you use the car-train you can stay in your car during the journey and later the direct link trains will come from a number of major cities. These will provide a relatively easy route for disabled walkers and will have wheelchair spaces.

You can, of course, travel by coach or train to the channel port; by ferry, hovercraft or SeaCat to get across the water and then by coach or train on the other side. Each of these routes and each transfer involves some problems.

Undoubtedly the easiest car ferry route is the one from Dover to Calais. The ferries operating all have lifts and wheelchair loos and there are frequent crossings. It doesn't matter much if you miss a ferry and if you turn up really early you might catch an earlier one.

Transport information for people with disabilities is available from **Tripscope**, The Courtyard, Evelyn Rd, London W4 1JE, *Tel:* (081) 994 9294. Tripscope offers information on journeys of any distance – local, long distance or international. The information is free of charge and they will phone you back if necessary. Wherever you are starting from they can advise on the easiest and the cheapest ways of travelling and about the problems you may meet.

We have organised this chapter to describe travelling by:
— car: using the tunnel, various ferry routes or the hovercraft/SeaCat short crossings
— coach
— train (which will shortly get easier with the opening of the tunnel)
— air

We are looking at things largely from the point of view of someone making their own plans and bookings. Remember that if you are arranging your trip through a tour company it is essential that you make your needs clear and check that they can organise things to your satisfaction.

TRAVELLING BY CAR OR MINIBUS

General advice

If you already travel around by car or minibus you will be used to the facilities available in this country. In particular most motorway service stations have some wheelchair accessible facilities, although not all provide access to the main restaurant. We are not attempting to include a detailed guide to UK facilities since the variety of starting points and routes could be enormous. The *AA Guide for Disabled People* has useful information.

If you are taking your car abroad, all the usual precautions apply. Make sure it has been serviced and is in reasonable nick. Use the AA 5-star insurance package or an equivalent (also see the write-up on Insurance) and get a Green Card from your own car insurance company. The green card establishes that you have third party insurance, as required by law in France. **The AA or RAC Continental Handbook is full of useful advice and information.** If you are taking a minibus it will need a tachograph and various EEC regulations apply. Get details well in advance from the AA or RAC.

Hints on driving in France are included in the chapter on *Getting around in Paris*. For the ferry crossing see the section on cross-channel ferries. The route from Calais to Paris is mainly by Autoroute A1 and the biggest service stations have wheelchair accessible loos. Going towards Paris the only service stations which have a wheelchair accessible restaurant are Assevillers and Ressons. On the way back Assevillers has a wheelchair accessible restaurant while Ressons has a wheelchair accessible buffet. A booklet *Guide des Autoroutes a` l'Usage des Personnes a` Mobilité Réduite* (Guide to the facilities on Autoroutes for disabled people) covers all French autoroutes and is available from the CNFLRH. A new edition was published in 1993 and it can also be obtained from Information-Communication, Direction des Routes, La Grande Arche, 92055 La Défense, Cedex 04.

Comparing the different crossings

There is a wide choice of routes and of methods of crossing the channel and what you want to do will depend on where you are starting from, where else in France you are going and your own particluar preferences and needs. As a generalisation the ferries offer a more accessible and fuss-free way of crossing than either Hoverspeed or SeaCat on the short route from Dover to Calais. Ferries also give you the choice of longer routes starting from other ports such as Portsmouth and Felixstowe. The opening of the channel tunnel increases the number of accessible options available.

If there are access problems on your intended route it makes it even more important to contact the company involved in advance and ask for appropriate information and assistance. Even on the main Dover-Calais ferries the operators ask that disabled passengers let them know 48 hours in advance if possible. It means that if there were a large number of disabled people wanting to use a particular crossing they could make appropriate staffing arrangements. In practice you'll probably be perfectly all right on this route if you just turn up and that is one of its advantages. Whichever way you go it is sensible to arrive in good time. Most of the operators like you to arrive about an hour before the advertised departure time.

Most ferries have lifts linking the car deck to the main decks. The problem the loading officer has is that once the car deck becomes full (or parts of it become full) chair users may not be able to get between the vehicles to get to the lift. If you have special needs not met by the normal provisions or if a group of disabled people are travelling together it is advisable to contact the ferry company and discuss the practicalities with them. A point made by Stena Sealink is that ships are sometimes substituted on different routes. Hovercraft and SeaCat both have access barriers or problems between the car deck and the passenger areas so make sure that you are aware of them.

It is important to make your presence known to the loading officer. You can do this at the ticket check and more importantly confirm it when you are instructed to join a particular queue of cars. The key thing is that most passengers will go up the internal stairs to get to the car deck. Most passengers with disabilities will want to use the lift and you need to make this requirement known. Things are much easier with everyone at the port having a mobile radio. It could be sensible to display a prominent 'disabled' symbol in your windscreen to call attention to the fact that you will need to use the lift.

Car drivers and their passengers may not even need to get out of their cars before driving on board, provided that they have booked in advance and their documentation is in order. However, the time at the ferry port can give the opportunity for a break. The only occasion when you are likely to be asked to get out of your car is on disembarkation when you may be asked to do so by a customs official in the course of a customs search. With new common market procedures, this should become less common. However, you may well find it advisable to use the wheelchair loos in the terminal buildings as there will probably only be one on the ferry and if there are several chair users travelling you might find that it is occupied.

The internal steps on a ferry from the car deck to the passenger areas are usually narrow and steep and there may be quite a lot of them. If you have a problem because of a heart or chest condition or for any other reason, explain this briefly to the crew and they will let you use the lift.

We are not commenting on the relative cost of crossings since the business is very competitive and things will change when the tunnel opens. It is better for you to do your own research on this. Accurate price information is relatively easy to come by, but reliable access data is not. Disabled drivers will find that there are reductions available through the Disabled Drivers Association and the Disabled Drivers Motor Club whose details are given under *Useful addresses*. This can allow you to take your car without charge on some of the ferry routes but it takes a while to process the necessary application so allow a little time.

Ferry company contacts:

P & O European Ferries, Channel House, Channel View Rd, Dover, Kent, *Tel:* (0304) 203388.

Sealink, PO Box 29, Victoria Station, London SW1, *Tel:* (071) 834 8122 or (071) 630 1373 for group travel.

Sally Line, Argyle Centre York St, Ramsgate, *Tel:* (0843) 595522.

Olau Line, Sheerness, Kent, *Tel:* (0795) 580010.

For SeaCat and hovercraft crossings contact:

Hoverspeed Ltd, Marine Parade, Dover, Kent, *Tel:* (0304) 240241.

The routes described are:
— Folkestone-Calais using the Channel Tunnel
— Dover-Calais by ferry
— Short crossings by hovercraft or SeaCat
— Ramsgate-Dunkirk
— Newhaven-Dieppe
— Portsmouth-le Havre/Southampton-Cherbourg
— Sheerness-Vlissingen
— Felixstowe-Zeebrugge

Folkestone-Calais using 'le Shuttle' through the Channel Tunnel

As the tunnel is not yet open, this information is based on what we have been told. Eurotunnel have gone to considerable lengths to incorporate the needs of passengers with disabilities in their design. What they aim to do is to provide a turn up and travel service, with no reservation, between Folkestone and Calais. The Shuttle is primarily for passengers with their own cars. BR and SNCF will operate the services for through trains described later.

Frontier formalities will be the same as those at other places where people travel to and from France, but they will all be carried out at the point of departure. Thus in travelling in either direction you first buy your ticket then pass through the customs formalities of the country you are leaving and the immigration controls of the country you are entering, all on the same site. When you arrive you are free to drive straight off. The terminals at either end will have a range of facilities such as shops and restaurants and there will be the provision of loos for people with disabilities.

The shuttle carriages have two areas. A double deck section for normal cars with a height restriction on it and a single deck section which will take mini-buses and coaches. Some disabled people with adapted cars with high roofs may have to use the single deck section. *Perhaps the most important thing for many disabled people is that you will be able to remain in or near your car during the journey.* As the journey time is only 35 minutes you should be on the shuttle for less than an hour all told. The procedure cuts out all the business of loading and unloading that you have to go through with a ferry. Obviously one of the things you will need to take into account is the price of the crossing which has not yet emerged.

The principal requirement in relation to passengers with disabilities from Eurotunnel's point of view is that they should declare themselves on arrival. Our only comment on this is that it isn't quite as obvious or simple as it sounds. They will site the vehicles with disabled drivers or passengers in the lower deck of the front carriage which means that you'll get off first and, in the unlikely event of an emergency, Eurotunnel staff will have the right equipment to hand to help people get off.

There is provision for carrying up to five disabled people in the double deck section of the trains and up to ten in the single deck half. If there are large groups of disabled people wanting to travel they are asked to give advanced notice if possible.

No doubt as the opening gets nearer more details will emerge and it will be interesting to see how it all works out. Potentially the tunnel offers a route to the continent for disabled passengers with less hassles than the ferries. Eurotunnel are planning to publish a *Code of practice for the carriage of disabled passengers.* We hope that the high expectations outlined will be met.

Dover-Calais by ferry

This route is operated by both P & O European Ferries and Stena Sealink. Port facilities at both Dover and Calais have been recently modernised.

P & O European Ferries have a modern fleet of ships and all of those normally operating on the route have both lifts and wheelchair loos. Four vessels provide the service: the *Pride of Dover* and *Pride of Calais* each have three lifts (D100 W210 L210) and three unisex wheelchair loos (D85); the *Pride of Bruges* has two lifts (D84 W126 L196) and one unisex wheelchair loo (D81); and the *Pride of Kent* has two lifts (D86 W112 L198) and three unisex wheelchair loos (D75). Between them the lifts serve all the floors and the loos have flat access.

Stena Sealink operate a number of large ferries on the Dover-Calais route. These include the *Côte d'Azur, Fiesta, Stena Invicta* and *Stena Fantasia.* All these have large lifts, a wheelchair loo and reasonably good access. Sealink were unable to give us lift sizes and loo door widths. They highlighted the need to contact the company first before travelling and the fact that they sometimes switch ships around with the result that the facilities vary.

For road travellers the M2/A2 via Canterbury and the M20/A20 via Folkestone both provide motorway or dual carriageway links with the port and both link to the M25. Dover is by far the biggest and busiest of all the channel ports, being served by eight very large ferries – up to 38 sailings a day.

There is flat access everywhere via ramps or lifts. Each set of loos has a unisex wheelchair loo. All the public buildings have loop systems for people with impaired hearing. Seats in the restaurants are movable.

There is a Motorists' Information Centre at car assembly park B giving information on the European road network. A port plan can be provided and a leaflet for disabled travellers. For more information contact Dover Harbour Board, Harbour House, Dover, Kent CT17 9BU, *Tel*: (0304) 240400.

On your arrival, staff will fix a coloured sticker to your windscreen. This is done so that disabled travellers can be loaded on the ferry as close as possible to a lift. It also alerts other staff to the presence of passengers with special needs. *Make sure that you have this 'mark'.*

At Calais the car-ferry terminal and hoverport are directly connected to the A26 motorway network. The terminal building has flat access throughout. Some facilities, including the restaurant, are on the upper floors which are reached by lift (D80 W109 L140). There are wheelchair loos which are available to passengers travelling in both directions. For more information contact Le Directeur Général, Chambre de Commerce et d'Industrie de Calais, Hôtel Consulaire, 24 bd des Alliés BP 199, 62104 Calais, *Tel:* 21.46.00.00 *Fax:* 21.46.00.99.

En route to Dover

If you are taking your own car and either using a ferry or 'le Shuttle' which will run through the channel tunnel, you may be driving quite a way before you get to the coast. While we haven't undertaken a full survey of what is involved we can make a few suggestions.

Most motorway service stations have reasonable facilities and in particular loos for chair users. However, you must remember that there are still long stretches of motorway – **notably the M25** – which have no services.

The Farthing Corner services are on the M2, some 55km from Dover, between junctions 4 and 5. The wheelchair loo is on the London bound side, but can be accessed by going across the ramped bridge if you are going towards Canterbury/Dover. It uses the RADAR key scheme, but if you don't have a key you can get one from a staff member. The Little Chef at Harbledon, about 30km from Dover, has a wheelchair loo reached via the restaurant, as does the Esso Service Station on the M2, 5km short of Dover.

If you've come a really long way already you may want an overnight stop just before or after crossing. If you are looking for somewhere to stay Holiday Care Service have comprehensive listings of accessible hotels around the country and will know of some near Dover. The Travel Inn chain has recently adopted the standards of *Tourism for All* which includes criteria for people with disabilities. In their newer developments this includes wider sliding doors, space for side transfer to the loo and a lower, wider bath with grab rails. They have one at Sevenoaks, *Tel:* (0732) 884214 and one at Dover, *Tel:* (0304) 213339. For a complete list contact Travel Inn, Park St West, Luton, Bedfordshire LU1 3BG, *Tel:* (0582) 405680. At Dover there is a Forte Posthouse on the A2, about 5km from the town, with an adapted room which has a washroom with a shower and conventional shower tray. The loo has D70+ and ST70+. There is also a wheelchair loo (D70+ ST95) on the ground floor from the bar/restaurant.

If you find yourself in Dover with time to kill because you have got through more quickly than you expected, you may be interested in the **Dover White Cliffs Experience** which is in the city centre and well signed. It is a presentation of the history of Dover from Roman times and includes tableaux, videos, displays and an auditorium with a 15 minute presentation. You should allow well over an hour and expect to cover about 500m. The exhibition is on three floors; there is a lift (D80 W107 L140) by the entrance and another near the restaurant. It has a wheelchair loo (D70 ST70+) on the third floor near the restaurant.

On the French side

If you just want to get across the channel and stop you should consider the Formule 1 chain. They are basic, clean, and incredibly cheap at about £20 a night for three people. They have standard rooms adapted for people with disabilities and a loo and shower with flat access and plenty of space (D80+ ST150+). See the survey in the *Accommodation* chapter of a Formule 1 hotel outside Paris. They are all **exactly** the same. They have a hotel on RN1 called Calais Coquelles, *Tel:* 21.96.89.89. For information in Britain, *Tel:* (081) 741 1001.

You will find other suggestions for accommodation en route in RADAR's *Holidays abroad for people with disabilities* which is published annually.

Short crossings by hovercraft or SeaCat

Both the hovercraft and SeaCat offer shorter crossing times than the traditional ferries, but both have access problems. Both give you a fairly lively and potentially unpleasant ride when the sea is at all rough. They operate on a number of routes, therefore giving you more choice.

Hovercraft go from Dover-Calais. The hovercraft itself has some steps. It has a ramped entrance to the car deck and then +5 steps into the seating area on either side. Staff will help if needed. In the seating area itself there is space for one wheelchair at the front of each seating section and one or two by either central exit, six in all. Alternatively you can sit in aircraft-style seats. There is no wheelchair loo on board.

At the Dover 'hoverport' there is a wheelchair loo and the building has ramped entrances and exits. Calais hoverport also has ramped entrances and exits. The departure lounge has a wheelchair loo (D70 ST70) and this can be used on arrival if you need it.

SeaCat services run between Dover-Calais, Dover-Boulogne and Folkestone-Boulogne. There is no lift access from the car deck so you have to get out of your car before boarding and use the ramped passenger entrance. Disabled drivers will need to park early then wheel off the catamaran along the car ramp and use the foot passengers' ramp. The alternative is +19 steps from the car deck up to the top lounge level.

From the ramp there is flat access into the top level of the catamaran's passenger lounge and a staff operated lift avoids the −5 steps with handrails to a lower level. Wheelchair users can remain in their chairs. Alternatively you can transfer to open plan lounge seating or rows of aircraft-style seating. There is flat access to the bar, duty free shop, first aid room and wheelchair loo (D90 ST100 via the front of the loo). When disembarking at Boulogne there is another ramp with handrails but it is steep at times.

Ramsgate-Dunkirk by ferry

Sally Line operates two ferries from **Ramsgate to Dunkirk**. Sally's flagship the *Sally Star* has two passenger lifts which give access to all floors. Each lift can accommodate one chair user plus two other people. A wheelchair is carried on board and the vessel has one unisex wheelchair loo (D80). The *Sally Sky* has one lift, which also accommodates one wheelchair user and two other people, serving the cardecks and main deck with restaurant, brasserie and bureau de change. There is no wheelchair access to the bar, Duty Free mall or TV lounge. A wheelchair is carried on board and the vessel has one unisex wheelchair loo (D97).

Sally Line own and operate the ports at both ends of the route. The main facilities have flat or single step access and there is a wheelchair loo at both Ramsgate and Dunkirk. The contact number for additional information is *Tel:* (0843) 595522.

Newhaven-Dieppe by ferry

This route is operated by Stena Sealink. They have recently refurbished the two ferries operating. Both the Stena Londoner and Stena Parisien have lifts and wheelchair loos. Sealink were unable to supply us with details. The route has advantages for some in reducing driving distances. The terminal is to the south of the town centre, and you should allow extra time on your journey to drive through the town. We are told that the terminal at Newhaven has recently been thoroughly refurbished and that there is flat access and provision of a wheelchair loo. For further information contact Stena Sealink Line, Newhaven Harbour, Newhaven BN9 0BG, *Tel:* (0273) 516699. Apparently the facilities at Dieppe are due to be reconstructed during 1993 and these will hopefully be upgraded when this is done.

Portsmouth-le Havre/Cherbourg and Southampton-Cherbourg by ferry

P & O European Ferries operate the **Portsmouth-Le Havre** and **Portsmouth-Cherbourg** routes which are served by ships which have lift access and at least one unisex wheelchair loo, although we have no measurements for these. We are also told that these ships have some adapted cabins for disabled passengers.

Stena Sealink operate the **Southampton-Cherbourg** route and have a large cruise ferry the Stena Normandy. This has lift access, unisex wheelchair toilets and several en-suite cabins adapted for disabled travellers.

Portsmouth ferry terminal is situated at the end of the M275 which completely by-passes the built-up area. From the coast, the M275 leads onto the M27 and A3(M). There is flat access into the terminal building and to all the facilities inside. The car park is approximately 50m away. The terminal is fairly small and at peak times can become crowded. It includes all the usual facilities including wheelchair loos located in the men's and women's. For further information contact The Port Manager, Harbour Offices, Continental Ferry Port, George Byng Way, Portsmouth PO2 8SP, *Tel:* (0705) 297392.

Le Havre is well situated for going to Normandy or the Loire area and is within easy reach of Paris by motorway. The terminal can be reached without going through the centre of the town, although there's a longish drive through the docks area. The terminal is fully accessible with ramps and lifts and there are two wheelchair loos. There is no restaurant or shop. For further information contact Port Autonome du Havre, Terre-Plein de la Barre, BP 1413, 76067 Le Havre, *Tel:* 35.21.74.00.

Sheerness-Vlissengen by ferry

Olau Line have just two ships. The route from **Sheerness to Vlissingen** is not ideal for visitors to Paris, although both ports are close to the motorway network. **Access is generally good.** Both ships, the *Olau Hollandia* and *Olau Brittania* weigh 35,000 tons and have lifts (D80 W90 L105) linking all the decks. **Both have two special cabins for wheelchair users** with adapted showers and toilets.

Sheerness, used and managed by Olau Line, is conveniently situated for London, being only 15km off the M2 (exit 5). After one step at the entrance to the terminal building, there is flat access to all the facilities inside and these include the booking office, a newsagent's and a unisex wheelchair loo (D70+ ST70+). For further information contact The Passenger Manager, Olau Line (UK) Ltd, Sheerness, Kent ME12 1SN, *Tel:* (0795) 666666 for reservations or (0795) 580010 for administration.

Felixstowe-Zeebrugge by ferry

The Felixstowe-Zeebrugge route is operated by P & O European Ferries. We are told that the ferries operating all have lifts from the car deck, wheelchair loos and adapted cabins for disabled travellers.

Felixstowe is conveniently situated for travellers from the Midlands and East Anglia. The A45 is now a dual carriageway for much of the way and by-passes Ipswich. There is flat access throughout the terminal building and the car park is immediately outside. There are unisex wheelchair loos and a café with movable chairs. For further information contact The Passenger Terminal Manager, P & O European Ferries (Felixstowe) Ltd, The Ferry Centre, Felixstowe, Suffolk IP11 8TB, *Tel:* (0394) 604040.

Zeebrugge is only a few kilometres from the end of the Brussels-Ostend motorway. The terminal has flat access throughout. There is a unisex wheelchair loo by the restaurant. For further information contact P & O European Ferries, Doverlaan 7, B-8380 Zeebrugge, Belgium, *Tel:* 50.54.22.11.

TRAVELLING BY COACH

Coach travel is generally the cheapest but *this is not a method of transport we would recommend to most disabled people if simplicity and ease of access are important*. There are potential problems associated with the various transfers necessary en route, on and off ferries or hovercrafts. Operators are getting better at meeting special needs, providing you make careful enquiries when booking. Coaches don't necessarily use the most accessible routes. You must remember that there will be 3 or 4 large steps into the coach and that you probably won't have a particular seat reserved. Most seats have limited leg-room. In addition, there will only be a few stops en route. Despite the problems, if you use coaches and buses in this country then you will probably manage.

Hoverspeed runs a service from London to Paris using the hovercraft crossing and this is the one we surveyed.

The coach leaves from Victoria coach station at the London end. The station has flat access and, as part of National Express policy, disabled travellers can be met and transferred from one coach to another, though help is not provided for actually transferring onto and off the coaches themselves. If you arrive at Victoria train station it is a 600m walk south to reach the coach station. This route is flat apart from one or two road crossings.

The coach station has wheelchairs available for use to help with transfers and has two wheelchair loos: one at the arrivals desk and one by the disabled persons' 'help' desk.

At the Dover hoverport there is a wheelchair loo and the building has ramped entrances and exits. The Hoverspeed staff offer assistance with luggage and in getting between coach, hovercraft and coach. There is one coach for the English side of the trip and another for the French. Calais hoverport also has ramped entrances and exits. The departure lounge has a wheelchair loo (D70 ST70) and this can be used if you have just arrived, although you need to ensure the coach doesn't try to leave without you.

The hovercraft itself has a ramped entrance to the car deck and then +5 steps into the seating area on either side, which numerous staff will happily assist you with. There is space for one wheelchair at the front of each seating section and one or two by either central exit – six in all. There is no wheelchair loo on board.

TRAVELLING BY TRAIN

Getting on and off a train is generally easier than a coach, except that French railway platforms are commonly only a few centimetres above ground level, meaning that there are 3 or 4 steep steps to get up into the carriage. The British Rail routes from Victoria to Paris currently used are: Folkestone-Boulogne via the SeaCat, Dover-Calais via Sealink ferry and Newhaven-Dieppe also via Sealink ferry. If access is important, check the details under the cross-channel ferries section. Generally the Dover-Calais route is the most accessible.

With 24 hours notice British Rail (BR) can phone ahead to the English port and arrange for a disabled person to be met. They do not, however, take any responsibility for transferring someone from the train to the ferry – that is the responsibility of the ferry company. Similarly BR will make no arrangements for disabled passengers on the French side. The SNCF office in London will arrange that for you.

Many of BR's trains are old stock, thus chair users travel in the guard's van as the carriages are small. Carriages brought into service more recently have removable seats and wide doors so wheelchair users can ride in the compartments, but these do not run on all routes yet.

Our solo wheelchair surveyor did not have a very good trip. The booking staff were not very clued up about possible access difficulties and had no idea that they varied depending on the route taken. His journey was reasonably smooth from Victoria to Dover, but he was not allowed to get on board the ferry using the easiest method, ie via the lift from the car deck. It may well be that the car deck was full by the time the rail passengers arrived, making it impossible to get to the lift. Consequently he was carried up the steps into the ferry. On board it was crowded and, although the Sealink ferries from Dover all have a wheelchair loo, the sliding door of the loo was stiff and heavy. On the French side he was taken down a gang plank and railway staff merely took him to the side of the train, clearly expecting him to get up out of the chair and walk on – the comment on the survey form at this stage was 'God give me strength!' He was eventually lifted on, but at the Paris end no one came to help him off and he had to collar a couple of British travellers to give him a hand...

Perhaps this paints slightly too black a picture. Someone travelling with friends would have less problems. It does, however, illustrate some of the hassles you may encounter. A person we spoke to at BR customer relations recently said, "It is BR policy neither to encourage nor to discourage wheelchair users from using the service."

SeaCat

SeaCat catamaran services run between Dover-Calais, Dover-Boulogne and Folkestone-Boulogne. Our surveyor travelled via Folkestone to Boulogne. SeaCat offers a relatively quick, efficient and fuss-free route from London to Paris with trains that link close to the catamaran at each end. It is reasonably accessible if you can get on and off the trains. A problem is that it can be an uncomfortable crossing in rough weather. The service runs twice a day throughout the year, but may be cancelled if the weather is extremely windy.

Link trains leave from platforms 1 or 2 at Victoria. At Folkestone Harbour there are women's and men's wheelchair loos on the platform and wheelchairs available for use. From the platform there is flat access to the check-in desk about 50m away and to board the catamaran itself there is a 40m-long ramp with handrails. Staff at Victoria told us that if you need assistance being pushed up the ramp it is best to ring in advance and they will arrange for help at both ends.

From the ramp there is flat access into the top level of the catamaran's passenger lounge and a staff operated lift avoids the −5 with handrails to a lower level. Wheelchair users can easily remain in their chairs; otherwise you can transfer to open plan lounge seating or rows of aircraft style seating. There is flat access to the bar, duty free shop, first aid room and wheelchair loo (D90 ST100 via the front of the loo). When disembarking at Boulogne there is another ramp with handrails, but it is steep at times and it is some 500m to the baggage lounge, passport check and trains. The French trains at Boulogne have 3 large steps up into the carriage from the low-level platform. You arrive at Gare du Nord from where there is flat access to the taxis, but not to the métro (see Gare du Nord section). The whole journey takes about six and a half hours.

For information and bookings on the rail route contact British Rail Continental Enquiries, Victoria Station, London, *Tel:* (071) 834 2345 or for SeaCat crossings contact Hoverspeed Ltd, Marine Parade, Dover, Kent, *Tel:* (0304) 240241.

The **Disabled Persons Railcard** which offers substantial fare reductions in Britain does not apply to boat-trains, ferries or to the French railway system. A sighted person accompanying a blind traveller will, however, go for half price.

The principal enquiry points are **BR Continental Enquiries**, Victoria Station, London SW1, *Tel:* (071) 834 2345 and **SNCF** (French Railways), 179 Piccadilly, London W1, *Tel:* (071) 493 9731 or (071) 491 1573.

Using the Channel Tunnel

BR/SNCF services to and from Paris via the Channel Tunnel

During 1994/95 a number of new services should become available, making it much easier for the disabled traveller to get to Paris. All of these will use similar rolling stock which we will describe. However, unlike the shuttle, people with disabilities, and more specifically *anyone who would have a problem getting on and off the train and sitting in a conventional seat, will need to book in advance*. The number of wheelchair spaces, for example, is limited and French stations have a much bigger drop from carriage to platform than British ones.

The core service will be direct trains to and from London and Paris with a journey time of less than four hours. This will operate to and from Waterloo International and the Gare du Nord.

In addition there will be direct services from places like: Edinburgh, Newcastle, York and Peterborough; Manchester, Crewe, Stafford and Milton Keynes; and Birmingham and Coventry. These should be operational by 1995.

Finally there will be overnight services, planned to start late in 1995, from Glasgow via principal stations en route and from Swansea via Cardiff and Bristol.

On the day-time services, it will be essential to book wheelchair spaces and appropriate assistance in advance. *One problem we see with this quite restricted facility* is that the chair spaces may be booked by someone who really doesn't mind transferring which would block off the booking for someone else who really cannot comfortably transfer. It depends on how much these spaces are used as to whether it's a problem.

Getting on board at most BR stations would be via a portable ramp if you find it difficult to get up the steps. At the Gare du Nord, in common with other French stations, getting on and off will be via a portable platform lift because the height difference between the carriage and the platform is quite considerable. It may be more than a metre, whereas in Britain it is less than half a metre. **On each train there will be two allocated wheelchair spaces in the first class area,** although charged at second class rate. **Nearby will be a wheelchair loo** which will have space for side transfer. Obviously you can transfer to a seat if you prefer, but you may then be seated in the second class area away from the larger loo.

On the overnight services the sleeping cars have been designed so that there is one adapted compartment for a chair user which can be used either as a single or a twin. It has an en-suite loo and washroom designed for chair users.

At the principal stations involved there is adequate wheelchair access to the platforms, though if you are coming from somewhere other than London, you would be sensible to check. At Waterloo International there will be escalators or moving inclined walkways. There will also be lifts. **The separate terminal buildings will include new wheelchair loos**. A survey of the Gare du Nord is included in the *Getting around in Paris* chapter. **Waterloo is served by the Carelink wheelchair accessible bus service linking main line London railway stations.** The Gare du Nord links up with the RER, important parts of which are accessible (described in detail in the chapter on *Getting around in Paris*).

The question of price concessions for disabled passengers is still under discussion. Account must be taken, in BR's view, of the additional engineering costs of providing facilities for passengers with disabilities. A wide range of requirements has been considered, including the need for colour contrasts and induction loops where possible. At this stage we are, of course, only passing on the information received from BR, as there is currently no experience of these services. They should make travelling for people with disabilities to certain destinations considerably easier.

TRAVELLING BY AIR

This can be the simplest and is certainly the quickest way to go. It is also, of course, fairly expensive. The chief disadvantage is that you finish up 20km outside the centre of Paris without transport. If hiring a car is a possibility you can solve two major problems; getting into Paris itself and getting around once there.

For many years airport authorities and airlines have made better provision for disabled travellers than organisations in charge of other forms of transport. Help is available at most airports for both chair users and disabled walkers and if you find distances a problem you can either borrow a wheelchair or ride on one of those fancy motorised buggies which are used at the big airports. Airports are, however, big and busy places and often the signposting and information services are inadequate. **Free information leaflets for disabled people for most UK airports** are available from the British Airports Authority Publications Department, Gatwick Airport, Horley, West Sussex and from the Air Transport Users Committee, 2nd Floor, Kingsway House, 103 Kingsway, London WC2B 6QX, *Tel:* (071) 242 3882.

British Airways fly direct from Belfast, Birmingham, Bristol, Edinburgh, Glasgow, Manchester, Newcastle, London City Airport and London Heathrow. Should a wheelchair passenger be travelling unaccompanied, British Airways offers a complementary 'Meet and Assist' service; meeting you on arrival and offering assistance with all airport procedure onto the plane. This service should be requested when you make your reservation. You can travel with wet cell batteries for an electric wheelchair providing they are properly prepared for carriage and British Airways offer advice on this.

Air France have direct flights from Birmingham, Bristol, Edinburgh, Glasgow, Manchester, Southampton, London City Airport and London Heathrow. Any disabled passengers must inform Air France of the nature of their disability when making the flight reservations and the company doctor will decide whether the passenger must be accompanied on board the aircraft. Air France enlists the services of specialised firms to accompany the passenger through the airport procedures and onto the aircraft. Wheelchairs are transported free of charge, but wet cell batteries are not accepted. Disabled children cannot travel unless accompanied.

Although provincial airports may be closer to where you live, they are naturally much smaller than the London ones and there will probably be steps up into the aircraft. Procedures for coping with disabled passengers will vary, and if you are lucky there will be a fork lift truck to get you up to the aircraft door.

If you are travelling from London by public transport there is an accessible rail link from Victoria to Gatwick and lifts from Gatwick station to the airport concourse. Public transport linking Heathrow with major rail terminals is via the wheelchair-accessible Airbus service, from Victoria and Euston stations, *Tel:* (081) 897 3305. Facilities at both airports are basically good, although both get congested at peak periods and any hiccup in the system such as air traffic control problems causes disproportionate confusion. There are long distances involved.

Heathrow airport has four terminals. British Airways fly to Paris from terminal 4 and Air France from terminal 2. The easiest way to arrive at Heathrow is by car or taxi. One in every three taxis at Heathrow is now wheelchair-accessible, *although many disabled walkers find the traditional black cab presents unique problems, as there is no easy access to the main seats*. If your knees are not strong or, if you can't bend easily, you have to crawl in and it's most undignified. Passengers and luggage can be dropped off right outside the terminal buildings, although a car is allowed to stop but not park. The short term car parks are some 100 to 200m from the terminals with reserved disabled spaces located close to entrances and lifts. They are expensive if you want to park for more than a few hours. The long term car parks are about a kilometre outside the main area and are linked to the terminals by a courtesy minibus. Car park reception can arrange for a coach which will take wheelchair users to the terminal building. If your vehicle is over 2m high you must use the long term car park anyway.

Heathrow is served from Victoria and Euston rail stations by the Airbus which stops at each airport terminal. London's Underground network has two stations for Heathrow on the Piccadilly Line, one serving terminals 1, 2 & 3, the other terminal 4. Unfortunately access to underground stations in the centre of London is very difficult, involving escalators and stairs.

At Heathrow terminals 1, 2 & 3 there is an escalator to and from the tube platform. Help buttons to call for assistance are located on each side of the 'up' escalator to get someone to operate the lift. From the station you may have to go at least 500m, although some of it is on travelators.

Terminal 4 can be reached with lifts and only 200m distance. The station is directly under the terminal and there is a help point on the left-hand side as you leave the station concourse.

There are wheelchair loos in every terminal, but they vary somewhat in accessibility. There are long distances to walk, although there are wheel-chairs readily available for anyone who finds this difficult. Motorised buggies are also available to disabled walkers for getting to and from the departure lounges once you pass the security checks.

Assistance from your arrival at Heathrow until you board the plane and vice versá can be arranged via the **Travel-care** service, *Tel:* (081) 745 7495. Our surveyors found this to be excellent; one of our chair users was met on the plane from Paris, escorted through the system, put on a coach to Poole and had his parents phoned by the representative to confirm which coach he was on in order to be met on arrival.

If you are in need of assistance and unable to find any passenger service staff you can call one from the **help points** situated outside the Terminal buildings. From these help points you can call a porter, for a £5 charge, or for other passenger services. There is also an accessible **help bus**, *Tel:* (081) 745 5185, to facilitate transfer between the central bus station and the terminals. Heathrow publishes a leaflet containing information for people with special needs available from Heathrow Travel-care, Room 1214, Queen's Building, Heathrow Airport, Hounslow, Middlesex TW6 1JH, *Tel:* (081) 745 7495.

Gatwick airport has two terminals called North and South linked by an accessible rapid transit train. The arrangements for car parking are similar to those at Heathrow with dropping off points in front of each terminal in addition to short and long stay car parks which have bus links with stepped access to the terminals. Accessible taxis are available from Gatwick Airport Cars, *Tel:* (0293) 562291. The British Rail station is adjacent to South terminal and leads via a lift onto the check-in concourse from where you should take the connecting service to North terminal. All buses and coaches stop at the coach station located on the ground floor at South terminal. There are unisex wheelchair loos located throughout both terminals. Courtesy phones to the handling agents are available for disabled passengers at entrances to both terminals and by the parking bays for disabled people.

Gatwick airport publishes a leaflet *Welcome to Gatwick* containing information for disabled people which is available from Gatwick Passenger Information, Public Affairs Department, PO Box 93, Gatwick Airport Ltd, Gatwick, West Sussex, RH6 0NH. Gatwick information is available on *Tel:* (0293) 535353.

Stansted airport only has one terminal and is used by Air UK to Paris. In terms of parking it similarly has a set-down area, short and long stay car parks. In the short stay car parks, spaces are reserved for disabled travellers with courtesy information telephones. Access to the terminal is by lift or ramp. The long stay car park has frequent courtesy buses equipped with wheelchair lifts. The railway station is located beneath the Terminal Forecourt from where lifts and ramps ensure easy access to the terminal itself. The coach station is located in front of the Terminal Forecourt giving easy access to and from the terminal by lift and ramp. Assistance inside the terminal can be arranged in advance by telephoning the Customer Services Department, *Tel:* (0279) 662041. Wheelchair loos are located throughout the terminal and satellite. Stansted publishes a passenger information leaflet, *Tel:* (0279) 662714.

Paris has two major airports; Roissy, Charles de Gaulle in the north and Orly in the south. If you are flying in from Britain you will fly to Charles de Gaulle and it is not a good idea to take a cheap ticket to Beauvais airport which is some 100km north of Paris.

Roissy, Charles de Gaulle airport, in Paris is newer and smaller than Heathrow. It has much the same range of services, but access to public transport is much more difficult. There is flat/ramped access everywhere and the inclined travelators are quite exciting. There are several wheelchair loos and a number of courtesy telephones with a special number for disabled passengers needing assistance. At Roissy the RER station with lift access to the platforms is about 2km from the terminals. There is a bus connecting the two terminals and the RER which has a spacious interior but is inaccessible to wheelchair users because of two large steps. You may like to organise one of the accessible minibuses to meet your flight and take you to your hotel. Details of these are given in the chapter on *Getting around in Paris*. If you do this, make sure that you arrange a very clear meeting point by a numbered entrance.

Terminal 1 where you arrive on British Airways is circular, and hence meeting someone is not as easy as it sounds. The marked 'meeting point' is on the arrivals level by exit 36. Terminal 2 where you arrive on Air France is even more complicated, and is split into three separate sections, with another one opening soon. You need to find out which part you are using if you arrive or leave from this terminal. The parts are 2A, 2B and 2D with 2C opening soon. We are told that special arrangements can be made by the airport administration to transfer wheelchair users to the RER station, but we have no experience of this. A free information leaflet about the airport in English and including some information for disabled passengers is available from **Aéroports de Paris, Servicing Marketing Passengers, Orly Sud 103, 94396 Orly Aérogare Cedex**. Special contact numbers for disabled passengers at terminal 1 are *Tel:* (1) 48.62.28.24 and at terminal 2 *Tel:* (1) 48.62.59.00. Note that a new TGV station is under construction near the airport, which will incorporate the RER station. This is due for completion in 1994/95, and it is to be hoped that it will ease access problems. The key thing is the provision of an easy and accessible link from the terminals to the station.

Orly airport, located south of Paris off the A6, has two terminals. The West terminal is for internal flights and the South terminal for international flights. The airport is not directly accessible by rail because the Orly RER station has dozens of steps. There is, however, a bus service which runs from opposite the RER station at Denfert-Rochereau to Orly. Each terminal has an underground car park with access via a huge lift to the terminal and each car park has well signposted disabled parking spaces with assistance phones next to them. A shuttle service connects the two terminals and, like the RER shuttle bus, has 2 steps with handrails through a wide door into the bus. Wheelchairs are provided by the airport authorities and it is neccessary to transfer onto these chairs in order to get onto the plane. They will not allow you to use your own chair.

The South terminal, *Tel:* (1) 49.75.77.48 – disabled travellers' information, *Tel:* (1) 49.75.30.70 – has six floors connected by eight large lifts with one wheelchair loo on each of the basement, ground and first floors. On the first floor, opposite gate M, is Girt Air which is the reception desk for disabled travellers. This desk provides wheelchairs and any assistance that a disabled person needs. All the shops and cafés are accessible.

The West terminal, *Tel:* (1) 49.75.78.48 – disabled travellers' information, *Tel:* (1) 46.75.18.18 has three floors and four large lifts which go to all floors. There is one unisex wheelchair loo at each end of the first floor. Also on the first floor at gate W is the reception for disabled travellers which can provide wheelchairs as well as assistance. All the shops and cafés have flat access.

A few tips

You may have to wait for a time before **getting off the plane** and the system is frequently bureaucratic. The major problem is that 'handling' is normally the responsibility of the airport, not the airline staff, and there are sometimes strict procedures. Even if you are travelling with friends they may not be allowed to lift you as this is, in principle, the airport's responsibility. It is the old *"what happens if something goes wrong...we'd be responsible"* syndrome and sometimes people's wishes and even common sense go out of the window. It is often possible for those who are totally reliant on their own wheelchair to use it to reach the cabin and to have it immediately accessible to them on disembarkation. Nowadays more airlines are understanding about how difficult and uncomfortable it can be to use an airport chair instead of one designed for a person's individual needs.

If you need help getting on or off the plane it is essential to tell the travel agent when booking and it is advisable to telephone the airline as well and check the arrangements a day or so before departure. The International Air Travel Association (IATA) has produced a standard medical information form (MEDIF) on which to define what help you require. In some situations, for example if you have a chest condition or if you are recovering from an operation, medical clearance is required and your doctor will need to complete the form. Some airlines issue a standard Frequent Traveller's Medical Card (FREMEC) to people with a stable condition who travel by air. This does not make prior notification unnecessary, but it does reduce the administrative hassle.

- **When you book your flight** tell your travel agent what your disability is and what your needs are.

- **Carry a letter from your doctor** and maybe have a copy stating that you are fit to fly – particularly if you are travelling alone.
- **Travel light and take an absolute minimum of hand luggage.** The ideal way to travel is with one's hands empty of everything except a good book and a newspaper, with a pocket full of English and French small change, together with any necessary documents and medicines.
- **Put a label and luggage tag on your wheelchair and remove anything that will come off**, eg arms, footrests and cushions. Ideally take a soft, empty bag to put these in.
- **Arrive in good time and make your needs known at the check-in desk.** Ask what the procedure will be and then you will have the chance to discuss things.
- **Use one of the airport loos before departure** – make sure the airport staff give you time to do this.
- **If you cannot walk far** arrange for an airport wheelchair or motorised buggy to take you from the check-in to the departure lounge. It can save a lot of trouble and some airports are big.

Check your wheelchair on arrival for any damage in the luggage handling system. British NHS chairs are not really built for this kind of handling and are liable to damage, special light-weight chairs even more so. In our experience a chair gets damaged on about one journey in ten. If there is damage report it at the time and make sure that your complaint is registered.

The flight from London to Paris takes less than an hour so there should be no problems arising because you can't get to the loo. Remember that the cabin staff have to handle food on the journey and it is not part of their job to deal with incontinence aids. It is essential to get proper medical advice if you are in doubt about any aspect of flying and if your doctor wants further information he or she can contact the Medical Service, Heathrow Airport, *Tel:* (081) 745 7047.

Accommodation

Your trip to Paris will be much more enjoyable if you can find a good place to stay. When choosing your accommodation the most important factors to weigh up are the cost, where it is and how easily you can get about. Atmosphere and that special something called 'ambience' are also important, but they are not easy to describe and what appeals to one person may not appeal to another. If you're going to have trouble getting around the city, the position of your base will be particularly important and you may have to be prepared to pay more for centrally situated and accessible accommodation. If, on the other hand, you can travel around by car, taxi or RER, then a wider range of good and cheaper accommodation will be available to you. You may also like to check out the availability of the various adapted taxis (see the *Getting around* chapter). It goes without saying that visitors with their own cars will find the provision of a hotel car park to be enormously valuable.

Paris offers a wide range of accommodation with many more cheap places to stay than London. However, much of it is not readily accessible, which discriminates inevitably against the disabled visitor. We have tried to look for reasonably priced places and have found several that offer good value and are fully accessible. **The important thing is that we have visited all of them and are therefore confident about the accuracy of the information.** You will appreciate that we couldn't possibly survey all the hotels in Paris and we only visited those where we had an indication from questionnaires or elsewhere that the access and facilities might be particulary suitable. We were also looking for as wide as possible a spread in terms of location so that you can find somewhere close to the main sights or stay a little more cheaply in areas around the city.

Although most visitors will stay at conventional hotels, other sorts of accommodation are available. Our list includes some hostels, one of which is exceptionally good, and we also surveyed three camp sites for those who want to stay in caravans, dormobiles or under canvas.

Note that we have included the Euro Disney resort hotels in the section on the Euro Disney theme park.

There are a number of fairly new hotel chains in France who reckon to provide a small number of adapted rooms for disabled guests in each of their hotels. Most have hotels in or around Paris and several offer reasonably priced accommodation. *We tried to get the companies to explain exactly what their provision is and what their design criteria are when they say that they have 'adapted' rooms.* **The results were not entirely satisfactory** and when we carried out some checks to see if the information was accurate we regrettably found that it was not. This especially applied to the possibility of sideways transfer in the bathroom attached to an adapted room which companies had said was possible when it certainly wasn't.

The other thing we found was that, although a number of the chains have British agents, these had no detailed information about access. In addition, in two cases where we made a booking through the agent there was a substantial extra cost involved. Compared with booking directly with the hotel we paid about an extra £15 on top of £35 for a room. So when making enquiries it's worth asking about any booking charge.

The one thing that is impossible to assess is the reception you will be given by the management and staff. In most places people will probably be helpful and understanding, but attitudes can depend on who is on duty at the time, how busy they are and whether they've had good or bad experiences with previous disabled guests.

We have divided the hotels into those inside and outside the boulevard Périphérique. All the hostels are inside and all the camp sites outside, except for the Bois de Boulogne site. We have used price bands to indicate relative costs. Room charges vary with the time of year and in some hotels different rooms cost different amounts. **The banding indicates clearly whether the hotel is inexpensive (A/B), medium priced (C/D) or expensive (E)**. The FGTO listing will give you up-to-date prices. **The bands we are using** are based on a room for two people, including breakfast and service charge, and basic figures are based on 1992 prices.

They are:

A	up to 300Fr
B	300-450Fr
C	450-600Fr
D	600-750Fr
E	over 750Fr.

The main ways of arranging your accommodation are through a travel agent or by direct negotiation. If your requirements are specific then there's great advantage in doing it directly, providing you can communicate your requirements to the hotelier or hostel manager. If you deal through a travel agent then your message and requirements will probably get passed along through a series of intermediaries and there's more chance that the information will get scrambled. There are accommodation booking kiosks at the main Paris stations and at the Office de Tourisme in the Champs Elysées, but they are most unlikely to have any reliable information about access.

The places we recommend from those we surveyed from the point of view of facilities for disabled guests are:

The FIAP hostel "Jean Monnet"; the Campanile Italie Gobelins (av d'Italie); Climat de France (av du Professeur André Lemière); Grand Hôtel de France (bd de La Tour Maubourg); Ibis (rue de Bercy); Mercure Paris Montmartre (rue Caulaincourt); Urbis Lafayette (rue La Fayette) and the Formule 1, Noisy-le-Grand (bd du Rû-de-Nesles).

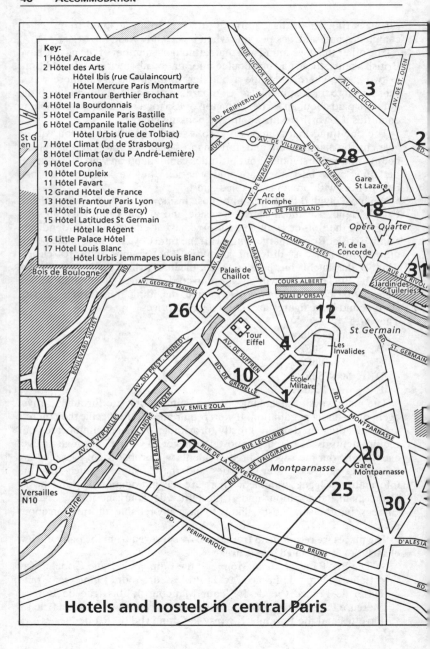

Key:
1 Hôtel Arcade
2 Hôtel des Arts
    Hôtel Ibis (rue Caulaincourt)
    Hôtel Mercure Paris Montmartre
3 Hôtel Frantour Berthier Brochant
4 Hôtel la Bourdonnais
5 Hôtel Campanile Paris Bastille
6 Hôtel Campanile Italie Gobelins
    Hôtel Urbis (rue de Tolbiac)
7 Hôtel Climat (bd de Strasbourg)
8 Hôtel Climat (av du P André-Lemière)
9 Hôtel Corona
10 Hôtel Dupleix
11 Hôtel Favart
12 Grand Hôtel de France
13 Hôtel Frantour Paris Lyon
14 Hôtel Ibis (rue de Bercy)
15 Hôtel Latitudes St Germain
    Hôtel le Régent
16 Little Palace Hôtel
17 Hôtel Louis Blanc
    Hôtel Urbis Jemmapes Louis Blanc

Hotels and hostels in central Paris

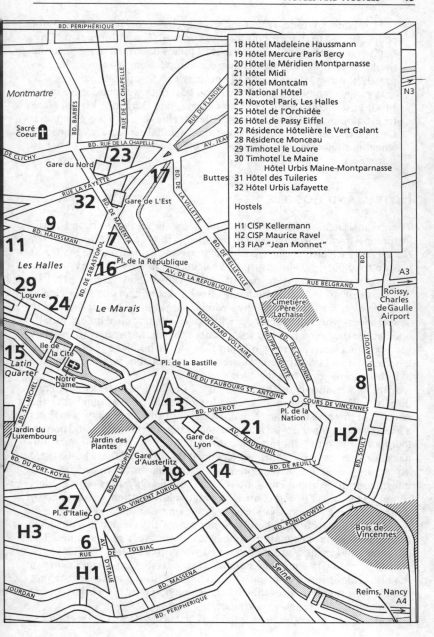

18 Hôtel Madeleine Haussmann
19 Hôtel Mercure Paris Bercy
20 Hôtel le Méridien Montparnasse
21 Hôtel Midi
22 Hôtel Montcalm
23 National Hôtel
24 Novotel Paris, Les Halles
25 Hôtel de l'Orchidée
26 Hôtel de Passy Eiffel
27 Résidence Hôtelière le Vert Galant
28 Résidence Monceau
29 Timhotel le Louvre
30 Timhotel Le Maine
     Hôtel Urbis Maine-Montparnasse
31 Hôtel des Tuileries
32 Hôtel Urbis Lafayette

Hostels

H1 CISP Kellermann
H2 CISP Maurice Ravel
H3 FIAP "Jean Monnet"

The Hôtel Arcade (rue Cambronne) has special advantages for people willing to share rooms for three or four. The bathrooms are tiny, but if you negotiate the use of the staff toilets described in the write-up the hotel can provide good value accommodation. You must be prepared, however, to sort out and put up with a few problems.

If you want a 'wheel-in' shower, the best ones we found were in the FIAP hostel "Jean Monnet"; the Corona (cité Bergère); Little Palace (rue Salomon-de-Caus); and Madeleine Haussmann (rue Pasquier). Outside the centre there are two chains that make a feature of having a wheel-in shower in their 'adapted' facilities and these are Balladins and Formule 1.

HOTELS AND HOSTELS

The main source of information about hotels in and just around Paris, including current prices and a list of facilities, is the *Guide des Hôtels, Paris, Ile de France* which is updated each year and is available from the FGTO. It lists up to about 1,600 hotels by arrondissement and by category. It's the best place to go to get an idea of prices and of how large a hotel is. Alternatively several of the guidebooks on Paris comment on the hotels and their location, and these may give you an idea of the style or ambience. Travel agents will tend to deal only with a particular group of hotels, usually ones where they can negotiate a discount or through an agency where they get a booking fee. They may, of course, know the hotel if one of their reps has visited it and stayed there. However, they probably won't have looked at it through the eyes of a disabled visitor.

Although hundreds of the hotels listed in *Guide des Hôtels* for Paris display a disabled sign among their list of facilities, we found that the criteria for this classification were not nearly rigorous enough; you may get a friendly reception, but you may also encounter tiny lifts, steps and narrow loo doors. From the information gathered either by our postal questionnaires or by our survey teams, we reckoned that many of these hotels were not at all suitable for accommodating a wheelchair user. In contrast, the information given about Paris hotels in the booklet *Où ferons-nous Étape?*, compiled by the APF, was consistent with the information we obtained by visiting. The list was not as extensive as the one you will find here.

The main obstructions in hotels are steps, small lifts, cramped bathrooms and narrow doors. The majority of hotels in Paris are in old buildings. The advantage of getting a ground floor bedroom (abbreviated to **GFB** in the listings below) with a minimal number of steps is that there is no worry of the lift breaking down or being a hassle to get into. In most cases we have included the dimensions of the lifts and some hotels or hostels have more than one lift, which is good insurance.

Nearly all the hotels we have listed have flat access from the reception to the lounge, bar, dining room and other public rooms. **Many small hotels in Paris don't have restaurants** and will only have breakfast rooms. Breakfast in bed is usually available and in some places the bedroom is the only place where you can have breakfast.

Public loos within the hotels were generally small and hidden away and we have only included details of the more accessible. Parking facilities are only mentioned if there is a car park exclusive to the hotel or very close by, as parked cars pack nearly all of Paris' roads, especially in the centre, and you certainly can't count on being able to park at the kerb right outside your hotel.

Very little has been mentioned about the spaciousness of hotel rooms, because nearly all of them provide enough space for a chair user to manoeuvre inside. If you come across one that is a bit cramped it is nearly always possible to re-arrange the furniture to create more space in the right places.

The hotels listed have only a few bedrooms which are suitable for a disabled visitor. To give yourself the best choice of good, accessible accommodation it is advisable to plan your trip in advance, make the necessary enquiries and book as early as you can. It is also a good idea to book for an off-peak period if you can manage it since a less crowded hotel can only improve your comfort.

If you are booking directly, ie not through a tour operator, we suggest you choose the hotel which you think best suits your requirements and then write a letter to the management, booking the period you want to stay and enclosing an international reply coupon. We have tried to cut the information down to the basic essentials relevant to most disabled people, but if we have missed out something you need to know or if the accuracy of certain information is particularly important for you we suggest that you include a number of clear and brief questions for the manager to answer. It may be useful to refer to the information in this guide, showing that you have some basic details which you want confirmed, together with some additional enquiries related to particular needs. Remember that the door widths and other details given won't apply to all the rooms in the hotel. Check when you book. You may need to know about door widths or handrails or other details or to know whether the hotel can cater for a special diet. *In making enquiries explain what you need and why, but try to concentrate only on the essentials and, above all, be brief.* People will only get confused if you ask too many questions or give them too much detail.

You may find the following format and translation useful:

Monsieur le directeur,
   I would be grateful if you would let me know the price for a stay of .... nights, from .... to ....
   I would like to reserve .... single rooms/double rooms/twin-bedded rooms with WC/bath/shower.

As I use a wheelchair/cannot climb steps/cannot walk very far, I would be grateful if you could also give me the following information:

- Is there parking space or a garage adjoining the hotel?
- Are there any steps at the entrance? If so, how many?
- How big is the lift? (Width of door:......cm, size of cabin:......cm by ......cm)
- Is there access without steps to bedrooms, toilet, bathroom, and dining room?
- My wheelchair is 70cm wide. Can I get to the WC and basin adjoining the bedroom?

I look forward to hearing from you, yours sincerely, etc.

Monsieur le directeur,

Je vous serais obligé de me communiquer vos tarifs pour un séjour de .... nuits, commençant le .... et se terminant le ....

Je voudrais réserver .... chambres à un lit/chambres à grand lit/ chambres à deux lits, avec WC/bain/douche.

Puisque je suis en fauteuil roulant/je ne peux pas monter les escaliers/ je ne peux pas marcher très loin, je vous serais obligé si vous pouviez me donner les renseignements suivants:

- Y a-t-il un parking ou des garages contigus à l'hôtel?
- Y a-t-il de marches à l'éntree? S'il en est ainsi, combien?
- Quelles sont les dimensions de l'ascenseur? (largeur de la porte....cm, et de la cabine:....cm par....cm)
- Y a-t-il accés à plain pied aux chambres, à la toilette, à la salle de bain et à la salle à manger?
- Mon fauteuil roulant est large de 70cm. Puis-je accéder aux toilettes et à la cuvette situées à côté de la chambre?

Je vous remercie en avance pour votre assistance. Veuillez agréer, monsieur, mes salutations distinguées.

Hostels

CISP Kellermann, 17 bd Kellermann, 75013 Paris. *Tel:* (1) 45.80.70.76 *Fax:* (1) 43.44.45.30.

The hostel has a large car park outside and flat entrance. It is a basic bed and breakfast hostel, catering mainly for groups. Most of the food comes pre-packed from machines. The snack bar on the ground floor has a split level and mainly fixed seating. There are no GFBs, although the lift (D78 W85 L120) goes to some adapted first floor bedrooms. Bedrooms (D80) have adequate space inside, but the two communal and shower complexes on this floor are poorly designed. The loo (D70+ no ST) is badly placed and one of the showers has two steps and a narrow door! The large amount of space would allow a chair user to take a shower using the flexible hose on

the bath for hair washing.
Price band A

      40%

CISP Maurice Ravel, 6 av Maurice Ravel, 75012 Paris. *Tel:* (1) 43.43.19.01 *Fax:* (1) 43.44.45.30.
It doesn't have a car park, but parking overnight is possible in the streets around. The entrance is ramped. The centre is accessible for exhibitions and meetings, but although listed with the wheelchair user symbol, the accommodation has poor access. It might be suitable for some disabled walkers as one group of rooms are reached via a small four person lift and the others via steps. There are no adapted loos or bathrooms and no GFBs.
Price band A/B

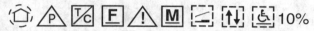 10%

FIAP "Jean Monnet", 30 rue Cabanis, 75014 Paris. *Tel:* (1) 45.89.89.15 *Fax:* (1) 45.81.63.91.
The hostel has no car parking of its own and the streets around are crowded. Because it has such good access we looked very thoroughly for parking, but the nearest we found was at least 200m away on boulevard St Jacques or boulevard Auguste under the métro. The nearest 'official' parking was some 500m away on the boulevard St Jacques. The hostel has been recently rebuilt and has an attractive entrance foyer with flat access. There are −3 steps to the café/bar bypassed by a lift on the right. Lifts (D79 W134 L134) go to the first floor restaurant, meeting rooms and bedrooms. Although there are no GFBs, **the hostel has eleven adapted bedrooms, each with four beds and about the most spacious loo (D70+ ST70+) and wheel-in shower en suite we've come across. The facilities for both chair users and disabled walkers are excellent** and the only problems are car parking and booking. At busy times it can be booked over six months in advance. A **wheelchair loo** (D70+ ST70+) is sited to the left of reception.
Price band B

Hotels inside the Périphérique

Hôtel Arcade**, 2 rue Cambronne, 75015 Paris. *Tel*: (1) 45.67.35.20 *Fax*: (1) 45.66.49.58.
Located close to the place Cambronne. Our surveying team stayed here.

Two doors have to be negotiated between the underground car park and lifts, so you may require assistance. There is flat access to the reception from the underground car park and main entrance. It is also flat to the restaurant and 'groups' breakfast room on the lower floor via a main lift. The bar can be reached by −3 steps or an outdoor ramp. The foyer by the bar has movable tables and chairs. Four lifts, including three main ones (D110 W125 L196) go to all floors. There are no GFBs or adapted rooms. The rooms (D78) have an identical pattern with twin beds and some have either one or two bunk beds that are mounted on the wall making the hotel quite cheap for three or four people staying sharing a room. The bathroom (D54) is cramped and access to the shower or loo is not easy.

However, between rooms 20 and 21 on each floor, by a bend in the corridor, there is an adequately accessible loo which is normally kept locked. The one we measured was on the sixth floor and was therefore between rooms 620 and 621. Basically all it has is a loo and a sink. Although the door (D65) opens inwards, there should be enough space (ST100+) for most chair users once it is shut again. The reason we have described all this in some detail is because if you can cope with this arrangement the hotel offers very good value for groups of four people and is well placed. Not all the staff know about these loos or their potential value to a disabled guest, but the keys are available to the duty staff if they know what to look for. What you may have trouble with is getting a room near one of these loos since their computerised booking-in system is a bit random and you'd need to get there early and negotiate. The public loos (D60 no ST) are in the basement on level −1.

Price band C

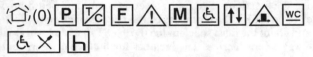

Hôtel des Arts**, 5 rue Tholozé, 75018 Paris. *Tel*: (1) 46.06.30.52 *Fax*: (1) 46.06.10.83.
The hotel has no parking facilities but there is some parking available in the street. The entrance is one step and access to the basement breakfast room is via a lift then +1−3 from reception. This lift (D70 W96 L81) goes to all six floors. There are four GFBs (D75) with bathrooms (D56 no ST) and no adapted bedrooms.

Price band B

Hôtel Frantour Berthier Brochant**, 163 bis av de Clichy, 75017 Paris. *Tel*: (1) 46.27.86.45 *Fax*: (1) 46.27.45.19.
The hotel has an underground car park with flat access to reception. The

L'Hôtel des Arts

entrance is up a steep ramp to a taxi drop-off point then flat into the hotel. Access to the restaurant, bar and all ground floor facilities is flat from reception. Six lifts (D77 W131 L118) serve all nine floors. It has no GFBs and surveyors were not able to see the two adapted rooms. Coach trips leave from the hotel. A low card telephone is available.
Price band C

Hôtel la Bourdonnais***, 111-113 av de Bourdonnais, 75007 Paris. *Tel*: (1) 47.05.45.42 *Fax*: (1) 45.55.75.54.
Public parking is 200m from the hotel, otherwise street parking is limited. The entrance is flat to reception. The breakfast room has a split level, although most of it is one step from reception. The restaurant, +1 with movable seating, is next door to the hotel. The lift (D69 W94 L107) goes to all six floors, but has +2 from reception. The ground floor is flat although it includes several (D66) doors. There are no GFBs. The largest bedroom (D75) on the other five floors has a bathroom (D57 ST73) with a standard bath.
Price band D

Hôtel Campanile Paris Bastille**, 9 rue du Chemin Vert, 75011 Paris. *Tel:* (1) 43.38.58.08 *Fax:* (1) 43.38.52.28.

On the corner of rue du Chemin Vert and rue St Sabin, the underground car park can be used with a 25Fr token from reception. There is flat access to the reception, lounge, restaurant, **wheelchair loo** (D70+ ST70+) and lifts. Two lifts (D88 W107 L143) serve all eight floors and the underground car park. No GFBs but the five adapted rooms (D78) have bathrooms (D88 no ST) with handrails for the bath.

Price band C

Hôtel Campanile Italie Gobelins**, 15 bis av d'Italie, 75013 Paris. *Tel*: (1) 45.84.95.95 *Fax*: (1) 45.70.73.06.

About 100m south of place d'Italie the hotel has a twelve-spacer underground car park. Access from the underground car park to reception is via a lift. Additional parking is available in a shopping centre across the road. The main entrance is ramped, but has a further +2 steps to reception. A single lift (D80 W106 L139) goes to all nine floors including the lower ground floor breakfast room which has movable tables and chairs. The two GFBs are both adapted as are two other bedrooms on the lower ground floor. All (D87) have bathrooms (D88 ST88) with handrails on the bath.

Price band B

Hôtel Climat de France**, 31 bd de Strasbourg, 75010 Paris. *Tel:* (1) 47.70.25.00.

Parking is possible in the Gare de l'Est about 500m away and suggested as there is none on the surrounding streets. The main entrance is flat through three heavy doors. Access is flat to reception and a cramped breakfast room. A single lift (D78 W148 L115) goes to all five floors. Two GFBs have their access restricted by several heavy firedoors. Two adapted bedrooms (D78) have a bathroom (D78 no ST) with standard shower, but no handrails. The rooms are small and somewhat cramped.

Price band C

Hôtel Climat de France**, 2 av du Professeur André Lemière, 75020 Paris. *Tel*: (1) 40.31.08.80 *Fax*: (1) 40.31.09.66.

Just off the large and busy place de la porte de Montreuil an underground car park has five wide spaces for disabled people and access is flat to reception from here via a lift (D76 W108 L140). It is −3 steps to reception using the main entrance, but flat through a side entrance on rue de Paris. Of

the six lifts one serves the underground car park, two (D80 W108 L140) serve the first floor restaurant and the other three (D110 W135 L155) go to all eighteen floors. Seven bedrooms (D87) have been adapted with bathrooms (D87 no ST) missing handrails. There is a well signposted public **wheelchair loo** (D70+ ST200+) on the first floor. Staff were extremely helpful when our survey team visited. Low telephones with induction loops are available. It's a big hotel so large distances may be involved.
Price band C

✗**Hôtel Corona***, 8 cité Bergère, 75009 Paris.** *Tel*: (1) 47.70.52.96 *Fax*: (1) 42.46.83.49.
Located in the cité Bergère Arcade, between "Quick" Hamburger restaurant and le Palais Theâtre, on the corner of rue Bergère and rue du Faubourg Montmartre. There are five parking spaces in front of the hotel, none of which are designated for disabled people. The entrance has one step to reception and from here it is flat to the lounge and breakfast room which has movable tables and chairs. There is no lift to other floors, but the one GFB (D85), +1 from reception, has a flat access bathroom (D90 ST130) which has a wheel-in shower although there is no seat.
Price band D

✗**Hôtel Dupleix****, 15 rue Dupleix, 75015 Paris. *Tel*: (1) 43.06.31.50 *Fax*: (1) 40.56.06.78.
Limited 'pay & display' parking is outside on the street. There is one step to the reception and then it is flat to the breakfast room and a lift (D58 W58 L109) goes to all six floors. Two GFBs have flat access; both (D67) have bathrooms (D75 no ST). Room 2 has a standard shower with a 13cm lip. The other room has a bath.
Price band B

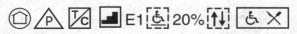

Hôtel Favart***, 5 rue de Marivaux, 75002 Paris. *Tel*: (1) 42.97.59.83 *Fax*: (1) 40.15.95.58.
The painter Francisco Goya lived here in 1824. Parking is difficult close to the hotel and an underground car park is over 500m away in the place de la Bourse with −16−3−3−7−1 steps to the lift. The hotel's main entrance has +1 and access is then flat to the lounge and breakfast room. The single lift

(D68 W135 L78) goes to all five floors. There are no GFBs and one so-called adapted bedroom (D69) on the first floor has a bathroom (D70 no ST).
Price band D

Grand Hôtel de France**, 102 bd de La Tour Maubourg, 75007 Paris. *Tel*: (1) 47.05.40.49 *Fax*: (1) 45.56.96.78.
There is minimal parking on the boulevard and the entrance has one step. Two lifts, one D79 W98 L140 and the other D60, serve all six floors including the basement breakfast room. Though no GFBs, there are two adapted rooms. We saw just one (D77) on the first floor which has a bathroom (D78 ST141) and a bath with handrails.
Price band B

Hôtel Frantour Paris Lyon**, 2 pl Louis Armand, 75012 Paris. *Tel*: (1) 43.44.84.84 *Fax*: 43.47.41.94.
Situated on a causeway northwest of the Gare de Lyon looking over boulevard Diderot. The hotel has no parking itself, but there is a short stay space for disabled people just outside the main entrance and a public car park opposite with flat access. The hotel entrance is flat. Access to the first floor restaurant and bar is flat from reception via one of three lifts (D78 W126 L145) which go to all seven floors. There are no GFBs, but each of the other floors has one adapted bedroom (D86) containing a bathroom (D89 no ST) and a bath without any handrails.
Price band C

Hôtel Ibis**, 77 rue de Bercy, 75012 Paris. *Tel*: (1) 43.42.91.91 *Fax*:(1) 43.42.34.79.
Rue de Bercy is very long and the hotel is just east of Palais Omnisports de Paris-Bercy, opposite rue Corbineau. There is an underground car park 50m southeast, but with no direct access to reception. The surveying team were unable to discover whether there was a lift to street level from the underground car park. The main entrance to the hotel is flat. There are +8 steps to the restaurant and bar from reception, avoidable by using a stair-lift, and a further five lifts (D90 W134 L150) go to all five floors. Despite having no GFBs, every other floor has an adapted bedroom (D91) with a bathroom (D76 ST85) including handrails for the bath. A public **wheelchair**

loo (D74 ST84) is in the men's on the restaurant/bar level.
Price band C

Hôtel Ibis**, 5 rue Caulaincourt, 75018 Paris. *Tel*: (1) 42.94.18.18 *Fax*: (1) 42.94.28.16.
Parking is available in a public underground car park next door with a small step and a lift (D80 W110 L140) to all levels. Access is flat through the main entrance to the ground floor bar and via a lift to the first floor restaurant. Three lifts (D82 W134 L140) serve all nine floors. There are no GFBs and surveyors were unable to see any of the eight adapted rooms. Standard first floor bedrooms (D77) involved +6 steps and bathrooms (D76 ST50). A public **wheelchair loo** (D76 ST50) is by the restaurant, but you will require a key from a waiter.
Price band C

Hôtel Latitudes St Germain**, 7-11 rue St Benoît, 75006 Paris. *Tel*: (1) 42.61.53.53 *Fax*:(1) 49.27.09.33.
Parking close to this hotel is extremely unlikely. The entrance has one step and there are no ground floor facilities. Two lifts (D80 W100 L140) go to all five floors. Four adapted rooms are on the third and fourth floors, but the surveying team were unable to see them and were told that special arrangements can be taken on board as long as the rooms are reserved well in advance. The Jazz Club in the basement has a **wheelchair loo** (D74 ST108) which is accessible throughout the day.
Price band E

Little Palace Hôtel***, 4 rue Salomon de Caus, 75003 Paris. *Tel*: (1) 42.72.08.15 *Fax*: (1) 42.72.45.81.
A car park 100m away has a steep ramp but there is some alternative metered parking in the street. The main entrance has +2 steps and it is flat to the restaurant and bar from reception. A single lift (D58 W72 L94) goes to all nine floors. There is one adapted GFB (D74) and its bathroom (D74 ST105) has a flat access shower.
Price band C/D

Hôtel Louis Blanc**, 232 rue du Faubourg St Martin, 75010 Paris. *Tel*: (1) 40.38.32.00 *Fax*: (1) 40.38.49.61.

On the corner of rue du Faubourg St Martin and rue Louis Blanc it has an underground car park with a lift up to reception. The main entrance has one step and once inside it is flat to the breakfast room. A single lift (D78 W120 L185) serves all five floors. Although no GFBs, there are three adapted bedrooms and the one (D86) seen by our survey team had a bathroom (D82 no ST). The bath had handrails. Public **wheelchair loo** (D70+ ST70+).
Price band C

 80%

Hôtel Madeleine Haussmann**, 10 rue Pasquier, 75008 Paris. *Tel*: (1) 42.65.90.11 *Fax*: (1) 47.42.89.76.
Off the junction with rue Chauveau-Lagarde there isn't any parking adjacent to the hotel, although some metered parking might be found in the place de la Madeleine. The entrance has one step and the basement restaurant is only reached by a flight of stairs. A single lift (D60 W83 L79) covers all other floors apart from the seventh. Two of the three GFBs are adapted (D75) with flat access to the shower in their bathrooms (D76 ST100+). There was no seat in the shower.
Price band C

Hôtel Mercure Paris Bercy***, 6 bd Vincent Auriol, 75013 Paris. *Tel*: (1) 45.82.48.00 *Fax*: (1) 45.82.19.16.
At the Seine end of the boulevard Vincent Auriol. The underground car park has twelve spaces which are allocated at the time of reservation. A lift provides flat access to all floors from the car park. As well as one step, the entrance has a door to avoid its revolving doors, but it was locked when we visited. It is flat to the restaurant with movable seating from reception and a ramp bypasses the +3 steps to the bar. Two lifts (D70 W107 L137) go to all seven floors. Each floor, except the ground, has an adapted room (D90) with a bathroom (D78 no ST).
Price band D

Hôtel Mercure Paris Montmartre***, 1-3 rue Caulaincourt, 75018 Paris. *Tel*: (1) 42.94.17.17 *Fax*: (1) 42.93.66.14.
Just south of Montmartre Cemetery a public underground car park is about 20m along the road with a lift (D80 W110 L140) and −1 step to street level. The hotel entrance is flat as is access to the ground floor bar and first floor restaurant via a lift. Three lifts (D81 W135 L143) go to all nine floors. There are eight adapted bedrooms, but no GFBs, and our survey team only saw one (D87) with bathroom (D86 ST154). The public **wheelchair loo** was

locked when we visited.
Price band D/E

Hôtel le Méridien Montparnasse***, 19 rue du Cdt René Mouchotte, 75014 Paris. *Tel*: (1) 44.36.44.36 *Fax*: (1) 44.36.49.00.

Next to the Gare Montparnasse the entrance is flat and the bar is +4 steps from reception. Of the eight lifts (D110 W200 L150) four go to floors one to thirteen and four to floors thirteen to twenty-five. There are no GFBs and our survey team were unable to see the three adapted rooms. A standard room (D90) had a bathroom (D68 no ST). A public **wheelchair loo** (D70+ ST70+) can be found on the ground floor.
Price band E

Hôtel Midi**, 114 av Daumesnil, 75012 Paris. *Tel*: (1) 43.07.72.03 *Fax*: (1) 43.43.21.75.
Located east of rue de Rambouillet the hotel has its own parking next door. The entrance has +1+2 steps with handrails and the dining area is −2 with handrails from reception. There is no lift. Of nine GFBs (D65) none are adapted and bathrooms (D88 no ST) are without handrails for the bath.
Price band C

Hôtel Montcalm***, 50 av Félix Faure, 75015 Paris. *Tel*: (1) 45.54.97.27 *Fax*: (1) 45.54.15.05.
Metered parking is on the street outside the hotel. The entrance has one step and there is flat access to the basement breakfast room via a lift. A single lift (D76 W116 L91) goes to all six floors. One of the three GFBs is −2−3 steps without handrails from reception. The one adapted room (D88) has a bathroom (D88 no ST). The bath has handrails.
Price band C/D

National Hôtel***, 224 rue du Faubourg St Denis, 75010 Paris. *Tel*: (1) 46.07.99.56 *Fax*: (1) 42.05.81.01.
Parking is available 500m away in the Gare du Nord underground car park (see Gare du Nord write-up). The hotel entrance has +2 steps and from reception it is flat to bar area and −16 with roped handrails to the breakfast room, although breakfast can be brought to the bedrooms on request. The two lifts (D65 W58 L85) cover all the upper floors. There are three GFBs,

but no adapted rooms. The GFBs (D67) have bathrooms (D58 no ST).
Price band C

Novotel Paris, Les Halles***, 8 pl Marguerite de Navarre, 75001 Paris. *Tel*: (1) 42.21.31.31 *Fax*: (1) 40.26.05.79.
The underground car park provides two spaces for disabled users and flat access to reception via a lift (D76 W99 L135). The main entrance is flat and a ramp bypasses +3 steps to the restaurant and +6 to the bar from reception. Three lifts (D80 W131 L149) go to all six floors. Although no GFBs, eight rooms have been adapted, but surveyors were not able to see these. Normal bedrooms were cramped. Public **wheelchair loo** (D70+ ST70+).
Price band E

Hôtel de l'Orchidée***, 65 rue de l'Ouest, 75014 Paris. *Tel*: (1) 43.22.70.50 *Fax*: (1) 42.79.97.46.
On the junction with rue du Château metered parking is crowded. The entrance has +2 steps and there is flat access to the breakfast room and bar from reception. A single lift (D78 W112 L105) serves all six floors. The lone GFB (D85) is adapted with a bathroom (D88 ST105).
Price band C

Hôtel de Passy Eiffel***, 10 rue de Passy, 75016 Paris. *Tel*: (1) 45.25.55.66 *Fax*: (1) 42.88.89.88.
Near place de Costa Rica, a multistorey car park is 50m away with large lifts to all floors. The hotel's main entrance has one step, and flat access to the breakfast room with movable tables and chairs from reception. The single lift (D63 W91 L82) goes to all five floors. There are four GFBs: two (D67) are −2 steps with a bathroom (D56 no ST); one (D57 en route) is +2 with a bathroom (D56 ST100); the other was not seen.
Price band D

Hôtel le Régent***, 61 rue Dauphine, 75006 Paris. *Tel*: (1) 46.34.59.80 *Fax*: (1) 40.51.05.07.
At the rue de Buci end of rue Dauphine, parking in the street is difficult and the pavements are narrow and uneven. The entrance has one step and the basement breakfast room is down a steep spiral staircase of −20 steps,

although breakfast can be served in the bedroom at no extra cost. A single lift only serves floors one to six and the first floor is +22. There is one adapted GFB (D86) with a bathroom (D85 no ST).
Price band E

Résidence Hôtelière le Vert Galant, 41 rue de Croulebarbe, 75013 Paris. *Tel*:(1) 43.31.63.05.
Situated southeast of square René Le Gall, metered parking is available in rue de Croulebarbe and adjacent streets. The entrance has +1+1 steps and access to the adjoining restaurant and bar is +1 from the street. All the bedrooms are on the ground floor via +1+1. They have D64 and the bathrooms are small, with no space for ST.
Price band C

Résidence Monceau***, 85 rue du Rocher, 75008 Paris. *Tel*: (1) 45.22.75.11 *Fax*: (1) 45.22.30.88.
At the Villiers métro end, metered parking is available on rue du Rocher. The entrance has one step and access to breakfast room is flat from reception. A single lift (D82 W109 L139) goes to all three floors. The three GFBs (D87) have bathrooms (D76 no ST) without handrails.
Price band D

✳**Timhotel le Louvre****, 4 rue Croix-des-Petits-Champs, 75001 Paris. *Tel*: (1) 42.60.34.86 *Fax*: (1) 42.60.10.39.
Just off rue St Honoré there is metered parking on the road outside the hotel. The entrance has one step and it is flat to the restaurant with movable chairs from reception. A single lift (D66 W90 L80) goes to all six floors. Of two GFBs, one (D73) is adapted with a bathroom (D77 no ST).
Price band C

Timhotel Le Maine**, 146 av du Maine, 75014 Paris. *Tel*: (1) 43.35.57.60 *Fax*: (1) 40.47.01.49.
On the corner of passage de la Tour de Vanves, parking available approximately 400m down the road. The entrance has one step and access is flat to the breakfast room and lounge from reception. One lift (D80 W108 L138) serves the first six floors and another (D68 W86 L96) goes to all seven. All

three GFBs (D76) are adapted. Their bathrooms (D78 ST90) have a bath with handrails.
Price band C

Hôtel des Tuileries***, 10 rue St Hyacinthe, 75001 Paris. *Tel*: (1) 42.61.04.17 *Fax*: (1) 49.27.91.56.
Parking is available in the multistorey car park with ramped access on place du Marché St Honoré about 200m from the hotel. The entrance is flat as is access to the breakfast room from reception. One lift (D70 W90 L80) goes to all four floors. There are no adapted rooms. Of the three GFBs (D60), it is +1+1 steps to two and +5 to the bed itself in the other. All have bathrooms (D60 no ST) without handrails.
Price band D/E

Hôtel Urbis Lafayette**, 122 rue La Fayette, 75010 Paris. *Tel*: (1) 45.23.27.27 *Fax*: (1) 42.46.73.79.
By place Franz Liszt, no parking is available on rue La Fayette itself, although there is metered parking on surrounding roads. Two multistorey car parks can be found adjacent to the St Vincent de Paul church. It is flat into the hotel and to the bar and dining area, both with movable tables and chairs. The garden at the back is −1 step. The lift (D80 W110 L210) serves to all seven floors. Three GFBs (D83) have been adapted with bathrooms (D130 ST96). The bath has handrails.
Price band B

Hôtel Urbis Jemmapes Louis Blanc**, 12 rue Louis Blanc, 75010 Paris. *Tel*: (1) 42.01.21.21 *Fax*: (1) 42.08.21.40.
On the east bank of the St Martin canal, metered parking is on the busy street. The entrance is flat and access to the breakfast room with movable tables and chairs is flat from reception. A lift (D81 W104 L129) goes to the first seven floors and there are stairs to the eighth. There are no GFBs, but our survey team saw one (D77) of the two adapted rooms which had a bathroom (D79 no ST) with handrails for the bath. A public **wheelchair loo** is on the ground floor.
Price band B

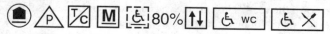

Hôtel Urbis Maine-Montparnasse**, 158-160 rue du Château, 75014 Paris. *Tel*: (1) 43.22.00.09 *Fax*: (1) 43.20.21.78.

At the avenue du Maine end of rue du Château there is metered parking in front of the hotel. The entrance has one step and it is flat to the breakfast room and bar from reception. A lift (D70 W100 L75) covers all the floors. Two rooms were adapted, but the surveying team was unable to see them. The standard bedroom (D66) had a bathroom (D57 no ST) without handrails.

Price band B

Hôtel Urbis**, 177 rue de Tolbiac, 75013 Paris. *Tel*: (1) 45.80.16.60 *Fax*: (1) 45.80.95.80.

On the corner of rue de Tolbiac and passage Foubert parking is available in surrounding streets. The main entrance has −4 steps, but it is flat from passage Foubert. Flat access is also possible via a lift from reception to the basement breakfast room. One lift (D82 W140 L160) goes to all the floors. The two GFBs are both adapted as is one first floor room. All (D80) have a bathroom (D80 ST123). A public **wheelchair loo** (D70+ ST70+).

Price band C

Hotels outside the Périphérique

Hôtel Balladins*, 9 rue de l'Université, 93167 Noisy-le-Grand. *Tel*: (1) 45.92.24.55 *Fax*: (1) 43.03.39.02.

Just north of the A4 it has a seven space car park with one space allocated for disabled people. Ramped access from rue de l'Université bypasses the +1+4 steps and there is flat access to the restaurant with movable tables and chairs from reception. The lift (D79 W108 L142) goes to all four floors. We saw one of the three adapted bedrooms (D79) and its bathroom (D81 no ST) has a flat access shower with seat. A **wheelchair loo** (D70+ ST70+) is in the foyer.

Price band A

Hôtel Campanile**, 1 allée Edmé l'Heureux, 94340 Joinville-le-Pont. *Tel*: (1) 48.89.89.99 *Fax*: (1) 48.89.76.49.

To the west of the Bois de Vincennes in the quartier des Canadiens this hotel has an underground car park with −2−8−8 steps to reception. The main entrance has one step and from reception it is flat to the restaurant

Hotels outside the Périphérique

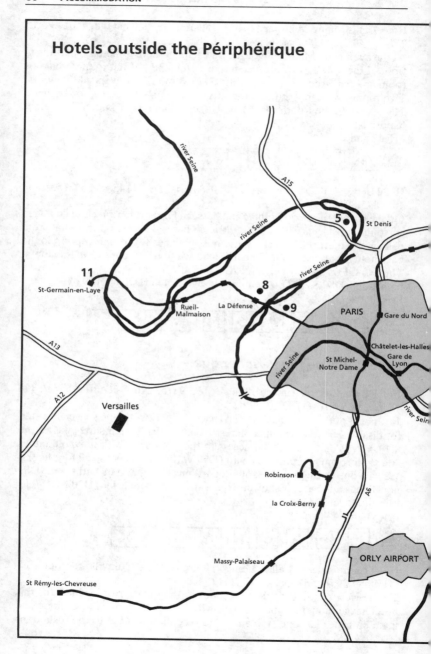

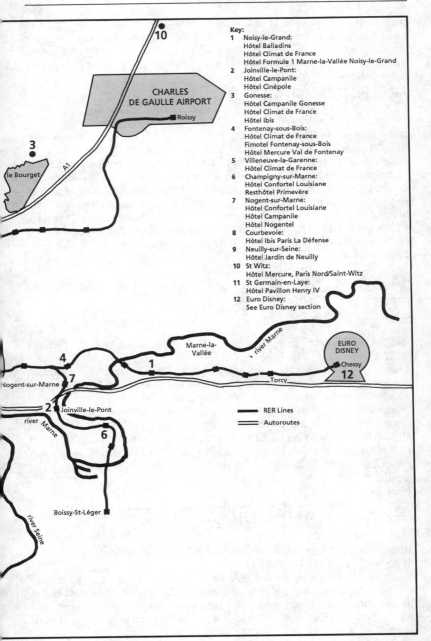

Key:
1 Noisy-le-Grand:
   Hôtel Balladins
   Hôtel Climat de France
   Hôtel Formule 1 Marne-la-Vallée Noisy-le-Grand
2 Joinville-le-Pont:
   Hôtel Campanile
   Hôtel Cinépole
3 Gonesse:
   Hôtel Campanile Gonesse
   Hôtel Climat de France
   Hôtel Ibis
4 Fontenay-sous-Bois:
   Hôtel Climat de France
   Fimotel Fontenay-sous-Bois
   Hôtel Mercure Val de Fontenay
5 Villeneuve-la-Garenne:
   Hôtel Climat de France
6 Champigny-sur-Marne:
   Hôtel Confortel Louisiane
   Resthôtel Primevère
7 Nogent-sur-Marne:
   Hôtel Confortel Louisiane
   Hôtel Campanile
   Hôtel Nogentel
8 Courbevoie:
   Hôtel Ibis Paris La Défense
9 Neuilly-sur-Seine:
   Hôtel Jardin de Neuilly
10 St Witz:
   Hôtel Mercure, Paris Nord/Saint-Witz
11 St Germain-en-Laye:
   Hôtel Pavillon Henry IV
12 Euro Disney:
   See Euro Disney section

CHARLES DE GAULLE AIRPORT
Roissy
le Bourget
A1

Marne-la-Vallée
river Marne
EURO DISNEY
Chessy
Torcy
Nogent-sur-Marne
Joinville-le-Pont
river Marne
Boissy-St-Léger
river Seine

━━━ RER Lines
═══ Autoroutes

with movable tables and chairs. A single lift (D110 W189 L137) goes to all eight floors. There are no GFBs and the survey team was unable to measure the adapted bedroom on each floor which is said to have a large bathroom and handrails. A public **wheelchair loo** (D70+ ST70+).
Price band B

Hôtel Campanile Gonesse**, ZAC de la Grande Couture, 95500 Gonesse. *Tel*: (1) 39.85.79.99 *Fax*: (1) 39.85.22.31.
Situated in an industrial estate on the outskirts of Gonesse it is badly signposted. The ground level car park outside the hotel has two spaces for disabled people. The entrance is ramped and it is flat to the dining area from reception. The first floor is only accessible up a spiral staircase with handrails. At least five GFBs are in a separate building across a car park which has flat access. Our survey team saw one of the two adapted rooms (D76) which has a bathroom (D76 ST100) without handrails.
Price band A

Hôtel Campanile**, quai du Port, 94130 Nogent-sur-Marne. *Tel*: (1) 48.72.51.98 *Fax*: (1) 48.72.05.09.
11km east of Paris off the river Marne by the Pont-de-Nogent. Surveyors did not see the parking, but were told that the hotel had 'closed' parking with two spaces allocated for disabled guests at an extra charge of 25Fr. The entrance is ramped to bypass +8 steps and from reception it is flat to the restaurant with movable tables and chairs. The lift (D79 W109 L136) covers all nine floors. There are no GFBs and the four adapted bedrooms on floors two to five need to be reserved in advance. The one (D85) seen has a bathroom (D90 ST83) with handrails. Public **wheelchair loos** are on the ground floor.
Price band B

Hôtel Cinépole**, 8 av des Platanes, 94340 Joinville-le-Pont. *Tel*: (1) 48.89.99.77 *Fax*: (1) 48.89.43.92.
South of the A4, to the east of Bois de Vincennes, it has an underground car park accessible via lift. The entrance is flat and from here it is flat to the breakfast room which is also used for evening snacks and has movable tables and chairs. Access to the patio is an awkward

+1−2 steps. One lift (D76 W105 L141) covers all thirteen floors. The two GFBs (D90) have a bathroom (D89 no ST) with a standing shower.
Price band A

Hôtel Climat de France**, 18 av Rabelais, 94120 Fontenay-sous-Bois. *Tel*: (1) 46.76.21.98 *Fax*:(1) 48.76.25.96.
Located near the France Telecom building on a steep hill there is a car park next to the hotel. The entrance is flat, as is access from reception to the restaurant and bar with movable tables and chairs. Although there is no lift, the hotel has twenty-one GFBs. One of the two adapted bedrooms (D80) was surveyed and had a bathroom (D83 ST100+) without handrails.
Price band B

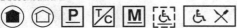

Hôtel Climat de France, rue d'Aulnay (RN 370), 95500 Gonesse. *Tel*: (1) 39.87.42.44 *Fax*: (1) 39.85.00.91.
Poorly signposted, it is on the right of the N370 heading from Gonesse to Villiers-le-Bel. The ground level car park has an allocated space for a disabled visitor. The hotel's entrance is flat and it is also flat from reception to the restuarant. There is no lift and of nineteen GFBs, three (D77) have been adapted with a bathroom (D77 ST100+).
Price band A

Hôtel Climat de France**, 5 rue du Ballon, ZI les Richardets, 93160 Noisy-le-Grand.
Tel: (1) 43.05.22.99.
About 7km east of the Bois de Vincennes it has ample car parking and a space for disabled people. It is +1 to the reception and restaurant with movable tables and chairs. There are no lifts as the twenty-five GFBs are +1 in separate buildings. Two rooms (D83) are adapted and have bathrooms (D78 no ST) with handrails for the bath. Our surveyors were told that a new building with a **wheelchair loo** would open in September 1992.
Price band B

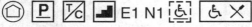

Hôtel Climat de France, bd Charles de Gaulle, 92390 Villeneuve-la-Garenne. *Tel*: (1) 47.99.56.00 *Fax*: (1) 47.99.88.66.
9km north of Paris, west of the Ile-St-Denis, the ground level parking has one space for disabled visitors. The dining area and reception are +1.

Again, bedrooms are in a separate block which is flat from the car park. They have at least twenty GFBs, two of which are adapted (D77) and have bathrooms (D78 ST80) with handrails.
Price band B

Hôtel Confortel Louisiane**, ZAC du Plateau, rue Alexandre Fourny, 94500 Champigny-sur-Marne. *Tel*: (1) 49.83.01.42 *Fax*: (1) 49.83.98.69.
15km east of Paris the hotel is badly signposted and has a large car park with two spaces designated for disabled people. It is flat via a ramp to reception and the restaurant has movable tables and chairs. Although there is no bar, drinks are available on request. It has no lift. None of the nine GFBs (D77) are adapted, there are firedoors en route and the bathrooms (D58 no ST) are cramped. A **wheelchair loo** is available in the hotel.
Price band B

Hôtel Confortel Louisiane**, rue de Nazare, ZAC du Port, 94130 Nogent-sur-Marne. *Tel*: (1) 43.24.32.32 *Fax*: (1) 43.24.02.08.
Located on the waterfront it apparently offers an underground car park accessible by lift, but it was under repair and not seen by the survey team. A ramp allows flat access to reception, bar and the restaurant with movable tables and chairs. A lift (D79 W106 L137) goes to all six floors. Floors one to five have an adapted room and our surveyors saw room 108 (D86) which has a bathroom (D89 ST95) with handrails and a flat access shower. A **wheelchair loo** (D70+ ST70+) is available.
Price band B

Fimotel Fontenay-sous-Bois**, 2-4 av du Val-de-Fontenay, 94120 Fontenay-sous-Bois. *Tel*: (1) 48.76.67.71 *Fax:* (1) 43.94.08.87.
Just off the A86, 10km east of Paris. It doesn't have a car park of its own, but a free municipal underground car park is −18 steps with handrails from the back of the hotel. The main entrance to the hotel is flat and access to the restaurant with movable tables and chairs and bar is flat too. The lift (D80 W109 L140) goes to an adapted room on each of the six floors. Unfortunately our surveyors were not able to see them. A public **wheelchair loo** can be found in the foyer to the left of reception by the lifts, although it was totally blocked with equipment when we visited.
Price band B

Hôtel Formule 1, Noisy-le-Grand*, bd du Rû-de-Nesle, 93160 Noisy-le-Grand, Marne-la-Vallée. *Tel:* (1) 43.04.10.22.
This hotel chain is not staffed in the normal way and is geared to 'automated' convenience. Apart from the times when the reception is open, there are no staff there at all, and no courtesy phone for calling anybody.

The hotel is just off the Champs exit of the A4 and 100m from RER Line A station Noisy-Champs, which is only accessible by escalator. If driving, turn left over the motorway bridge, go about 800m to a roundabout and the hotel is off to the right on the second exit. Parking is available outside, but it is on a slope. It is flat to reception and the small breakfast area; there is no restaurant or bar. The reception is open 06.30-10.00 and 17.00-22.00. If reception is shut on arrival, place your credit card in the machine and you can choose to be spoken to in French or English; however the keyboard is at 135cm and angled upwards. If you have pre-booked using your credit card, the screen will tell you your room number and the six digit code which you punch in to a keyboard by the door to enter the hotel and then another one by your room. **You should make a record of the number, and you should certainly not leave the hotel without it, as getting back in may prove difficult.** Of forty GFBs, three are adapted, but you must ring in advance to book one of these. Similarly, booking is essential if you want a standard ground floor room, as there is no lift to the first floor and the computer may allocate you a room on either floor because it doesn't ask access questions! The standard bedrooms are basic with a double bed, single bunk and washbasin, and are not big enough for a wheelchair because the beds are fixed. The adapted rooms have simply had their beds rotated so that the door and gap to get in are over 80cm. There is a loo (D70+ ST100+) and shower combined, with a sliding door. There is no seat of any kind available throughout the entire building to put in the shower.
Price band A

Hôtel Ibis Paris La Défense**, 4 bd de Neuilly, 92400 Courbevoie. *Tel*: (1) 47.78.15.60 *Fax*: (1) 47.78.94.16.
Located near La Défense, parking is available in the Des Saisons car park behind the hotel which is entered by −1−5 steps and a lift goes to all levels. The hotel entrance is flat to reception and the split-level bar. One of the three lifts (D75) which go to all fourteen floors provides flat access to the first floor restaurant. There are no GFBs, and the thirteen adapted (D77) rooms, one on each of the other floors, have bathrooms (D77 ST143).
Price band C

Hôtel Ibis**, RN2, Patte d'Oie de Gonesse 95500. *Tel*: (1) 39.87.22.22 *Fax*: (1) 39.87.03.93.

14km out of Paris off the N17, the ground level car park has two spaces for disabled visitors. The entrance is ramped and from reception it is flat to the breakfast room. A lift (D80 W110 L140) goes to all three floors. The two GFBs are adapted (D77) and have bathrooms (D77 no ST) with handrails for the bath.

Price band B

Hôtel Jardin de Neuilly**, 5 rue Paul Déroulède, 92200 Neuilly-sur-Seine. *Tel*: (1) 46.24.51.62 *Fax*: (1) 46.37.14.60.

Between the north side of the Bois de Boulogne and avenue Charles de Gaulle, it has no hotel parking of its own. The entrance has +1+9 steps with handrails. It doesn't have a restaurant or bar. The single lift (D62 W96 L77) serves all five floors. The one GFB is +3. The four adapted rooms (D69) are on the first and second floors and the one we saw has a bathroom (D75 no ST) with a low level bath only 36cm high.

Price band C

Hôtel Mercure Val de Fontenay***, av des Olympiades, 94120 Fontenay-sous-Bois. *Tel*: (1) 49.74.88.88 *Fax*: (1) 43.94.17.73.

Two spaces are designated for disabled guests in front of the hotel. Access is flat to the reception and bar. A ramp bypasses the +3 steps to the split-level restaurant. The garden patio is −1 from reception. Two lifts (D80 W100 L135) go to all eight floors. There are no GFBs. We saw one, room 412 (D86), of the four adapted bedrooms which has a bathroom (D80 ST70+) but with no handrails on the bath. A public unisex **wheelchair loo** (D70+ ST70+) is in the foyer area by the telephones.

Price band D/E

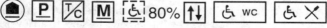

Hôtel Mercure, Paris Nord/Saint Witz, rue Jean Moulin, 95470 Saint Witz. *Tel*: (1) 34.68.28.28 *Fax*: (1) 34.68.22.81.

East of junction 7 on the A1, it has ground level parking with two spaces for disabled visitors. The entrance is flat, but the restaurant is +3 steps without handrails from reception. The outside swimming pool is −2 from reception or via a very steep cobbled ramp from the car park. Single lift (D77 W134 L122) goes to all three floors. Of twenty-seven GFBs two are adapted

(D80) and their bathrooms (D80 no ST) with standard baths.
Price band C

 N3

Hôtel Nogentel***, 8 rue du Port, 94130 Nogent-sur-Marne. *Tel*: (1) 48.72.70.00 *Fax*: (1) 48.72.86.19.
Situated on the waterfront, ground level parking is available in front of the hotel. The entrance has one step and from here it is flat via lift to the third floor restaurant and second floor grill which both have movable tables and chairs. The two lifts (D70 W107 L142) go to all seven floors. There are no GFBs and the two adapted rooms (D76) have bathrooms (D89 no ST). One adapted room has handrails on the bath (No 416), the other (No 412) did not.
Price band D

 E1

Hôtel Pavillon Henry IV****, 21 rue Thiers, 78100 St-Germain-en-Laye. *Tel*: (1) 34.51.62.62 *Fax*: (1) 39.73.93.73.
At the southeastern end of the château gardens, parking is available at the front of the hotel. The entrance has a flat gravel path and there is flat access to the restaurant and patio from reception with a stunning view of Paris in the distance. Two lifts (D79 W108 L145) cover all three floors. There are no GFBs or adapted bedrooms. The standard bedrooms (D76) have bathrooms (D56 no ST).
Price band E

 (0)

Resthôtel Primevère**, 201 rue Marcel Paul, ZA des Grands Godets "Le Plateau", 94500 Champigny-sur-Marne. *Tel*: (1) 47.06.46.47 *Fax*: (1) 47.06.81.28.
Parking is available in the hotel ground level car park with one space for disabled visitors. Access is flat through the entrance to the restaurant and bar with movable tables and chairs. The hotel doesn't have a lift and of six GFBs one is adapted but we were not allowed to see it. There is a public **wheelchair loo**, but this also was not seen by the surveying team.
Price band A

 wc

CAMPING

Camping can provide a relatively carefree and inexpensive way of finding holiday accommodation and your visit to Paris might be part of a more extensive holiday. Various companies can offer pre-pitched and well-equipped tents on good sites and we mention some of these.

To be honest we do not recommend the central Paris site in the bois de Boulogne. In our experience it's overcrowded, noisy, not particularly pleasant and the facilities for people with disabilities are minimal. The site with the best facilities is camp Davy Crocket which is attached to the EuroDisney resort. This is more expensive than other sites, but it offers a great deal more. Also worth considering are the sites at Champigny-sur-Marne, Choisy-le-Roi and Maisons-Laffitte. Unfortunately we only managed to visit a few of the sites during our survey, as it took a long time to get around them. Consequently much of the information in this particular section depends on what we have been told either by the companies running package camping holidays or by the site organisers.

One encouraging thing we have found is that companies are increasingly holding basic access data for customer information about their sites. The kind of information is fairly basic, but nonetheless useful. Eurocamp, for example, were able to highlight the differences between their three sites in the area in such a way as to indicate the possible problems for campers with disabilities.

We have listed three sites, about which we received details, from **La Fédération Française de Camping et de Caravaning**.

They are described as having basic facilities in the Paris region, although they're not particularly close to Paris itself:

La Ferte Vidame, 28340 Eure-et-Loir, is 30km southwest of Dreux. *Tel:* 37.37.64.00. It's a two star site on an area of 1 hectare.

Camp Municipal du Moulin d'Orgissel, 60120 Breteuil, is some 28km northwest of Clermont in Oise. This small two star site covers a quarter of a hectare.

Camp Municipal de Pierre le Sault, 77167 Bagneaux-sur-Loing, is some 40km south of Melun. *Tel:* 01.04.31.10. A large two star site of 3 hectares.

In 1985 new regulations were introduced about the facilities that have to be provided for visitors with disabilities. These include, in particular, a minimum number of accessible loo and washroom cubicles; the proportion is one per hundred camping places for a two star site. In their official sites listing, those satisfying the minimum requirements for these facilities are listed as meeting Classé Norms 1985. The Fédération publish an annual comprehensive listing for France called *Guide Officiel Camping Caravaning*, but it's not particularly user-friendly and the less comprehensive *Michelin* camping guide may prove easier to use.

Eurocamp Travel, Canute Ct, Toft Rd, Knutsford, Cheshire WA16 0NL. *Tel:* (0565) 633844. They have tents pitched on a considerable number of sites throughout Europe. Here are three sites in the Paris area for which they hold reasonably detailed access information:

Camping Domaine d'Inchelin, St-Illiers-la-Ville. There are no special facilities here and the loo and washblocks involve a step. The camping area is generally flat, there is flat access to the bar and the roads are tarmac.

Camping La Croix du Vieux Pont, Berny-Rivière. The camp area is flat with tarmac roads. The washroom blocks are ramped with a special washing cubicle for a chair user. There would be access problems to the bar and the loo in the restaurant is described as inaccessible to wheelchair users.

Camping Près de la Fontaine, Govaix. The site is flat. Facilities include a washblock with toilets and other facilities specifically designed for people with disabilities. The bar and restaurant are also easily accessible for wheelchairs. Other things being equal, this is the site that Eurocamp would recommend out of the three.

French Country Camping, 126 Hempstead Rd, Kings Langley, Hereford WD4 8AL. *Tel:* (0923) 261311 or 264068. They are a daughter company of Eurocamp. They use two sites in the Paris area, both of which comply with minimum French standards in respect of amenities for disabled visitors. The company say that neither is particularly suitable, although both are on firm level ground and have adapted toilets with unstepped access. The sites are:

Camping des Granges, 77320 La Ferté Gaucher. *Tel:* (1) 64.04.00.91.
Parc de Séjour de l'Etang, 10 chemin des Bellevues, 95690 Nesles-la-Vallée. *Tel:* (1) 34.70.69.34.

Sunsites, Canute Ct, Toft Rd, Knutsford, Cheshire WA16 ONL. *Tel:* (0565) 625555 or 625549. Here is one of their two sites near Paris:

Prés de la Fontaine, Provins, southeast of Paris, 78600 Maisons-Laffitte, *Tel:* (1) 39.12.21.91. It is on the banks of the Seine in an attractive and leafy suburb of Paris about 22km north of Versailles. The four star site covers 6.5 hectares and is flat with tarmac roads. There's one washroom block which has a shower and loo designed for chair users. It's also not far from some of the accessible RER stations on Line A which goes to St-Germain-en-Laye (see the *Getting around in Paris* chapter).

Here are the other sites we managed to survey:

Camping Paris Est le Tremblay, 80290 Champigny-sur-Marne. *Tel:* (1) 43.97.43.97. This three star site is only 14km outside Paris, towards Marne-la-Vallée. It is huge, occupying some 8 hectares. To find the site, follow the

Pont de Joinville exit off the A4, and you'll find that there are signposts all the way. Reception is +6+4 steps across some gravel. The area is flat with tarmac roads leading to rough paths with pitches all around. There are adapted facilities for people with disabilities.

Camping Parc des Sports de Choisy, 94600 Choisy-le-Roi. *Tel:* (1) 48.90.92.30. Take the D38 off the N186, and this 7.5 hectare three star site is on your left. Although not well signposted, it's attached to the Centre International de Séjour in the Parc des Sports making it a big complex. There are +4 steps to reception, but apart from this the facilities are excellent. There are tarmac roads throughout and the washblock has **wheelchair loos** (D70+ ST70+) and large flat access showers. Other facilities are in the Auberge de Jeunesse next door, but this is not particularly accessible; it has +3+5 steps at the entrance, although the management say that they have a ramp which would have to be quite steep. There's a further +3 to the restaurant in the Auberge.

Camp Davy Crockett, Euro Disney. This is about 2km from the theme park. There are nearly 100 camping emplacements, each with a picnic table and barbeque. Some of the site seems to be more designed with the motor caravan in mind than for campers with tents, but we were assured that the latter is possible. The site is big and well wooded, with tarmac roads and a regular bus to the EuroDisney resort. The facilities for washing, access to washing machines and for wheelchair loos are all excellent. There are four **wheelchair loos** (two in the men's and two in the women's), similarly four showers and four large washrooms, all for disabled guests (D120+).

The camp has a large number of cabins each of which has +3 steps for access with a right angle bend, making it difficult for a chair user. Inside they are reasonably spacious, except that the one we saw had a 55cm door to get into the loo/washbasin area. None of the cabins currently had adaptations for disabled guests.

There is a small 'village' on site with a farm full of animals, which could be a lot of fun for children, as well as a shop and a delightful indoor heated swimming pool. Access into the pool is down shallow gentle steps, which would be helpful to many people with disabilities. The village has occasional ramps to bypass single steps, but they are not always available. The village restaurant has **wheelchair loos** (D70+ ST70+) as has the pool. The only problem with Davy Crocket is that it's relatively expensive compared with other sites. It would be much cheaper than staying in a hotel, assuming that you already have the use of camping gear and the facilities are certainly much better than you would generally encounter at other camp sites.

You can book yourself into Davy Crockett through a number of agencies, including the **Camping and Caravanning Club**, Greenfields House, Westwood Way, Coventry CV4 8JH. *Tel:* (0203) 422024 *Fax:* (0203) 694886 for the club's Carefree booking service.

Getting around in Paris

Getting around in Paris presents a few problems, similar to those in other big cities. Much depends on whether you are able to use public transport or taxis, or on whether you have brought your own transport.

Paris has its own public transport authority, the **RATP** (Réseau Autonome du Transport Parisien). They are responsible for virtually everything in the city, including the métro (underground), the RER (suburban express trains) and the buses; even the Montmartre funicular comes under their authority. One advantage of this is a common ticketing system and the availability of short term passes which entitle you to use any part of the system.

Almost the only wheelchair friendly system is the **RER** (Réseau Express Régional) railway, and those limited sections of it which are accessible to chair users still present some slight difficulties. Full details are given later, but access to the platforms is via service lifts at selected stations and one step, of somewhat variable height, will get you into the carriage.

Paris has an active development programme for its public transport. A wheelchair accessible tramway is operating just to the northeast. This links St Denis with la Courneuve, Drancy and Bobigny. A longer tramway is planned to open in 1996 running close to the Seine, where it loops south on the west side of the city. The route will go from la Défense following the rive gauche via St Cloud, Sèvres and ending initially at Issy-Plaine. A later development will take it inside the boulevard Périphérique on the south side of the city. An exciting and extensive development across the centre of Paris called the Météor is also due to open in 1996. It should provide a wheelchair accessible train link from Tolbiac in the southeast through the Gare de Lyon and Châtelet-les-Halles to the Madeleine. There are ambitious plans through to 2015 to improve and extend the train network.

The other possibility, if you haven't brought your own transport, is to use taxis or a wheelchair-accessible minibus, of which there are just a few.

If you can face the prospect of driving in Paris and can bring your own car, this will give you maximum flexibility and the possibility of touring in other parts of France as well. (See driving section in this chapter.)

It is important to consider where you stay in relation to getting around. It may be worth choosing hotels within walking or wheeling distance of the main sights, which is why we have included a location map in the hotels section. An alternative option which could cut the cost of your stay is to use a cheaper hotel just outside Paris which has adapted rooms and is near an accessible RER station. Then you can go in to Châtelet-les-Halles, St Michel, the Gare du Nord, Gare de Lyon or la Défense, all of which are fully accessible – provided the lifts work! You can then do your sightseeing from there.

ADVICE FOR PEDESTRIANS

Even if you manage to find a hotel in the very centre of Paris or if the RER station is right next to where you want to go, you'll still have to cross some roads. From our experience, including a few lucky escapes, there are some things of which you should be aware.

Most obviously, when crossing the road, **look left** first. Anyone from a left-driving country will find that they instinctively look right and then begin to cross. This is particularly important if someone is being pushed in a chair because the chair user is the first to be exposed to the danger from an oncoming vehicle.

On a similar note it is vital to appreciate that *the markings on the road that look like zebra-crossings don't give priority to pedestrians as they do in Britain*. If you step onto them, traffic won't stop but will expect **you** to jump! The markings are often at places where you are supposed to wait for the accompanying traffic lights to stop the traffic. *If in doubt give way to traffic*.

At traffic lights, *when the lights are green for a particular direction, both cars and pedestrians have priority in that direction*. This means that pedestrians have priority over traffic turning either right or left, which is different from what people are used to in Britain.

Note also that there are relatively few dropped kerbs in Paris.

TAXIS AND ADAPTED MINIBUSES

There are plenty of taxis in Paris and there are ranks at most major road junctions and near major sights. You are more likely to get one at a rank than by hailing them in the street.

The taxis are ordinary cars and reasonably easy to get into if you can transfer to a seat. Most of them are four-seaters and hence can only carry three passengers. Our experience of using them was somewhat mixed. Sometimes there was no problem, at other times we met a distinct reluctance to carrying a wheelchair user. Drivers made excuses and some said they wouldn't take anyone in the front seat for safety reasons. When there's a language problem as well it is more difficult to be insistent. Some drivers charged extra for carrying the chair as luggage.

Our survey teams normally consisted of two able-bodied people and one chair user, and on a couple of occasions they very nearly gave up trying to get a taxi after being turned down several times. However, persistence paid off and our experience was that you will always get one in the end. We also met some friendly and helpful drivers who were somewhat disgusted with their colleagues.

Our surveyors who were disabled walkers had no problems, although they sometimes met a reluctance to go outside the central area. Prices are in line with what you would expect and are not excessive, particularly if shared between two or three people.

Most of the drivers do not speak English, so you may have to write down where you want to go. If you've got a street plan and are obviously following the route yourself, you're less likely to be 'taken for a ride'.

Taxi charges are based on the time of day and whether you are inside or outside the boulevard Périphérique. The tariff basis will show on the meter display in the taxi and there are three categories, **a**, **b** and **c**. These apply as follows:

— **a**; from 06.30 to 20.00 inside the Périphérique, except on Sundays.
— **b**; from 20.00 to 06.30 inside the Périphérique on weekdays, and all day on Sundays.
— **c**; at all times outside the Périphérique.

As with taxis everywhere, there is a surcharge for extra luggage, and a 10% tip is normal. The normal basis for charges if you order one by telephone is that you pay for it to get to you as well as for your journey. This will apply to the specialised services which we list below.

An alternative to a standard taxi is to use a specially adapted vehicle suitable for a chair user, who can then stay in their chair.

There are at least six companies operating and these are:

— **Aihrop**, 4 passage Saint-Antoine, BP 164, 92504 Rueil-Malmaison. *Tel:* (1) 47.51.50.50 *Fax:* (1) 47.51.14.76. This is the largest organisation offering specialised transport. They say that they have two vehicles which can be used to get to and from the airport – which could be extremely useful – but as far as we can tell, they do not have small vehicles available for occasional taxi-type hire. They operate a number of wheelchair-accessible bus services in Paris and in some of the surrounding towns like Coignières, Montreuil, Suresnes and Torcy. These services are limited and geared towards residents, not visitors. They have wheelchair-accessible buses available for hire to groups.

— **Assistance et Transports Adaptés pour Grands Handicapés (ATAGH)**, BP 198, 75926, Paris Cedex 19. *Tel:* (1) 40.05.12.15 *Fax:* (1) 47.31.51.23. They have three adapted vehicles for occasional hire/use. They are Express or Trafic Renault, and can take either one or two chair users, plus some able-bodied companions.

GiHP, 98 rue de la Porte Jaune, 92210 St Cloud. *Tel:* (1) 47.71.74.90 *Fax:* (1) 46.02.21.46. This company has four taxi/minibuses in Paris. They provide a good and reasonably cheap service. The vehicles are fitted with a pull-out ramp which measures 2.5m long and 69cm wide. Inside there are three wheelchair user spaces and four seats. We used this service and found it to be entirely adequate; the chairs were well clamped and our particular driver spoke sufficient English. As we only booked the day before, we were well pleased – but if you are going to depend on it for sightseeing, you would be well advised to book in advance. St Cloud is just outside the centre south of Rueil-Malmaison and the comments made under PMR (below) about where you stay also apply to GiHP.

— **le Kangourou**, 92500 Rueil-Malmaison. *Tel:* (1) 47.08.93.50. They have four adapted vehicles for disabled passengers which are able to carry one or more people in chairs.

— **TGVHD**, 92150 Suresnes. *Tel:* (1) 45.06.53.19. They have a Ford Transit which can take up to three chair users and two other passengers. Suresnes is just past the bois de Boulogne, near Rueil-Malmaison.

— **PMR Transport**, 20 rue Gambetta, 92500 Rueil-Malmaison. *Tel:* (1) 47.49.37.40 *Fax:* (1) 47.49.10.24. Rueil-Malmaison is just outside the centre of Paris, past the bois de Boulogne and southeast of la Défense. If you were planning to make extensive use of this service it would be sensible to stay on that side of the city, since the vehicle is charged from its point of departure. The same is true of GiHP. PMR have three vehicles: a Renault Trafic which can take up to three chair users, a Renault Nevada and a Renault 25, and these can take either one chair via a ramp or have an extending and pivoting seat to facilitate transfer from a wheelchair.

These vehicles could be of enormous value in getting you to and from the airport if you fly. Remember that this means quite a long journey for them so check the cost. If you are planning to make use of them on a daily basis, we would suggest that you plan your itineraries to minimise the cost. Most of the companies with these adapted vehicles are to the west or southwest of the city in Rueil-Malmaison, Suresnes and St Cloud. If using them frequently you would minimise the cost by staying in a hotel on that side of the city as they would have a shorter drive to pick you up. As there are only a tiny number of adapted vehicles, if you are depending on one of them to get around, you would be wise to make advanced reservations to avoid disappointment. You could get the minibus to take you somewhere in the morning, do all the sightseeing you want to do in that area and then arrange a pick-up in the afternoon or evening. You can probably even modify the details on the day, depending on the weather. If you were in Paris for a week, then five such points could be:

— The Eiffel Tower and a boat trip on the Seine
— Notre Dame, Ile de la Cité and the river banks
— The Orsay Museum and/or the Louvre
— La Villette

— Montmartre, or possibly the Champs Elysées.

With suitable use of the map and deciding what kind of places you want to visit, you can produce your own list and you may like to look at our *recommended itineraries* for a bit of guidance. If you have confidence in organising precise rendezvous points, then you could arrange a 'drop off here, pick up there' journey. If you try this, you need to be clear about the meeting point. You could agree it by pointing it out to the driver en route to your drop-off point in the morning.

You can get further and updated information from the APF or CNFLRH if you need it (see the section on French organisations for disabled people in *General information*).

DRIVING

Driving in Paris itself is undoubtedly a bit hairy and not recommended if you are of a nervous disposition or if you have no experience of big city driving. If your only experience is of country driving, you might be wise to test yourself out in London or your nearest major city and see how you cope.

One of the big problems is simply finding your way around – not made any easier with the numerous one way systems. **Good maps are essential and a competent navigator is invaluable** to read ahead and describe the junctions you're coming to. Again, one thing to take into account in organising your visit is that during July and August many Parisians leave the city for their annual holidays. Although the weather may be a bit sticky, the traffic is *much* reduced, making driving around and finding places to park considerably easier than at other times.

The basic driving rule is to keep to the right! There really is nothing to it (famous last words) as long as you are sensibly cautious especially at complicated junctions and roundabouts. Take it very easy when you first get there.

You will find it useful to read the AA or RAC Continental Handbook for details of local rules and for the significance of roadsigns. The French apply the 'priority to the right' rule. This means giving way to any traffic which is on your right, for example entering a roundabout, unless your right of way is clearly marked. The use of the priority is currently being modified and some roundabouts are being marked to cancel this priority. On main roads marked with a yellow diamond you have right of way, but it ends at named villages and towns – ie at the sign with the name on it – and the priority starts again when you leave – where the name appears again with a red line through it. However, the priority to the right principle is deeply engrained in French drivers' psyche, so take care and, if in doubt, be cautious.

Be particularly careful about keeping right after coming off a stretch of motorway, filling up with petrol, stopping for a picnic or driving on the left down a one-way street. These are the times when you might forget or get confused. Reverting unconsciously to the left can be both dangerous and expensive.

In general the road marking makes it perfectly clear where you should be and perhaps the most difficult manoeuvre is a left turn across oncoming traffic. Something you won't have come across in Britain is the use of the flashing amber light. Basically it means 'proceed with caution' (ie watch out!) and is used extensively on traffic lights at night where there will often be flashing amber lights in both directions. Also note the French use of the filter on the right, sometimes seemingly against the lights, and remember that pedestrians almost invariably have priority over turning traffic. Large intersections, roundabouts or squares may include more than one set of lights so be prepared to stop half way across on occasions – one tip is to keep an eye on traffic ahead and follow previously charted routes!

Boulevard de Clichy

One trick which eases the problem of navigating across central Paris is simply to head straight for the one-way mini freeways either side of the Seine, called the Rive Gauche and the Rive Droite. They are generally well signposted, which is more than can be said of the rest of Paris. So long as you identify the correct turning-off point, you can head directly for your destination. This may sometimes take you a little way out of your way, but should reduce or even eliminate the number of difficult junctions involved. Alternatively, of course, you can do the same thing using the motorway ring, the boulevard Périphérique, but this may take you quite a lot further round. The Périphérique does get clogged up sometimes during rush hours, near autoroute turn offs or when there are repairs. Although it might seem sensible, you may find driving in the inside/slow lane of the Périphérique a bit frightening because of the large amounts of traffic joining it. Our drivers found it safer to remain in the second lane whenever possible.

Paris traffic moves fast and some of the roads are quite wide. Until you are fairly confident, you would do well to steer clear of place de la Concorde and place Charles de Gaulle, at either end of the Champs Elysées. It is necessary to be fairly sharp and to be conscious of giving 'priority to the right'. Apart from the fact that Paris drivers can be a bit pushy, our surveyors found driving relatively straightforward. This was in spite of the fact that most were young and relatively inexperienced.

Parking

Parking is a chaotic business. There are a large number of both multi-storey and underground car parks marked on the main maps. Unfortunately most of them do not have a lift going to street level. As we have said in the text, often the only way to get out of a car park if you cannot use the stairs is to take the route that the cars take. If you do this you need to be sensibly cautious. If the vehicle is being driven by an able-bodied driver then the best thing may be to drop off the passengers in the street somewhere before parking underground. Note that most car parks are for a standard height car. If your vehicle has an elevated roof be particularly careful and remember that your choice of parking spot will be even more limited.

Some parts of Paris are extremely congested and a car park at your hotel can be a valuable facility. There are large meter areas. A fair amount of illegal parking also goes on despite the army of traffic wardens with their distinctive turquoise uniforms.

Orange badges for disabled drivers and passengers do now apply abroad in other EC countries. There is a leaflet called *The orange badge scheme, reciprocal parking arrangements for disabled and blind people in Europe*, which should be available through RADAR. Responsibility in France for parking concessions rests with the local, not national, authorities. In Paris you are exempt from parking meter charges if you have an orange badge and should also benefit from a 75% reduction in car parking charges. This presumably applies at local authority, not private, car parks. There are no general concessions or exemptions from parking regulations. The police are required to show a degree of tolerance and consideration for parking by vehicles which are used by identifiable disabled people.

All this means that it is well worth bringing your orange badge, even if you are only a passenger in the car. If you haven't got a badge or have left it behind, it may be worth having an 'international symbol' to display. It gives no rights in law, but will probably be respected, so long as it is not misused. In the useful phrases section we suggest one or two things you could say on a note left on the windscreen.

We can only say that our survey teams managed to park or stop quite near their various objectives and if parking in a spot where it is not strictly allowed they simply left a note on the windscreen. It is obviously essential to ensure that no obstruction is being caused to other road users. It is easier to explain things if the vehicle has an identifiable disabled user, although that is not always possible, as your disability may not be 'obvious'. Adapted vehicles are easily identifiable, but if you are in an ordinary car, the explanatory note and use of the orange badge are important.

Hiring

An alternative to bringing your own car or minibus is, of course, to hire one in France. Hiring hand-controlled cars is discussed in the *General information* chapter. If you fly out, it is ideal to collect and return your hired vehicle at the airport, taking all the access problems out of travelling. Be prepared for a bit of a wait though while your documentation is sorted out. Note that the minimum age for hiring a car is usually 21 and you should have a clean driving licence. Some companies operate a minimum age limit of 23 or 25. Avis excepted, most companies have an upper age limit of 60 or 65.

Fly-drive packages generally concentrate on destinations further away than Paris, but if you are also going further afield you may consider this.

By Bus

There is an excellent bus network and a particularly good feature is that there is a map inside each bus showing the route and the bus stops are all prominently named. We have not made a detailed survey of the system since the access problems involved are well understood. For most chair users and some disabled walkers buses are not a practical proposition as they usually have either two or three steps at the entrance. They can be jerky and you might have to stand if they're crowded. However, using buses avoids the huge number of steps you're likely to encounter on the métro. **One unexpected thing is that you cannot pay cash for your fare on a bus. You have to get some métro tickets which are valid for buses as well**. The RATP

(Paris Public transport Authority) have some reasonable maps of the system, but it takes a bit of getting used to. You may be lucky and find some convenient routes near your hotel.

If you are hard of hearing you might be wise to write down your destination to show the conductor since then you can be sure he or she knows. If you are partially sighted and need to be told when to get off, again it might be worth having it in writing if your French is not up to asking.

By Métro and RER

The Parisian underground system is renowned for being both extensive and efficient. Thirteen métro lines operate around the city and four RER lines provide connections to surrounding districts.

Métro

The whole system is highly automated with ticket machines and automatic barriers. This means there are very few staff. On the one hand this makes for a kind of efficiency, but on the other hand it results in a moderate crime problem. You should watch out for pick-pockets. The shortage of staff also means that there's often no one around to help or advise about the easiest ways of doing things.

The main métro system is basically inaccessible and journeys commonly involve dozens and possible hundreds of steps – some of the interchange stations are huge. For people with disabilities we don't really recommend the métro as there are generally easier ways of getting around. If you can manage the two or three steps buses should be a lot easier, if a little slower.

The entrance and exit barriers on the métro can be a problem, although there is sometimes a bypass in the ticket hall which a staff member can open. Finally, just to make life even more difficult, some of the escalators are too narrow to take a wheelchair. The chair user with intrepid friends and a desire for excitement can use the system, but it requires a lot of effort. The French may boggle, but they won't stop you – unlike in Britain where someone would find a regulation preventing you!

There are a variety of tickets available. All tickets are valid for the métro, buses and central RER. You can buy a single journey ticket or a *carnet* (packet) of ten tickets at a substantial discount. There are weekly and monthly passes for which you need two passport size photos and which you can only get at major stations. There are also *Paris Visite* passes valid for three days or five giving unlimited travel. The whole system is 'zoned' so the larger the area you want your pass or tickets to include, the more they will cost. For travel on just one day, like the Travelcard in London, you can buy a *Formule 1* ticket, again giving unlimited travel. Its price varies depending on how many zones you wish to include. All these tickets cover **all** forms of transport in the appropriate zones: the métro, buses and RER.

RER

The RER has four lines with standard colour markings on the RATP maps:
— **A** (red) runs west-east serving St-Germain-en-Laye, Vincennes and EuroDisney.
— **B** (blue) runs north-south going near Charles de Gaulle airport and to St Rémy-les-Chèvreuse.
— **C** (yellow) runs north-southwest and along the south bank of the Seine serving Versailles and Orly. The stations involve lots of steps and getting on the trains involves steps as well. The line is basically difficult for most people with disabilities.
— **D** (green) runs north from Les Halles and uses double decker trains which have +7 or −3 steps with handrails to the upper and lower decks respectively, although there is space between these two levels for a chair user without steps. Although it is the newest line, many of the stations are old and it serves no great tourist attractions. It is not regarded by the RATP as being accessible and they are not planning to upgrade it.

RER lines A and B are wheelchair accessible in parts. The RER has far fewer stations in the centre of Paris than the métro, but stretches further into local neighbouring regions. It is useful for the visitor because it goes to within a 2km bus ride of Charles de Gaulle airport, to several central stations, to St Germain, to Vincennes and to EuroDisney. It is a good system and could help you save a number of taxi fares. There are escalator links from street level right down to the platform at some stations.

A significant number of stations have service lifts to get you from street level right down to the platform. This makes the RER of potential value to both the wheelchair user and disabled walker. Our survey teams made extensive use of it, once we had established where the lifts were. The lifts are not only available for use by a wheelchair user, but also by any disabled person who would have trouble using the escalators. They are not public lifts so you will have to use the emergency intercom marked as *Appel* from the platform to attract the attention of a member of staff. In practice, disabled walkers might run into problems of perception by the staff of your disability and need, but if you do, just be quietly insistent.

Our experience also provides some cautionary tales. **Two separate incidents demonstrate the variability in attitude:**

During one visit, we were staying near Nanterre-Préfecture station which we happened to know has a lift to the platform. When our survey team, consisting of a chair user and two able-bodied people, set out to use it, the station staff disclaimed any knowledge of its existence and a member of staff had to be shown where it was! On this occasion we only used the lift from the level of the ticket office down to the platform, but when we made the same journey the following day we were shown a second lift that went from the street level down to the ticket office. After that we used the station every day. The incident illustrates the need for well-researched access data, which many able-bodied people consider to be a rather pedantic pursuit. It also shows that it pays to be persistent, since we could easily have been put off by the initial statement, "No, there isn't a lift here". We have been told at other stations that there is no lift when we *know* that there is one because we've used it!

Another incident shows a more positive side of the RER staff. When using Forum les Halles, which has a complex lift system, a surveyor using pidgin French managed to explain the need to use the lifts. Two staff members explained that the lift was broken, but they gave us assistance down the escalators and even phoned through to the destination station to warn them of our imminent arrival so that a member of staff was on hand to operate the lift when we arrived there.

The RER is useful. It is fast and efficient because it has far fewer stops than the métro. The trains are spacious and there is only a small step, normally about 20cm, up into the carriage which has sliding doors. The step to the platform can be more like 50/60cm on the section from Roissy to Gare du Nord on line B, but these stations are not regarded as being accessible anyway as they all involve steps.

If you are in a chair wishing to use the stations with escalators, the universal narrow automatic barriers may mean that you have to be lifted over them and the exit doors will be too narrow. There are normally one or two exits/entrances that can be opened by the staff and these are usually in the main ticket halls where people come in. Big stations have several exits and it may be a question of finding the right ones that lead through the ticket hall. Some exits bypass it and go straight to the street. It is almost certainly worth using the help point intercom and asking which exit to use if you are in any doubt.

In central Paris there are lifts at Châtelet-les-Halles, St Michel (for Notre Dame), Gare de Lyon, Gare du Nord, Denfert-Rochereau and la Grande Arche de la Défense. At Les Halles you need to use two lifts: one under control of the RER personnel and one service lift (see *Sights*).

Below is a list of wheelchair accessible stations and a diagram showing the journeys possible:

Line A
  Stations with flat access: Boissy-Saint-Léger; Chessy (EuroDisney)
  Stations with lifts: Saint-Germain-en-Laye; Le Vésinet-Le Pecq; Le Vésinet Centre; Châtou-Croissy; Rueil-Malmaison; Nanterre-Ville; Nanterre-Préfecture; La Défense; Châtelet-les-Halles; Gare de Lyon; Vincennes; Fontenay-sous-Bois; Nogent-Sur-Marne; Joinville-le-Pont;

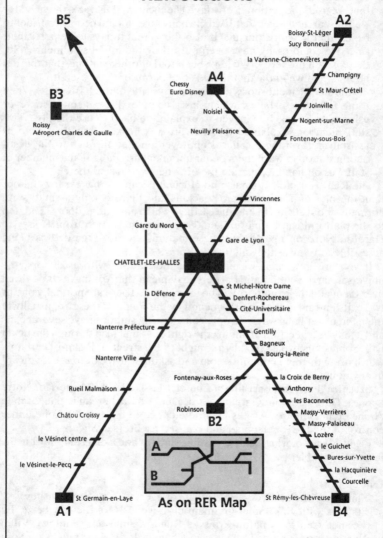

Map showing fully accessible RER stations

As on RER Map

St-Maur-Créteil; Champigny; La Varenne-Chennevières; Sucy-Bonneuil; Neuilly Plaisance; Noisiel.

Line B
    Stations with flat access: Bourg-la-Reine; Fontenay-aux-Roses; Robinson; La Croix de Berny; Massy-Verrières; Lozère; Le Guichet; Bures-sur-Yvette; La Hacquinière; Courcelle-sur-Yvette; St-Rémy-les-Chèvreuses.
    Stations with lifts: Roissy, Charles de Gaulle Airport; Gare du Nord; Châtelet-les-Halles; St Michel; Denfert-Rochereau; Cité Universitaire; Gentilly; Bagneux; Antony; Les Baconnets; Massy-Palaiseau.

For further information and an updated map contact RATP, Service du Développement Commercial, 53 quai des Grands Augustins, 75006. *Tel:* (1) 40.46.40.48 *Fax:* (1) 40.46.43.92.

The following detailed information on stations in central Paris is particularly for disabled walkers who may want to know where they can be sure of finding escalators and it can be useful to chair users if they arrive at a station and find that the lift is out of action. Going via the ticket hall there is always a route by which you can bypass the normal narrow exit doors with the help of a staff member. In the bigger stations some exits go directly to the surface bypassing the ticket hall and if you are a chair user able to get up escalators (as described in the chapter on *General information*) beware – you could get stuck unless you take the route which bypasses the barriers.

Auber (line A) has a lift on only one platform, in the direction of Étoile. This takes you to an upper level where the ticket office is. From here there are four large lifts which will take you to street level. Travelling in the other direction is not so easy as there is no lift to and from the ticket office and the platform for Châtelet and Nation. There are −22 steps from the ticket office and then an escalator.

Châtelet-les-Halles (lines A and B) is thoroughly described in the les Halles write-up. There is escalator access from platform (level −5) to ticket hall (level −4). To bypass the barriers you need to find the information point. There are then escalators to all the other levels and right up to ground level. *We include two extracts from the les Halles write-up which are relevant to the RER.*

    If you come by RER, you'll find that a help/alarm point is provided on each platform for people with disabilities. The main access up is by escalator and if you need to use a lift then find the help point and use the intercom. A staff member will come along and take you by lift to level −4 where the huge ticket hall is. You will then need to ask to be taken to an upper level again, because the main route upwards is still by escalator. You will be taken to a service lift and can be dropped off at any level from −3 up to ground level. (There's a detailed description of how to find the lift at level −4, if you are not escorted, in the *Sights* chapter.)

To get back on to the RER from street level (ie level 0), if you can't use the escalators down to levels −4 and −5, you need to find the junction between rue Rambuteau and rue Mondetour. Go into the complex through the arched entrance, following the direction of Mondetour. There are +3 steps, but there's a ramp to your right to bypass them. Go just 25m towards the Flunch restaurant, with the vowel sculpture just beyond on your right and the grotty service entrance is on your left, just before the double doors to Flunch. It looks rough and you won't want to go in, but the lifts are just 20m inside which will take you back to level −4 for the RER ticket hall. Once there you find the information point and staff will get you down to the platform.

Cité Universitaire (line B) only has an escalator on the south bound side. Going towards the centre of Paris there are 13+15+20 steps with handrails. Both platforms have a service lift to bypass the steps. Again, use the help-point intercom to get up from the platform and ask a staff member to operate the lift to get down to the trains.

Denfert-Rochereau (line B) has no escalators. There are two platforms, each with 17+17 steps. The station does, however, have two service lifts and these can be used if you call up a staff member on the alarm/intercom system from the platform. The lifts come out at street level just off the ticket office. You would similarly have to ask a member of staff for assistance to go down to the platform.

Étoile (line A) has a number of exits. It has no lift. For escalators to street level use the Champs Elysées exit on either side. Similarly to get back down with escalators, use the entrance on the corner of the Champs Elysées. A gate en route will enable a chair user to by-pass the ticket and exit barriers if you follow these directions.

Gare de Lyon (line A) has escalators up and down to all the levels which are slightly complicated, because some trains go from an upper part of the station: the RER platform is on level −2; the ticket hall is on level −1; taxis and cars go from ground level (0); and the SNCF platforms 1 to 19 are one floor higher on level 1. The only set of escalators from level −1 to ground level (0) are in front of the ticket office next to the métro access. A reasonably well signed service lift goes from level 0 down to the RER on level −2.

Gare du Nord (line B) has several escalators from the line B platform up to the line D platform, followed by further escalators to a split level and then a single escalator up to street level for buses, taxis and cars. Note that there is no down escalator to the split level and it can only be reached by −30 steps with handrails. A reasonably clearly signposted service lift bypasses the steps and escalators, linking street level with the line B platform.

Luxembourg (line B) has no lifts. The exit from both platforms is by escalator up to street level. However, to get down to the trains there are −13−9 steps to the ticket hall and then escalators to the platform on both sides.

Nation (line A) has a stair-lift for the direction of Marne-la-Vallée. Use the entrance on the corner of place de la Nation and avenue de Trone. To the right of this entrance there is a flight of steps, marked exit only, with a call intercom at street level. There are two stair lifts taking you to an intermediate level. From this there is a lift to the platform for Marne-la-Vallée or an escalator if you want to go into Paris. The normal route for passengers (and the route if the lifts are not operating) is via −21 steps and then an escalator to the ticket office level. From there it is −30 and then an escalator to the platform. Getting out from the station involves the reverse procedure.

Port-Royal (line B) has wheelchair stair-lifts on the platform leading out of Paris towards Gentilly. One goes from the platform to the ticket hall and the other from the hall to street level. On the platform for Châtelet and central Paris there are escalators up but steps down. For pedestrians, the normal access is by −19 steps to the ticket office and then −11−18 to the platforms. For getting off the platforms there are escalators up all the way to street level.

St Michel-Notre Dame (line B) has a new lift on the single central platform with access right up to street level. The lift is located in rue Xavier-Privas on the corner with quai St Michel. It is not very obvious, but has a call intercom to contact station staff. For walkers, we tried every entrance to the station, but all involved about 20 steps and seemed to go via the line C platforms. Use of the lift is thus essential for anyone who would find steps a problem.

Vincennes (line A) has a lift at the end of each platform which goes up to ground level behind the ticket office with a call button and intercom at both levels. Alternatively there are escalators from platform to street level in both directions.

By SNCF train

There is an extensive network of surface railways in and around Paris and the SNCF (Société Nationale des Chemins de Fer Français) are responsible for the long distance trains. One disadvantage of French rail travel is that getting on board usually involves bigger and more awkward steps than people are used to in Britain.

The main central stations are all accessible because they are terminals and don't have any rails to cross. Chair users may need to use one of the portable hydraulic lifts which are available at some of the big stations in order to get on to the train itself.

On the SNCF some stations in the Paris region are said to be accessible with the provision of lifts. The RATP are currently republishing a leaflet *Handicap et déplacements en région Ile-de-France*, but only in French. The rail map in the old edition was tiny and difficult to read, but there was a list of stations with lifts. A braille version was also available, but included only a small part of the information.

Paris Stations

Major Paris stations tend to be broadly similar with access to SNCF platforms, either by ramp or lift. Getting into the train carriages is somewhat variable. They tend to have much bigger steps than you may be used to in Britain, especially at intermediate stations. **The fact that you can get on the train unaided doesn't necessarily mean that you can get off**; there might be a much bigger step. For chair users there are small hydraulic lifts available in principle. Other facilities such as paper shops, cafés and loos are generally accessible, although stations are inevitably busy places, especially at certain times. Signposting is generally poor and you may have to ask several times to get the information you want. For access to many of the facilities you have to rely on the staff and, if you are not confident with your French, it would pay to learn a few relevant phrases.

The stations listed here are all SNCF terminals:

Gare d'Austerlitz, 55 quai d'Austerlitz, 75013. *Tel:* (1) 45.84.14.18 or 45.84.91.70. It serves southwestern France and Spain. It has good access for SNCF trains, but both the RER and métro have many steps. There is a small car park with six spaces for people with disabilities some 30m away on the quai d'Austerlitz. This gives flat access to the station itself and there is flat access inside with the usual bars and restaurants etc. The information desk inside the office opposite platform 16 offers assistance onto the trains and has two wheelchairs for use. A unisex **wheelchair loo** (D76 ST52) exists in the women's loos behind the ticket offices on the left-hand side when entering the station from quai d'Austerlitz.

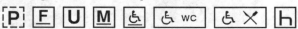

Gare de l'Est, pl de 11 Nov 1918, 75010. *Tel:* (1) 40.18.88.72 or 46.07.17.73. It serves Strasbourg, Champagne and southern Germany. An underground car park has four chair user spaces. It is on the left of the main entrance on place de Nov 11 1918 with lift (D96 W165 L95) access to platform 10. There is a pay and display car parking on rue d'Alsace and rue place de 11 Nov 1918 with ramped kerbs and from here it is flat into the station. The taxi rank is at the main entrance. Inside the station, access to all the usual facilities is flat or ramped. The ticket offices are on the rue d'Alsace side of the station as is a unisex **wheelchair loo** (D70+ ST175). There is an office which offers assistance to people with disabilities and they can arrange help for journeys as far as London. Although it has a 'disabled persons' sign on the door, it is not well signposted and you will find it next to the wheelchair loo. There are wheelchairs available and a low level phone near the rue Faubourg St Martin exit which has −6 steps with handrails.

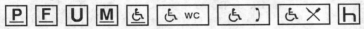

Gare de Lyon, pl Louis-Armand, 75012. *Tel:* (1) 40.19.17.19 or 43.43.33.24. This is the TGV terminal in southeast Paris. The TGV is the French high-speed long distance network and lines from here serve Burgundy, the Alps, Provence and the Riviera. Renovation work means that some details will change, though hopefully for the better. It is split into an upper and a lower level with a large lift to the RER. A ramp from rue de Chalon leads to both a short stay car park and a long stay underground car park, from which there is flat/ramped/lift access to the upper level. Flat access can be gained to the upper level from the taxi bay on rue de Chalon, while the taxi bay on rue Bercy gives flat access to the lower level. The lift (D78 W92 L136) on the upper level is located near the entrance for platforms 5 to 19 and is near the left luggage on the lower level. If you need staff assistance to use the lift, there are information desks on the upper level near track M and on the lower level by the RATP kiosk near the exit. The station has the usual facilities, snackbars and the like which are generally accessible. Wheelchairs are available from the upper information desk, by the boulevard Diderot entrance. There is a **wheelchair loo** (D85 ST105) on the upper level, next to the lift at the entrance for platforms 5 to 19.

Gare Montparnasse, 17 bd de Vaugirard, 75015. *Tel:* (1) 40.48.04.78. It serves Brittany and southern Normandy. For level C the taxi rank has ramped access from boulevard de Vaugirard to platform 24 and there is a ramped exit to platform 1 from rue du Cdt-René-Mouchotte. The ticket office near platform 1 has a counter designed for wheelchair users and will display a small Union Jack card if an English speaker is present. The station has five levels – métro, underground car park, A, B and C, in ascending order. Trains leave from levels A and C. One lift (D80 W115 L115) serves all levels except the métro and another lift (D90 W100 L140) serves levels

A, B and C. From place Bienvenue there is a flat entrance to level A where there is a low level phone as well as some shops. Luggage lockers are on level B whilst platforms 1-24 are on level C. A **wheelchair loo** (D70+ ST70+) is situated on level C at the boulevard de Vaugirard entrance next to the information desk where wheelchairs can also be borrowed. The métro station underneath is huge; it has dozens of steps and long distances to walk, so be warned!

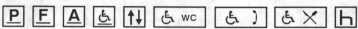

Gare du Nord, 18 rue de Dunkerque, 75010. *Tel:* (1) 45.26.94.82. This is the station serving England, northern France, Belgium and northern Europe. There are taxi bays on rue de Dunkerque and from here it is flat into the station. The underground car park entrance is also on the rue de Dunkerque and there is a lift up to the station level. At the time of surveying, much of the ground surface was bumpy with temporary floors due to renovations. All 16 platforms and station facilities – shops, restaurants with movable chairs, sandwich bars etc – are on one flat level. The ticket and left-luggage offices are 50m from platform 3 at the west end of the station, to the left as you enter from rue de Dunkerque. Here the fairly high international counter has an induction loop. A disabled persons information service is signposted, but staff denied any knowledge of it. It should be mentioned that there is very little seating and the signposting is typically deceptive. Some of the automatic ticket machines are on a raised level and the ramp installed may be too awkward for some chair users. The RER can be accessed by service lift (D200 W200 L200). There is a unisex **wheelchair pay loo** (D80 ST90) right at the east end of the station.

Gare St Lazare, 13 rue d'Amsterdam, 75008. *Tel:* (1) 42.84.88.00. It serves locations west of Paris. Most apparent obstacles can be bypassed. An underground car park on rue de Londres has a lift to place de Budapest. The main entrance to the station, with a misleading wheelchair sign, has +1+7 steps followed by an escalator. A better alternative can be found on the rue Amsterdam opposite the place de Budapest; it is flat/ramped from there to the first floor of the station and the platforms, ticket office and luggage lockers are all on this level. There is a unisex **wheelchair pay loo** (D75 ST86) on this floor opposite platform 19. Most of the shops are on the ground floor and have flat access from the road, but are only connected to the platforms internally by the stairs and escalators.

RIVERBOATS

Like so many of the great cities, Paris has built itself up on the banks of a river and a trip along the Seine, as well as being a relaxing approach to sight-seeing, is one of the best ways to take in much of what the city has to offer. Many of the main sights are on or near the river and in the evenings the floodlighting shows some of the facades at their best. Several major companies operate huge sight-seeing riverboats along the Seine and the standard trip takes about an hour. Two such trips were surveyed.

Bateaux Parisiens. *Tel:* (1) 44.11.33.44. Boats leave from a quai just east of the Pont d'Iéna near the Eiffel Tower. There is a riverside car park and there is a ramp from here to the ticket office. In the summer it can get quite busy. There are steps down to the quai from the pont d'Iéna, but it is possible to go a slightly longer way round using the road. There are +2 steps onto the boats, but a ramp is available to bypass these at the other end of the boat. Although the seats are fixed, there's plenty of room for a few people using chairs. The boats vary a bit in their suitability.

Bateaux Mouches. *Tel:* (1) 42.25.96.10. **These boats are larger and far more accessible.** They leave from the north (Rive Droite) side of the river near the pont de l'Alma, east of the Eiffel Tower. There is a clearly marked taxi pick-up point and car park beside the ticket office with a ramp to the boat. Access onto either the upper or lower decks is flat. You will have to request to be on the top deck if you so desire, but it has no cover and there are −11 steps with handrails on the left side only to reach the lower deck which is awkward if it rains! Meanwhile, entry to the lower deck with indoor and outdoor sections is through a 76cm gate and via a steep gradient ramp. The lower deck is flat with a 66cm entrance to the inside, although it can be widened if necessary. Boats have no refreshment facilities on board and only a tiny loo with a 46cm door at the back. *This trip is highly recommended and our surveyor had no problems with his chair.*

The smallest boats are the Vedettes de Paris operating from near the Pont-Neuf. Access is poor in that you either have to go down about 50 steps or make your way down a long ramp to the bumpy and partly cobbled lower quai on the Ile de Cité. There are 3 or 4 steep steps down into each boat.

Sights and interesting
spots

The sights are presented in alphabetical order, split between those in and near the centre and others which are much further out. We have used French names as the basis for the listing, as these are what you will see signposted. However, the various alternatives are cross-referenced and if you can't find something, try the index. *If you want to identify small areas with varied things to see and do, which can be visited easily with a minimum amount of walking or wheeling, have a look at the itineraries first*, then have a look back at some of the detailed write-ups in this chapter.

CENTRAL PARIS

Arc de Triomphe, pl Charles de Gaulle, 75008. *Tel:* (1) 43.80.31.31 (Michelin Guide Principal Walk 2). Located in the place Charles de Gaulle at the top of the Champs Elysées, this Napoleonic arch is one of the major landmarks. Commissioned by Napoleon some 200 years ago to celebrate France's military achievements, it was not exactly designed with disabled people in mind. It is included in the Champs Elysées *recommended itinerary*. The island on which the arch is located can be reached in two ways: either by risking life and limb crossing one of the most chaotic junctions in Europe; or by using the subway, from the Champs Elysées or avenue de la Grande Armée, which is −26 steps from ground level into it and +30 to get out in the centre of the roundabout. There are a number of underground car parks down the Champs Elysées, the nearest being at the junction with George V, with lift access.

If you are successful in reaching the arch, there are no barriers at the base and it is possible to see the Tomb of the Unknown Warrior with its eternal flame of remembrance. The stone base of the arch serves well as a bench. From here you can see up and down the Grand Axis to the place de la Concorde one way and the Grande Arche de la Défense the other. On a clear day it is impressive.

The ascent to the viewing area at the top is only possible for intrepid walkers and those in narrow chairs with a sense of adventure and strong friends. There is a large lift, but it is not always working and, even if it is, there are +2 steps to the lift and a further +46 at the top because it does not go all the way. There are some quite narrow and awkward turns to negotiate. The alternative is +146 steps which are narrow (69cm) with even more awkward bends. Loos (inward opening D53) can be found in the pedestrian subway.

It is almost certainly better to go and see the excellent views from the more accessible Tour Montparnasse, Grande Arche de la Défense or Eiffel Tower.

Detail from the Arc de Triomphe

Apart from the Champs Elysées, which has its own special ambiance, there aren't many other 'sights' nearby and, if you are only in Paris for a short time, you might find it easier to see the Arch from a car or taxi. It is an experience to drive or be driven around the famous roundabout which is called Étoile or place Charles de Gaulle. If you are driving around it, *beware* – there are twelve roads which go off like the points of a star, making it extremely chaotic. The technique for driving is to head in with confidence, because you have got right of way over every vehicle on your left. Head for the centre and go round as far as you need – you can even do a complete circuit once you have got to the centre. After that it will be a fight to get off again, since everything entering the roundabout has right of way over you. Just be patient and wait for suitable gaps.

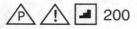 200

Arènes de Lutèce (Lutetia Arena), rue des Arènes (Michelin Guide Additional Walks, near the Mosque). A genuine Gallo-Roman arena now forming a small attractive park which provides a sheltered spot, ideal for a picnic and interesting in its own right. The streets around offer some metered parking. The entrance is flat and there is flat access to the arena itself and to some seats on the right overlooking the entire structure. The ground is fairly rough, but the whole place is small, so there's not far to go. Alongside the Arènes is the Square Capitan, with ramped access bypassing the 6 or 7 steps, providing an enormous children's sandpit which is very sheltered like the Arènes. Plenty of seats are available.

Army Museum *see* Invalides, Hôtel des

Art Moderne de la Ville de Paris, Musée d' *see* Musée d'Art Moderne de la Ville de Paris

Art Naïf Max Fournay, Musée d' *see* Montmartre

Basilique du Sacré Cœur *see* Montmartre

Beaubourg *see* Les Halles *and* Pompidou Centre

The **Bois de Boulogne** (Michelin Guide Principal Walk 25) is a huge park to the west of Paris which occupies almost 900 hectares. It includes the Longchamp and Auteuil racecourses, several lakes, the Jardin d'Acclimatation, the Parc de Bagatelle and the National Museum of Popular Arts and Traditions. Most of the park is accessible by car and parking is easy. The road system has many one way routes. Once out of the car there are numerous "walks", but few dropped kerbs. The park provides a welcome haven from the hustle and bustle of Paris without being far from the centre, although a lot of traffic uses the main roads. It is perhaps worth noting that parts of the Bois de Boulogne have recently got a rather bad reputation, so a little discretion is sensible, and visiting after dark is generally not advised. Most of the time, as a casual visitor, you'll probably not notice anything amiss. There is an excellent map of the park and its attractions in the Michelin Guide.

The **Bagatelle** can be found in the northwest of the park. These are the grounds and formal gardens of an earlier substantial château and a good plan appears in the Michelin Guide. Two reserved parking spaces for disabled people are located at both east and west entrances. A ramp allows for flat access from both directions to the gardens which contain an outdoor restaurant. The Trianon and the Orangerie have occasional art exhibitions. Entrance to the Trianon is by +9+9 steps at the front but only +3 at the rear. You may have a problem with the gravel paths, a few steep gradients and there are occasional steps. A **wheelchair pay loo** (D80 ST70+) is situated by the western gate and staff assistance is needed to open it. There are a number of benches and a thorough visit will involve about 1km.

 80%

Jardin d'Acclimatation (Children's Amusement Park), Carrefour des Sablons, *Tel:* (1) 40.67.90.82. The garden measures approximately 600m by 300m and is situated on the northern boundary of the Bois off the Carrefour des Sablons. It exists primarily as a children's amusement park and on some days there are special events. There is a small zoo with a typical Norman farm, an art museum (**Musée National des Arts et Traditions Populaires**), a workshop for children (the **Musée en Herbe**), a bowling alley and an adventure playground. Sometimes there are puppet shows. A miniature railway goes to Porte Maillot. Parking is possible on the road outside or in a limited number of parking bays at the entrance. The main entrance is flat and inside paths are gravel or tarmac with slight inclines. There are numerous benches although most are up 1 step. The least obstructed entrance to the bowling alleys is +2−4 with handrails from the Porte Madrid. There is a further +2 to the café inside and bowling alley loos (D70 no ST) are −14. There are numerous shopping kiosks throughout the gardens and the main restaurant is +2. There is another set of loos (D narrow) by the water wheel which are +1.

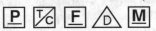

Musée National des Arts et Traditions Populaires has an entrance with +1+5 steps.

 E6

Botanical Gardens *see* Jardin des Plantes

Centre for Science and Industry *see* La Villette

Cernushi Museum *see* Musée Cernushi

Chaillot Palace *see* Palais de Chaillot

Children's Amusement Park *see* Bois de Boulogne

Church of St Gervais-St Protais *see* St Gervais-St Protais

Church of St Séverin *see* St Séverin

Church of St Sulpice *see* St Sulpice

Cimetière de Montmartre *see* Montmartre

Cimetière de Montparnasse *see* Montparnasse

Cité des Sciences et de l'Industrie *see* La Villette

Cluny, Hôtel et Musée de (Hôtel de Cluny and its Museum), 6 pl Paul Painlevé, 75005. *Tel:* (1) 43.25.62.00 (Michelin Guide Principal Walk 19). Two buildings, one containing the remains of some Roman baths dating back to 200 AD and the other being one of the few private houses in Paris dating back to the 15th century, have been combined to make up this sight. They now form a museum with some exceptional exhibits including stained glass and a unique collection of mediaeval tapestries. Access inside is limited and it was recently decided not to install a lift because of the age and fragility of the building. There is an excellent diagram of the layout in the Michelin guide and we refer to the room numbers used there.

Parking may be possible on meters in place Paul Painlevé and the surrounding roads. There are 30m of cobbles in the courtyard before you get to the main entrance where +3 steps give you access to rooms I to VI. To get from V down to VII and VIII there are −14. The only other rooms involving small numbers of steps are IX, X and XI which can be reached through a door and +1−5 without handrails into room X on the other side of the courtyard. From room X there are −3 into IX without handrails and +2 into XI without handrails. Room XII is accessible only by −15 with handrails from XI or −7−1 with handrails from VII. To get to the first floor the +7+8+12 with one handrail near the ticket office are less slippery than the +7+16+11 with handrail from room XI. The museum is about 150m in length and there are plenty of seats. Loos (D60 no ST) are −20 from the ticket office. Behind the museum there is a garden, Square de Cluny, looking down onto boulevard St Germain with a flat entrance from street level and seats.

The Roman baths which are only open once a week were not surveyed. The staff said that they contained steep steps with no handrails.

 E3N40+ 🚻 10%

Conciergerie, la *see* Palais de Justice

Dali Museum *see* Musée de Dali

La Défense (Michelin Guide Principal Walk 27) is an exciting and unique new development to the west of porte Maillot. The buildings appear to have been part of a competition in architectural adventurism. While it is first and foremost an international business centre, it is still a very interesting place to see. The whole complex makes an interesting visit with great contrasts between the ultra modern Grande Arche and the huge bustling shopping and restaurant area Quatre Temps. The area is included in the *recommended itineraries* chapter, based on the detailed description here.

The area is run by EPAD (Établissement Public d'Aménagement de la Région de la Défense) set up in 1958. EPAD have their offices at 1 place de la Coupole, la Défense 6, Courbevoie 92400, *Tel:* (1) 47.96.23.30. The development is part of a grand design associated with the Grand Axis, beginning at the Louvre, along the Champs Elysées, and through the Arc de Triomphe.

La Défense is the new business centre of Paris and is characterised by futuristic architecture, notably the Grande Arche which dominates the skyline. Although it is a brand new complex, access has been surprisingly badly thought out and working out the potential ramped/lift routes was a minor nightmare for our surveyors. Nevertheless, there are ways to get around, even for the electric chair user, but they are not signposted nor are they obvious.

If you come on the RER, there is lift access from the platform to the ticket hall and foyer, which is huge. If you go past the Exit E sign there is a well hidden lift just alongside the SNCF information/reservation office which will take you right up to the Parvis which is the main open air concourse. The lift has a call button and intercom to summon someone to help you use it. If you want to go to the Grande Arche, the route is signed and also described in its own write-up below. If you want to go to Quatre Temps from the RER use the signed exit from the ticket hall, then go across part of the underground car park at level −1 for about 70m, following the signs for les Arcades and, once through another set of doors, you will find some lifts on your left to take you up into the complex. If you start from the Parvis, use the ramped entrance well over to the left at Porte de la Poste to avoid the +3+3 stepped split level which you can see in front of you. Remember that to get back to the RER you either use the Arcade lifts to level −1 which is the ticket hall level, or the lift from the Parvis by Info Défense.

Arriving by car you will come round the boulevard Circulaire which goes right round the La Défense area. As you come from Neuilly, central Paris, you will pass the Novotel on your right. The signposting is quite difficult to pick up, because there is so much of it. Various parking/business areas are numbered from 1 to 8 and parking for the Grande Arche and Quatre Temps is signed in sector 7, so the one you want is some way round. When you find it you have to choose between Park A (left) and Park B (right). It is probably best to choose Park B, from where the lifts will bring you up in the middle of Quatre temps.

It is essential to write down the number of your parking area and remember its colour. The park is about the size of Wembley stadium, or feels like it, and there are four levels underground. Each level has its own colour and sectors are defined by numbers. If you don't remember the number of your spot, you really could spend hours looking for your car. There are a few reserved places for people with disabilities, but it is a tiny number and when we surveyed they were all occupied. Exits from the car park are reasonably well signed, but with names that don't mean anything unless you know what they relate to on the surface – they are fine for locals and almost useless for visitors. We hope that the diagram of Quatre Temps will help to clarify where you are likely to finish up.

Grande Arche de la Défense, *Tel:* (1) 49.07.26.26, is an enormous, hollow cube 106m high offering a superb view of the skyline over Paris. The hollow part is so big that it could contain the towers of Notre Dame and it is as wide as the Champs Elysées. From the top, the Grand Axis of boulevards and major buildings – the Arc de Triomphe, Louvre, Concorde and Champs Elysées – is clear, but what you may not expect is the other alignment with the Eiffel Tower and the Tour Montparnasse.

The Arch is located at the west end of La Défense central boulevard. It is impossible to miss.

If you have come on the RER and used the lift to the Parvis, you will be very close to the Info Défense building which houses an exhibition following the development of the complex. At the front of the Arch you will see +54 steps without handrails. However, a wheelchair accessible route is fairly well signposted from where you are; it goes down a ramp and through some doors where you turn left past an RER exit. You then reach the central column under the Arch where some escalators will take you up to the ticket office level. Just past the escalators is a main lift shaft with a call button and intercom point. It is about 300m from the Info Défense to the lift. Be warned: you may have to be patient at this point and/or send someone up to the ticket office to demand attention.

If you come via Quatre Temps and the underground car park there, use the porte de la Poste exit from level 1, make your way across the

Parvis to the Info Défense building and then follow the same route. Coming from the car park this way you would cover at least 400m to the Info Défense.

Tickets are sold on the main platform under the Arch. There are four lifts each taking about sixteen people which take you up to the level of the exhibition halls. From the lift exit there are +3+3 to the exhibitions, but temporary ramps are normally available, though you may have to ask the staff. Behind the lifts there was a somewhat congested bookshop and +6 or a wheelchair stairlift to bypass them. If you take this option, **it gives flat access to the unisex wheelchair loo (D70+ ST70+)** about 50m to your right at the end of the corridor. Men's loos are +10 and women's a further +10. If you turn left after the stairlift and go through the doors, there is another stairlift to bypass the +34 without handrails to the viewing area. They have provided a small raised platform to enable chair users to see over the parapet.

It is all quite good, but *chair users depend very much on finding a staff member to operate the special systems and there may be reluctance by staff to operate the stairlifts etc for elderly people and disabled walkers who might find all the steps, particularly the +34 to the viewing platform, far too difficult.* It is a place to consider coming to in an 'occasionally used' chair if you have one.

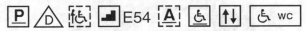

La Défense Central Boulevard runs from the Grande Arche and the Parvis to the Takis pond overlooking the pont de Neuilly. Beware of long distances, because the esplanade is over 1km long. Its length is deceptive because it is dwarfed by huge skyscrapers. In the centre of the boulevard the monumental fountain plays, with both illuminations and music at set times. At the far end, between the Arch and the centre of Paris, there is the Takis pond (already referred to) with a 'mirror' of water to reflect dozens of multi-coloured lights. On a clear day there is a magnificent view both back at the Arch and over Paris.

Les Quatre Temps is a huge shopping mall with some two hundred and fifty shops on three floors, over a massive car park. It is claimed that it is Europe's biggest shopping centre and is almost a small town on its own in the middle of la Défense. There is a massive hypermarket, with inclined moving walkways for trolleys and chairs. Elsewhere there are large branches of C&A and Toys R Us and many others. There are also dozens of cafés and restaurants, ranging from fast food joints to some really nice restaurants.

As described in the introduction to la Défense, there are four levels of car parking underneath. There are three big circular rotundas housing the groups of escalators for going up or down to all the levels. The lifts

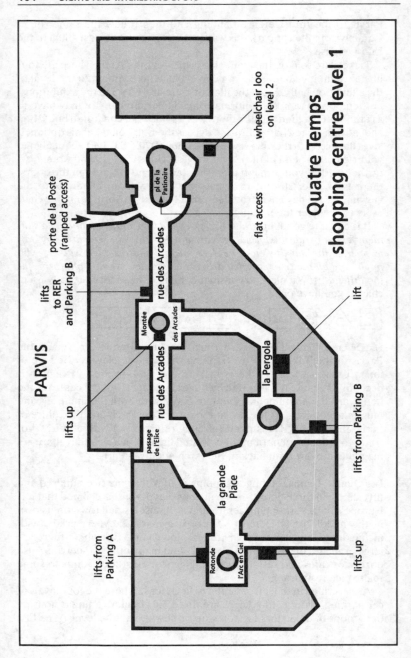

Quatre Temps
shopping centre level 1

PARVIS

porte de la Poste (ramped access)

lifts to RER and Parking B

lifts up

rue des Arcades

rue des Arcades

des Arcades

Montée

passage de l'Élice

la grande Place

lifts from Parking A

Rotonde

l'Arc en Ciel

lifts up

la Pergola

lift

lifts from Parking B

pl de la Patinoire

flat access

wheelchair loo on level 2

generally serve either the car parks, bringing you to the bottom level of the shopping mall, or they join the different floors of the shopping area. The Rotonde de l'Arc-en-Ciel is at the end nearest to the Arch and you will probably come up here from parking area A. However, there is no easy exit to the Arch, unless you can use an incredibly steep ramp up some 20 steps. Rotonde des Miroirs is part way along and the Montée des Arcades is central. Des Arcades is the rotunda which links to the RER ticket hall.

The only way in and out from Quatre Temps to the Parvis for a chair user is via the porte de la Poste. Note also that the only flat access into the place de la Patinoire inside Quatre Temps on level 1 is from the rue des Arcades end. Patinoire is a sunken area with a variety of stalls and everywhere there are steps to get down into it.

The lifts are marked on the plan. On either side of the Rotonde de l'Arc-en-Ciel at level 1 there are lifts to go up to the shops or down to the car park. Near the Rotonde des Miroirs at level 1 there is a lift down to the car park. At Montée des Arcades on level 0 there are lifts down to the RER at level −1 and to the car park with a separate lift up to the shops. There is a lift dedicated to Toys R Us from La Pergola, level 1. Lift dimensions were almost all D100 W180 L130.

The only wheelchair loo we found was off the Patinoire area on level 2 right at the far end of the building. The loo has a large cubicle, but included some bars on either side helpful to anyone with arthritis, which make side transfer difficult. **There are other wheelchair loos in the area**, one at the top of the Arch and **the other in the Hôtel Sofitel which is across the Parvis** and built into the side of the World Trade Centre (CNIT in the Michelin Guide).

There are several restaurants on level 2 of the Patinoire area.

World Trade Centre (CNIT). This is another huge building with shops and services. It is mainly geared towards the various exhibitions etc held there, but there is a huge public ground floor area before you get to turnstiles to go into an exhibition. There is an unsigned wheelchair loo on the ground floor, half-right as you come into the building from the Parvis. It is in the 'general' loos which are signed and, as you go in, the men's is on the left and the women's on the right. The wheelchair loo door is straight ahead, but it had a very low seat and looked as though it needed an attachment to raise it to a conventional height.

We found a wheelchair loo (D70+ ST70+) in the Hôtel Sofitel which is part of the complex; you need to go through the Trade Centre, as otherwise access is only via revolving doors, leave by the Soprite Esplanade which is half left from the main entrance, then turn left and the hotel entrance is about 50m away. Take the lift to the first floor –

there is no one there to stop you – turn left out of the lift and the loo is almost immediately on your left before you get to the reception desk.

Dome Church *see* Invalides, Hôtel des

Eglise du Dôme *see* Invalides, Hôtel des

Eglise de la Sorbonne (Sorbonne Church), 47 rue des Ecoles, 75005 (Michelin Guide Principal Walk 20). There is some metered parking in place Paul Painlevé to the north. The main entrance to the church has +6 steps, but this section is only open for temporary exhibitions and cultural events and was closed when our survey team visited. A double door to the left of the main entrance gives flat access to the Cour d'Honneur which is the main courtyard of the Sorbonne. From here you can see some interesting architecture including the façade of the church. The main entrance to the Cour d'Honneur is from the rue des Écoles and has +7. Visitors are advised to write in advance if they wish to see the church's interior.

 E6

Les Egouts (the Sewers), pl de la Résistance, 75007. *Tel:* (1) 43.20.14.40 or 47.05.10.29 (Michelin Guide Additional Walks and Sights). On the corner of Quai d'Orsay and Pont d'Alma, the sewers are one of the more bizarre tourist attractions, but draw large crowds and there is often a queue. There are over 2,000km of tunnels under Paris in a system originally engineered over a century ago of which you only see a tiny part. A visit is instructive, even if slightly smelly. Afterwards you may catch a whiff of something you recognise when you are wandering around various parts of Paris! A visit is included in the *recommended itineraries* as part of the Eiffel Tower and river trip suggestion.

There is some metered parking nearby on the other side of the Quai d'Orsay from the river. The entrance is −30 steps down a spiral staircase with handrails and the exit is +9+7+15 up a straight staircase with handrails. **The steps are avoidable by taking a large service lift**, but you have to ask about it at the 'caisse' (ticket office) which is −30. The exhibition is mainly on one level, with the exception of +2 to the galerie Belgrand and +9 to another gallery which at the time was exhibiting toilet seats! There is a 50m section of the museum that is only 50cm wide, but this can be by-passed. The loo (D65 no ST) is +9+1.

 E30 90%

Eiffel Tower *see* Tour Eiffel

Forum des Halles *see* Les Halles

Galeries Nationales du Grand Palais *see* Palais de la Découverte

Géode *see* La Villette

Gobelins, Manufacture des (Gobelins' Tapestry Factory), 42 av des Gobelins 75013, *Tel:* (1) 48.87.24.14 or 43.37.12.60 (Michelin Guide Additional Walks and Sights). Situated right by Gobelins métro, this factory is one of just four great tapestry workshops in France that have retained 17th century methods of production. Parking may be possible on the main road. The main entrance, approached across 50m of cobbles, has +3+1+5+11 steps. However, it is possible for the staff to open a door from avenue des Gobelins which affords flat access, but they ask for prior warning. You are now in the small workshop and the main workshop is across a further 250m of cobbles and +1 to a lift which we were told was large, but were not allowed to see. Unfortunately our surveyors were not allowed beyond this point. Commentary in French only, opening times are restricted and groups are preferred.

 80%

Grand Palais, Galeries Nationales du Grand Palais, av Winston Churchill, 75008. *Tel:* (1) 42.89.54.10 (Michelin Guide Principal Walk 2). Along with the Petit Palais, this formed part of the buildings for the 1900 World Exhibition. It is now an exhibition centre with a part of the building accessed from avenue Franklin D Roosevelt given over to a science museum called Palais de la Découverte. The museum is written up separately. The area comes into the *recommended itinerary* for the Champs Elysées.

The main part of the Palais is just one huge hall. From avenue Winston Churchill there is a ramped entrance and the hall itself is flat inside. Major exhibitions are often reached from the entrance in avenue du Général Eisenhower where there are +26 steps, but an alternative entrance is just to the left marked with the 'wheelchair' sign. Here there is a stairlift down to the basement, and this leads to a lift which goes to all floors inside.

 E26 90%

Grande Arche *see* La Défense

Halle St Pierre *see* Musée d'Art Naïf

Les Halles (Forum des Halles, Beaubourg), 75001. *Tel:* (1) 42.96.68.74 for administration (Michelin Guide Principal Walk 13). This is an ultra-modern development on the site of the old Central Market. Its main excuse for being called a 'sight' is because of its modern architecture on the surface and its three hundred shops plus and restaurants, two multi-screen cinemas, swimming pool, auditorium and a host of other things. Approaching it from elsewhere, and particularly as you look down on it, it looks rather like a huge art-deco flower coming up out of the ground. The main colours used are white and grey. Around the central focus is a large pedestrianised area full of shops and cafés. In the Forum itself the main development has been downwards and it is built in a huge hole in the ground around which various facilities have been built. Levels are defined by their minus sign, which says that they are below ground level. The RER station is at the deepest level at −5. Most of the shops, cafés, museums, exhibitions and auditoria are from levels −1 to −3. There are two levels above ground and from their upper terraces you can get good views over the whole area. Les Halles is part of a *recommended itinerary* including the Pompidou centre and Notre Dame.

Because of its complexity we will describe access in some detail and *we hope that the diagram of the largest level (−3) will help you find your way*. The main ways up and down are by escalator, but these aren't useful for everyone and consequently we made a thorough investigation of the lifts. *Please don't be put off by the length of the description. Once you have understood where the lifts are, access is really quite easy.*

Two important places are the office of the **Administration des Halles** which is on level −3, at the right angle bend in the rue de l'Arc en Ciel off porte Berger, shown on the plan. Its significance is that you can get a fairly clear, coloured isometric plan of the place, which should help you get round. The other important place is the **main security office** which is on level −2 by porte Lescot where the taxi pick up and drop off point is. The office is well disguised and is in room 206. It has an unlabelled red door and there is an intercom point quite high up to the right side of the door. If you have trouble, for example late in the evenings, getting to the service lifts we have described, this is the place to go for help.

If you arrive at les Halles at street level, things are relatively straightforward. The main lifts (D80 W170 L110) are from porte Rambuteau and porte Berger. The isometric diagrams you will see in the centre do show some of the lift routes with a thin black line, but they are not very clear and the lifts are not labelled on the diagram.

If you come by car we have described the route to the Parking Sud, which gives you flat access into level −3 via heavy doors. You approach this from République on the rue de Turbigo. Just past rue Etienne Marcel the road forks after the crossing and Parking Sud is reached by following the signs which say 2.35m, Pont Neuf, Autres Directions and Parking Forum. About 100m along the road veers to the right and Parking Sud is signed. There are a couple of spaces reserved for people with disabilities. Due to the size of the building it was helpful to record the number and colour of the area where we parked and where we entered the Forum itself. Parking Sud is signed from parts of the complex.

Taxis arrive and leave porte Lescot on level −2 and this point is reached through two heavy doors.

If you come by RER you will find that there is a help/alarm point on each platform for people with disabilities. The main access up is by escalator, so if you need to use a lift find the help point and use the intercom. With luck a staff member will come along and take you by lift up to level −4 where the huge ticket hall is. From here you will need to ask to be taken to an upper level, because the main route upwards is still by escalator, and you should be taken to a service lift which serves all levels from −3 up to ground level. On the whole this is fairly simple and with luck you will have no problems. If you are going to visit the Les Halles shops etc, we suggest you go to level −3 and go straight to the Administration Office (already described) to get a proper plan of the place.

Here is how to find the lift at level −4 without staff assistance or if you have been to the cinema. If you have come from the RER, take the porte Lescot exit, turn left down the rue de l'Orient Express, past the escalators and cinema on your left, towards the dead end with a large pillar on the left, then go through the unmarked doors furthest to the right and the lift is a short distance inside. From here the lift will take you to levels −3, −1 or to ground level (0).

However, *getting back on to the RER is a different story* . . . .

From street level (0), if you can't use the escalators down to level −4, you need to find the junction between rue Rambuteau and rue Mondetour. Go into the complex through the arched entrance, following the direction of Mondetour where there are three steps, but a ramp is on your right to by-pass them. Go just 25m towards the Flunch restaurant, with the 'vowel' sculpture just beyond on your right. The somewhat grotty service entrance is on your left, just before the double doors to Flunch. It looks rough and you won't want to go in, but the lifts are just 20m inside. Go down the corridor, turn left, and you will find the lifts which will take you back to level −4 for the RER ticket hall. Once there you find the information point and they will get you down to the platform.

From level −1, you need to find the right-angled bend in the rue Poquelin. The doors are set in a painted wall between the entrance to Jean Marc hairdressers and some Sortie Secours (emergency exit) doors. The lifts are about 20m along the corridor which bends to the right.

As the exit from these lifts at level −2 is into a private car park, this level is not really relevant. From level −3, find the junction/corner of rue des Piliers and rue Brève. The doors are between Pimckie and

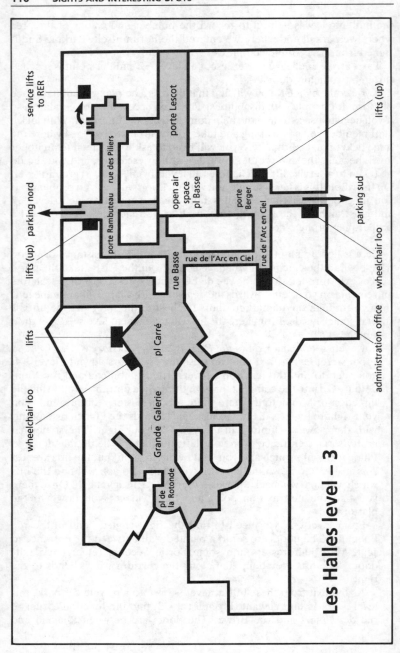

Les Halles level – 3

Forum Go Sport, labelled Couloir de Service. The lifts are some 15m along the corridor which bends to the right. They are marked in the diagram.

If you can't use the escalators, your most important facility is the lifts. We have already described three pairs of them which link levels 0, −1, −2 and −3 from porte Rambuteau and porte Berger (these names are used on each level) and the service lifts for getting to and from the RER.

Another pair of lifts (D77 W110 L140) links levels 0, −2, −3 and −4 (parking St Eustache). At level 0 they come up in the middle of the gardens, by the junction of allée St John Perse, allée Fredrico Garcia Lorca and allée André Breton (leading to porte Pont Neuf). The lifts are on the corner of Fredrico Garcia Lorca. At level −3 they are just off place Carrée towards the Parking St Eustache exit to the right of the loos. They are the only lifts going to the Auditorium des Halles on level −2 (see *Entertainments* chapter for further details) and are not shown on the isometric plans.

All these lifts are shown on the plan at level −3.

There is another service lift, which you may not have to use, from porte Berger level −1, behind the doors marked Couloir de Service, serving levels −3 and −4 in Parking Sud. On level −3 the lift entrance is near the loos and is marked Servitudes Techniques, whilst on level −4 it is opposite zone 83 and has red doors.

Access to most of the shops is flat, although a few around the central open space are up steps. The central open air space, place Basse at level −3, has +7 steps to get to it from the main level. On the whole this doesn't seem a great loss, although in the summer it may be nice to get out into fresh air.

In Fnac on level −3 at porte Lescaut on the corner with passage des Verrières there are music and entertainment booking desks for, amongst other things, the Auditorium des Halles and other nearby venues.

The **Videotèque de Paris** is on level −3 just off the Grande Galerie, close to place Carrée. There is flat access and a lift (D80 W98 L140) just past reception to bypass the steps and narrow ticket barriers. The videotèque has facilities for individuals to watch a selected video in the salle de consultation Pierre Emanuel from a library of over 4,000 films. You have your own screen and it is possible to view from a wheelchair. There are also other small viewing rooms, mostly with fixed seating, but the main one opposite the lift has two wheelchair spaces. There is a cafeteria with movable chairs and tables.

There are two cinema complexes, each with several screens. One is on level −4 and the other is the Gaumont on level −3. We asked at both and were told that there would be no problem for a chair user getting into any of the cinemas and they would be able to stay in their chair. The cinemas had flat access.

There are four wheelchair loos inside the Les Halles complex, all on level −3, and two close by outside:

inside   – level −3, place Carrée, just inside the entrance to the clearly signed loos; unisex

– level −3, by the entrance/exit to parking Sud; unisex, sideways transfer

– inside the Videotèque de Paris entrance, see write-up on level −3

– level −3, in McDonalds, on the corner of rue de l'Arc-en-Ciel and rue Basse; go left past the counter and walk through the restaurant, zig-zagging slightly. The loos have unmarked large cubicles (D70+ ST70+).

outside   – in the Kentucky Fried Chicken at the junction of rue Berger and boulevard Sebastapol. Turn left at the counter and zig-zag through the restaurant following the sign to the 'toilettes'. The unisex cubicle has sideways transfer

– in the Novotel hotel in place Marguerite de Navarre, opposite 19 rue des Halles. Access is flat through the main doors, turning left past reception, following the signs to the restaurant/bar and the loos are on the left before you reach the bar; unisex, with 86cm door and 71cm sideways transfer.

Hôtel de Cluny *see* Cluny, Musée de

Hôtel de Ville (Town Hall), pl de l'Hôtel de Ville, 75004. *Tel:* (1) 42.76.43.43 or 42.76.59.27 (Michelin Guide Principal Walk 9). This is the official residence of the mayor of Paris and the principal meeting place for the city's administrators. It has an attractive façade outside and the interior is quite grand in parts with delicate chandeliers and decorated ceilings. Because it is a 'working' building, visits are restricted, although there are City Council meetings to which the public are admitted and occasional exhibitions. It is mentioned in the *recommended itinerary* covering Les Halles and Notre Dame.

There is inevitably a fairly high level of security and for groups it is necessary to book a tour in advance, though a pre-arranged tour may still be cancelled at the last minute if there is an official visit. For individuals, tours are on Mondays at 10.30, but you must turn up at least ten minutes early or you won't be allowed in. Remember that it may take you several minutes to be directed to the correct entrance for disabled visitors.

There are plenty of dropping off points, but parking is tricky. There might be the odd metered space around the square. There is an underground car park with the vehicle entrance in the quai de l'Hotel de Ville, but it has an exit of +25. For groups that have arranged it in advance, it may be possible to park in the inner courtyard, but staff must have number plate details and the driver's name beforehand.

The entrance for the building and tour is on the rue de Rivoli and has +4 steps. Alternatively there is flat access via a side gate and a steep ramp. This takes several minutes to organise. The information desk is to the left. There are two exhibition centres, one on the rue de Rivoli and the other inside between the two inner courtyards. There is flat access to the first from the entrance hall. When we visited there was an exhibition about past Paris mayors and their residences. The second exhibition centre is +3 without handrails. It can be reached on the flat from an outside entrance on the rue de Laban.

The guided tour takes about an hour and there is a fair amount of seating around. Any steps en route are ramped and there are two lifts to the second floor (D139 W210 L150 and D80 W125 L160), making it possible to see most of the building.

There are two designated wheelchair loos, one in Exhibition Centre and one off the main corridor. We saw one (D80 ST61) on the ground floor.

Institut du Monde Arabe (Institute of the Arab World), 1 rue des Fossés St Bernard, 75005. *Tel:* (1) 46.34.25.25 or 40.51.38.38 (Michelin Guide Additional Walks and Sights). This is an interesting, high-tech building. It has amazing light-sensitive arab-style screens on the south side of the building. There is a good view of the Seine, towards Notre Dame. It contains a museum with a fine collection of art and artefacts illustrating the development of Islamic culture. There are often temporary exhibitions.

There is the possibility of street parking on meters. The main entrance is flat and there are six glass lifts (D80 W125 L130) which serve all the floors. The museum entrance is on the seventh floor and you can use the main lifts to reach the other floors in the museum. The ninth floor has a café, a fairly expensive restaurant and a terrace with excellent views. Note that there is a barrier around the terrace which is 105cm high. **The wheelchair loo (D85 ST90) is in the basement on level −2.** Temporary exhibitions are also held on this level.

Les Invalides, Hôtel des (The Invalides), 75007. *Tel:* (1) 45.55.92.30 (Michelin Guide Principal Walk 4). Located at the end of avenue du Maréchal Gallieni, the whole complex was originally built by Louis XIV for some 4,000 disabled soldiers and is a remarkable creation. Regrettably it didn't do much for its disabled residents, many of whom finished up begging, because all the state money was being spent elsewhere. The gold-plated Eglise du Dôme, housing the tomb of Napoleon, dominates the site, but there are impressive buildings and courtyards all round it. During the summer there are *Son et Lumière* performances in the courtyard, which should be quite impressive.

There is parking around the place Vauban and in the surrounding streets. There are two entrances into the complex. From place des Invalides in the north a 75m concrete path and 10m of cobbles lead directly into the large Cour d'Honneur at ground level. Here there are +5 steps to the gallery surrounding the courtyard giving access to the Musée d'Armée and the Eglise St Louis. You can avoid these +5 by using the south entrance from place Vauban with a 50m concrete path followed by a gravel path to the left of the Eglise du Dôme as you face it. The gravel path gives ramped access to the Cour d'Honneur, passes the Invalides café, which is +2 and contains the ticket office and a souvenir shop. The café has movable chairs and loos (D51 no ST).

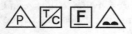

Eglise du Dôme (The Dome Church). The main entrance has +14 steps without handrails, but once inside the gallery is flat. Napoleon's tomb is obscured by a 95cm high barrier. To get level with the tomb in the crypt there are a slightly spiralled −17 and then −26 from the gallery. Other tombs are in recesses on the upper gallery which is +6 without handrails. The surface throughout is carpet and marble, and there are no seats in the building.

 E14 N43

Eglise St Louis (Church of St Louis des Invalides). Not a particularly interesting sight, but there is flat access from the gallery around the Cour d'Honneur, +5 steps from the courtyard, where you get into the museum. The only notable decoration is the captured banners over-hanging some of the galleries.

 E5

Musée de l'Armée (The Army Museum). There are galleries and exhibitions on both sides of the Cour d'Honneur and the collection of military hardware is one of the largest in the world. While there are some things to see on the ground floor, the museum has five floors altogether and a lot of steps. Although there is at least one service lift, and we suspect that there are others, our wheelchair surveyor was not allowed to use it. There are loos (D55 no ST) on the ground floor.

 E5 N100

There are **wheelchair loos** (D84 opens inward ST86) at the Aérogare des Invalides by the river near the Pont Alexandre III.

Jardin du Luxembourg *see* Luxembourg, Palais et Jardin du

Jardin des Plantes (Botanical Gardens), 57 rue Cuvier, 75005. *Tel:* (1) 40.79.30.00 (Michelin Guide Additional Walks and Sights). There is parking available at the Gare d'Austerlitz and from here there is flat access to the gardens, although you do have to cross the busy boulevard de l'Hôpital. All entrances to the gardens are flat, but inside the paths are gravel or tarmac and often uneven. There is a good map in the Michelin Guide. If you have difficulty using the loos in the gardens, the Gare d'Austerlitz has a wheelchair loo.

Zoo. *Tel:* (1) 43.36.54.26. This small zoo is in the northeastern quarter of the gardens and the main entrance is from the west end, on rue Cuvier. There are shallow steps or ramps to most of the animal houses; for example +3 to the Vivarium, +5+3 to the lions and tigers and ramped access to the reptile house. Most inside exhibits have handrails and there are plenty of animals outside which can be seen from the paths. Only squat loos (D62) exist in the zoo and are +1−12−2.

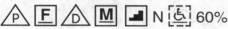

Mineralogical Gallery. *Tel:* (1) 43.36.54.26. Between rue Buffon and allée Hauy within the gardens. The main entrance has +12 steps, but inside there is flat/ramped access to most of the exhibits which are on a low level. Most exhibits also have braille descriptions. There are a further +3 to the section which includes a wheelchair loo (D90 ST109).

◢ E12 N3 ⟨&⟩ wc

Palaeontological Gallery. *Tel:* (1) 43.36.54.26. Situated just inside the Jardin des Plantes by the intersection of rue Buffon and boulevard de l'Hôpital. The entrance (D64) has +5 steps. There are +2 to main exhibits, +3 to ground floor shop and +20 to exhibits on the other floors without a lift. The loo (D56 no ST) is +3−8−16 with handrails, but the steps are slippery.

◢ E5 N20+ ⟨&⟩ 40%

Jardin des Tuileries (The Tuileries Gardens), 75001 (Michelin Guide Principal Walk 2). Located between the Louvre and place de la Concorde, these gardens provide a welcome retreat from the noise of central Paris and offer beautiful views of the Seine. Metered parking is available at the place de la Concorde entrance from which there is flat access throughout the gardens. There is also underground parking nearby. The paths are rough gravel and the whole park covers approximately one square kilometre.

The **Musée de l'Orangerie** in the gardens has +4 steps without handrails at the entrance, although there is an alternative side entrance with a lift. All floors of this small art gallery are accessible by lift (D87 W110 L200) and you may have to ask to use this at the reception. **There is a unisex wheelchair loo (D79 ST89) on the ground floor**. The highly visible ferris wheel has ramped access from rue de Rivoli.

Law Courts *see* Palais de Justice

Louvre *see* Musée du Louvre

Lutetia Arena *see* Arènes de Lutèce

Luxembourg, Palais et Jardin du (Luxembourg Palace and Garden), rue de Vaugirard, 75006. *Tel:* 42.34.28.60 or 42.34.20.00 (Michelin Guide Principal Walk 21). The Palais, situated on the rue de Vaugirard where it meets rue de Médicis, is the home of the French Senate, the upper house of parliament. The garden surrounding the Palais is beautifully laid out. The Medici fountain dates from the 17th century and is at the end of a long pool. The gardens are full of statues.

Metered parking is available at l'Observatoire, to the south of the gardens. There is also an underground car park on rue Auguste Comte with a lift which was not working when we visited. There is a flat entrance from place Paul Claudel, whilst most of the others involve a step or two. There is a lake and plenty of seats around the park. The path surfaces should not be too inhibiting. There are four public loos and **a unisex wheelchair pay loo (D70+ ST70+) located 100m inside the park from the place A Honnorat entrance on the south side.** It is not marked as a wheelchair loo.

La Madeleine, pl de la Madeleine, 75008. *Tel:* (1) 47.42.60.11 or 42.65.52.17 (Michelin Guide Principal Walk 5). Situated in the centre of the square this is a historic church, whose entrance facade resembles à Greek temple. There is a car park in the northwest corner of place Madeleine. You will have to fight your way across quite heavy traffic and then up +1+14+14 steps with handrails. It is flat inside except for the crypt. The crypt, including a chapel in which morning mass is celebrated, is reached by +3+1 and then a spiral staircase −15−11 with handrails from inside or +2+1−1 from the outside north entrance. There are no loos. It has an induction loop.

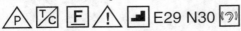

Maison de l'UNESCO *see* UNESCO

Monceau Park *see* Parc Monceau

Montmartre, 75018, (Michelin Guide Principal Walk 7). Montmartre is built on and around the only hill in Paris. A couple of centuries ago it was a village outside the city which had several windmills for grinding flour; hence the 'Moulin Rouge' and the 'Moulin de la Galette' which inspired many painters. Its reputation comes largely from the writers and painters who were attracted to the area. Now it is a mixture. There is still a village atmosphere at the top of the hill, and parts are really attractive. There are also streets with neon lights and strip clubs. Parts of the area, for example around place Pigalle, are decidedly sleazy. The Musée de Dali is nearby. Montmartre forms the basis of one of the *recommended itineraries*.

Montmartre is one of the most atmospheric, but unfortunately least accessible, parts of Paris, containing many hilly, stepped and cobbled streets. The streets can become very crowded with access restricted by shop displays and cafés which overflow onto the pavement. The best way to get to Montmartre is probably to take a taxi to just above the Sacré Cœur, as parking in the narrow surrounding streets is particularly difficult. Immediately in front of the Sacré Cœur there are over 150 steps up the steep hill. These can be bypassed by a highly accessible funiculaire (funicular railway) which goes from place St Valadon to the rue du Cardinal Dubois. Alongside the Sacré Cœur to the west is the place du Tertre, a bustling square of painters' and artists' galleries.

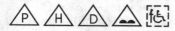

There are some superb views to be had from the hillside – a visit is worth it just to see these and to wander round looking at the artists' work.

Cimetière de Montmartre (Montmartre Cemetery), av Rachel. This is in a small bowl below the rue Caulaincourt, which passes overhead on a viaduct. It is a long way down from the hilltop and you would be advised to use a taxi or take the car, unless you are content to look down from the viaduct. Famous people including Émile Zola (a writer with a street named after him in almost every French town), Hector Berlioz (composer), Offenbach (composer), Nijinsky (ballet dancer) and Alexander Dumas (novelist) are buried here and there is an excellent cemetery plan in the Michelin Guide. It covers an area of approximately 500m by 300m and the entrance is at the end of avenue Rachel where street parking is available. The cemetery has a grid of paths, some cobbled and some tarmacked, which run in approximately 60m squares. It's a bit hilly. The tombs themselves are not all accessible from the main paths due to several steps, but there should be more than enough famous ones on view to satisfy your curiosity. Most of the tombs are grand and there is plenty of interesting stonework. There is nowhere to sit inside the cemetery, but there are benches on avenue Rachel. Men's (D58 no ST) and women's (D60 no ST) loos can be found just inside the gate on the left.

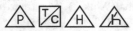

Musée d'Art Naïf (Museum of Naïve Art) and **Musée en Herbe (Children's Museum)**, 2 rue Ronsard, 75018. *Tel:* (1) 42.58.74.12 or 42.58.72.89. These two museums are housed in the **Halle St Pierre** at the bottom of the Montmartre hill. The building is on the opposite side of the steps from the funicular. Parking is quite difficult (see the Montmartre itinerary). The main entrance and ground floor Musée en Herbe are flat and have a café, gift shop and numerous low level displays. On the first floor the Musée d'Art Naïf Max Fourny is flat and can be reached by a lift (D79 W97 L190). **There is a unisex wheelchair loo (D77 ST97) on the first floor.** A lot of attention has been paid to the needs of people with disabilities, especially chair users, and our surveyors recommended this museum as being both interesting and fun for adults and children alike.

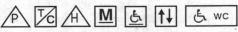

Musée de Montmartre (Montmartre Museum), 12 rue Cortot, 75018, *Tel:* (1) 46.06.61.11. There is very limited parking near this small museum exhibiting the history of the Montmartre area. The entrance has +3−1 steps with a 73cm door. There are four floors with between +8 and +17 steps between each floor. There is no lift and loos are in the basement −17.

 E4 N50

L'Office de Tourisme (Tourist Office), pl du Tertre, 75018. *Tel:* (1) 42.62.21.21. This contains a tourist information desk, bureau de change, and booking office for the Promotrain. The entrance has a step down. English is spoken.

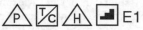 E1

Le Petit Train de Montmartre (Promotrain), 75018. *Tel:* (1) 42.62.24.00. Despite it being slightly expensive, we recommend this motorised 'train' trip if you can get on board. It gives a 45 minute guided tour of Montmartre and relieves the difficulty of getting around this otherwise very hilly area. It starts from place Blanche in front of the Moulin Rouge on the boulevard Clichy. Tickets can be purchased from the tourist office on place du Tertre or reserved by phone on the number above. *Watch out, because the carriage doors are only 40cm wide and 30cm above ground with no additional steps*. Transferring or getting into the little carriages presents problems, but with some help it would be possible for a good number of chair users and most disabled walkers.

Sacré Cœur

Sacré Cœur, Basilique du, pl du Parvis du Sacré Cœur, 75018. *Tel:* (1) 42.51.17.02. This huge white basilica dominates Paris' northern skyline. As explained above there is little opportunity for parking nearby, but there are taxi dropping-off points just below or just above the church itself. Whether you take a taxi or the funicular (see above) **there are +25 steps without handrails into the building.** The ground/main floor is all flat, so you can go round and see the mosaics and stained glass. The church is quieter than Notre Dame and has a more prayerful atmosphere. There is a small somewhat congested souvenir shop. Signposting inside is good. To get to the dome, you must first descend −40 to the crypt and then ascend +296 without handrails. The small loos are 40m outside the entrance, but are −13.

 E25 75%

Eglise St Jean l'Evangéliste (Church of St John the Evangelist), pl des Abesses (Michelin Guide Principal Walk 7). Designed by Baudot and completed in 1904, this church was the first to be built out of reinforced concrete and is architecturally interesting for this reason. Located at the end of rue des Abesses, there may be parking in front of the church and in the surrounding streets. The main entrance is +2 small steps. Inside it is almost totally flat except for +1 to a display area. The seating is movable.

 E2 N1 90%

Eglise St Pierre (St Peter's Church), 2 rue du Mont Cenis, 75018. *Tel:* (1) 46.06.57.63. Located just east of place du Tertre, it is the only remaining part of a great mediaeval abbey. There is very limited parking nearby. There is a step into a cobblestone courtyard and the entrance has a further +2. It is then flat inside the church, except for +3 to a small gift shop and information desk.

E3 N3 75%

Montparnasse, 75014 and 75015 (Michelin Guide Principal Walk 23) has a history somewhat similar to Montmartre. It developed on the debris from old quarries which formed a substantial mound and gradually it became a meeting place for musicians, sculptors, writers and poets. Unlike Montmartre, the mound has been levelled and the area has been extensively redeveloped, with modern buildings, a new station and a huge tower over 200m high. It is not a particularly attractive area and virtually the only 'sights' are the cemetery and the postal museum. If you want a good view of the city with easy access, then a good place to get it from is the tower's 56th floor.

There are wheelchair loos in the area in the gare Montparnasse and the Hôtel Meridian.

Cimetière Montparnasse (Montparnasse Cemetery), bd Edgar Quinet, 75014. There is a flat entrance from the boulevard Edgar Quinet where metered parking is available. The cemetery is very extensive and is crisscrossed by tarmac paths. The graves, including those of Baudelaire (writer), Guy de Maupassant (writer), César Frank (musician), and

Saint-Saens (musician), are tightly packed. The grave of Sartre (philosopher) and Simone de Beauvoir (writer) are close to the Edgar Quinet entrance where there is also a map showing the locations of other famous graves. The Michelin guide has a good map.

 80%

Tour Montparnasse (Montparnasse Tower), pl Bienvenue, 75015. This 200m high office building offers the most accessible "view" of Paris and is an alternative to the Grande Arche de la Défense and the Eiffel Tower. The underground car park has a lift (D100) to ground level followed by a step. Alternatively there are two other entrances into the tower's lobby: one from the north which is flat and one from the south which has +2 steps from ground level. The booking office for the express lift to the top of the tower is +8+8, but these can be avoided by using the lift (D100) in the Galeries Lafayette, part of the Centre Commerciale, next to the tower. The express lift (D110, W200, L150) leaves from the lobby and ascends to the 56th floor. The main viewing platform is here and affords a superb panorama. The window is only 70cm high making it at eye level for wheelchair users, although there is a 30cm ledge which makes it difficult to see directly downwards. A luminous frieze and annotated diagrams are provided to help you identify the major sites, but at a height of 120-170cm it may be above their sightline for many chair users. Part of this viewing area is reached via −3, but most of it is flat. There are some audio commentaries with earphones at a height of 110cm. The telescopes on the viewing platform are well above wheelchair user eye level. There is no seating except in the bar which is +6 from the viewing platform. The roof on the 59th floor offers an open-air view, but the +72−3 to get there poses something of a problem. There are loos (D57 no ST) on the 56th floor; alternatively there is a wheelchair loo in Gare Montparnasse.

 80%

Musée de la Poste (Postal Museum), 34 bd de Vaugirard, 75015. *Tel:* (1) 43.20.15.30. An imaginative museum, but not recommended for accessibility. We were unable to resurvey for this edition because it was shut for the summer period. Our previous visit had found a step at the entrance, and a lift (D65 W110 L95) to get you to the fifth floor where the first gallery was situated. After that there were a series of galleries with −6 steps in between each. The final descent was −10−10−10 back to the ground floor. None of the steps had handrails. It did not appear that the lift could be used to get to intermediate levels of the museum. There was a loo off a separate exhibition hall, +6 from the entrance. We hope that things will have changed, but please note that this information was not rechecked in 1992.

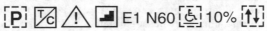

Mosquée (Mosque), pl du Puits de l'Ermite, 75005. *Tel:* (1) 45.35.97.33 (Michelin Guide Additional Walks and Sights). This was built in the 1920s and includes designs and decor from a number of countries. There is some non-metered parking on the street, but it tends to be fairly congested. Guided tours of the mosque leave every 20 minutes from the caisse (ticket office). The entrance has +2+3 steps without handrails and there are +4+5 into the first quadrant. From here there is a small step into the prayer area or −5−1−2−6 down into the Moorish style sunken garden which symbolises paradise. The loo (D61 no ST) by the entrance is −15.

Musée de l'Armée *see* Les Invalides

Musée d'Art Moderne de la Ville de Paris (Museum of Modern Art of the City of Paris), 11 av du Président Wilson, 75016. *Tel:* (1) 47.23.61.27 (Michelin Guide Principal Walk 24). This is in a large and somewhat confusing building called the Palais de Tokyo. It was built for the 1937 World Exhibition and houses a number of organisations. The modern art museum contains a collection representing the main trends of 20th century art. A famous exhibit is the picture *The Good Fairy Electricity* which represents the technicians and thinkers who have mastered this energy form. It is said to be the largest picture in the world.

Metered parking may be available on avenue du Président Wilson. There are two entrances; one from the riverside via +8+4+1 steps then +2+11+4; the other from avenue du Président Wilson which has +10+5. An earlier survey had identified a flat way in at the end of rue Gaston de St Paul, but this is a service/goods entrance. If the steps are a real problem, it might be possible to persuade them to let you in that way.

There are three floors connected by a service lift (D110 W240 L150) which you will have to ask to use. Many exhibits are in separate viewing rooms with split levels and numerous steps. Between the lower and upper ground floors there are two split levels: from the upper ground floor the Parvis Entrée is −22 and houses the cafeteria and Matisse room which is a further −3−5−4; the Dufy room is +18 from the upper ground floor and there are then a further +5+22 to the first floor. The loos (D60 no ST) are on the lower ground floor, which the lift does not go to.

We spoke to the museum curator/director who told us that by 1994 the museum would be adapted for access and have better facilities for people with disabilities. At the moment this building remains relatively inaccessible.

 E15 N20

Musée Cernuschi, 7 av Vélasquez, 75008. *Tel:* (1) 45.63.50.75 (Michelin Guide Additional Walks and Sights). This museum houses a collection of oriental, mainly ancient Chinese, art donated to the city of Paris by the banker Henri Cernuschi. It is in what was a house and so is quite small, but has some remarkable exhibits. It is located just outside the Parc Monceau off the boulevard Malesherbes. Parking is possible on surrounding streets, if you are lucky. A door at the main entrance can be opened if you ask, leaving +2 steps into the reception hall, from where there are a further +2 to a large lift serving both floors. Each floor is flat, although a few exhibits may be a bit high to be seen by a chair user. There is a loo (D68 no ST). When we suggested that the +2+2 at the entrance could be easily ramped we were told that this would "probably be done one day"!

 E2 N2

Musée de Cluny *see* Cluny, Hôtel et Musée de

Musée de Dali, 11 rue Poulbot, 75018. *Tel:* (1) 42.64.40.10. is a permanent exhibition of Dali paintings located slightly west of the avenue du Colviare in Montmartre. There is very limited parking available on surrounding streets. The main entrance has +2 steps but it is then −17−17 with handrails to the main exhibition area. There are loos (D66 no ST) located by the top of the exit stairs which are +20+15 from the exhibition level. There is a final large −1 drop to street level when leaving.

 E2 N34

Musée de l'Institut du Monde Arabe *see* Institut du Monde Arabe.

Musée du Louvre (The Louvre), 34-36 quai du Louvre, 75001. *Tel:* (1) 40.20.51.51 or 40.20.50.50 (Michelin Guide Principal Walk 1). The Louvre palace has had sections built in every century from the 16th to the 20th, making it the world's largest royal palace. It is a huge chateau which has been adapted to become one of the largest and finest museums in the world. It contains some very famous works of art. It also has some 18km of corridors and halls, so a visit can be quite daunting. Fortunately the controversial new pyramid entrance has made it more accessible than it used to be. Nevertheless, there are still problems. The reorganisation of the museum is not yet complete and only two of the exhibition areas are currently open: Sully and Denon. In a year or so's time the third area,

Richelieu, will be opened. The location of these sections is shown on the diagram. The museum will undoubtedly go through further stages of reorganisation when the new area is opened. The Louvre provides the basis of a *recommended itinerary*.

Arriving. There is an underground car park with its entrance in rue Marango under the Louvre des Antiquaires. This has a lift (D80 W120 L106) to street level where there is a small step. There is also metered parking in the place du Palais Royal. A huge underground car park is being built under the Jardin des Tuileries and this is due to open late in 1993. It will have several reserved spaces for people with disabilities and will provide direct underground access into the Cour Napoléon, the main hall under the pyramid.

The nearest car, taxi and coach dropping-off points are more than 50m from the pyramid, including the rue de Rivoli and the quai du Louvre. The nearest accessible RER station is Châtelet-les-Halles which is just over a kilometre away.

The Pyramid is the main entrance to the Louvre. It is an imaginative glass construction over the Cour Napoléon. The entrance is flat and wide. The main route down is by escalator. However, the design includes a remarkable piston lift called 'le Tube'. This does not have a lift shaft in the conventional sense, but rises on a huge piston from the floor of the reception area way below. The lift has an open top, so as you go up and down you can lean over the edge and look down. It has been beautifully designed, but there have been some problems with its reliability, which is not surprising considering that it is a unique piece of engineering. Hopefully the engineering bugs will get ironed out with time.

The **Cour Napoléon (Hall Napoléon)** is a huge area with ticket and information desks, restaurant, café, bookshop, giftshop, post office (D60), auditorium and wheelchair loos. There is free access to this area and it is worth a visit, even if you don't go on to see anything in the galleries.

When you arrive in the Cour Napoléon, go to the information desk and ask for the *Guide d'Orientation Visiteurs à Mobilité Réduite (Orientation Guide for Mobility Impaired Visitors)* which is available in both French and English. This should give you up-to-date information about which galleries are open and how to get there. It has diagrams showing the location of lifts and what they give access to. The three main parts of the museum are shown on the diagram and to identify what is on display the Louvre further subdivides each of these parts into numbered sections. In addition there is an identifying colour for each floor being used. The ground floor is shown in steely blue, the first floor in a dark maroon and the second floor in a darkish amber. It is worth spending a few moments getting to understand the system they use and the descriptions of where you can get to using various lifts since it will probably save you a lot of walking or wheeling.

The information desk also has a free *Guide du Visiteur a` Mobilité Réduite*, but this is only available in French. This gives a guided tour of the museum's highlights in the order in which they can be seen by taking various lifts. For further information, do not hesitate to contact the Louvre's disability officer, Anne-Marie Habdi, *Tel:* (1) 40.20.54.32. She seemed extremely helpful and is keen to improve the Louvre's services. She would be the person to contact if you wanted to arrange any kind of group tour or education session.

Disabled visitors and their immediate companions can have free entry to the museum. This normally applies to chair users, and we are not sure exactly what criteria they apply. You can borrow a wheelchair in the Cour Napoléon if you think it would be helpful and in view of the distances that's a good idea for some.

Temporary exhibitions are held in a hall off the Cour Napoléon which has −8 steps with handrails, but there is a wheelchair stairlift to bypass them.

The **Auditorium du Louvre.** *Tel:* (1) 40.20.51.51. Off the Cour Napoléon under the pyramid, it is used for concerts, 'colloques' (teach-ins), conferences and films. The entrance is flat but with heavy double doors. There is plenty of space at the top of the sloped seating for chair users.

A general point is to be wary of the polished wood and marble floors throughout the building as they can be rather slippery. There is some seating available in the galleries. Most exhibits are at wheelchair user height. The layout of the Louvre is confusing and the signposting is poor. Hence the orientation guide mentioned earlier is invaluable.

The museum is vast and it is impossible to see more than a fraction in one visit. If you plan your visit to see a sensibly restricted number of things and then come back a second time to see a bit more, you will probably enjoy what you do see twice as much. Just wait awhile in the Cour Napoléon and watch the blank faces of the people who have 'done' the Louvre in half-a-day if you don't believe us.

One thing to beware of is that the lifts tend to be carefully tucked away and they are not particularly well signposted. They are, however, marked on the orientation guide. Note that some of the standard guides are inappropriate for people with disabilities, in particular the *Guide for the visitor in a hurry* which really isn't much help because it takes you via numerous monumental staircases, of which there are legion.

The description here is based on the rooms open in December 1992 and, as we explained, these will change as the collections are re-arranged when the Richelieu wing opens. However, the objects described here are in their permanent position. The diagrams show firstly the relative positions of the three main areas. In the Cour Napoléon, after getting over your 'wonder' at its vastness and obtaining the leaflets we've mentioned, *what you need to do is to find lifts D and E*. These will get you up to the mezzanine level. We

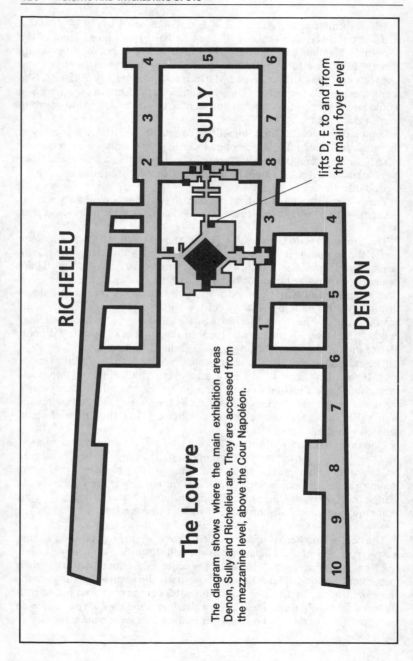

The Louvre

The diagram shows where the main exhibition areas Denon, Sully and Richelieu are. They are accessed from the mezzanine level, above the Cour Napoléon.

RICHELIEU

SULLY

DENON

lifts D, E to and from the main foyer level

Cour Napoléon mezzanine level

From the mezzanine you can go in one of three directions.

You arrive in lift D or E from the entrance hall below. The diagram shows the location of the key lifts for Denon and Sully (Richelieu was not open at the time of surveying).

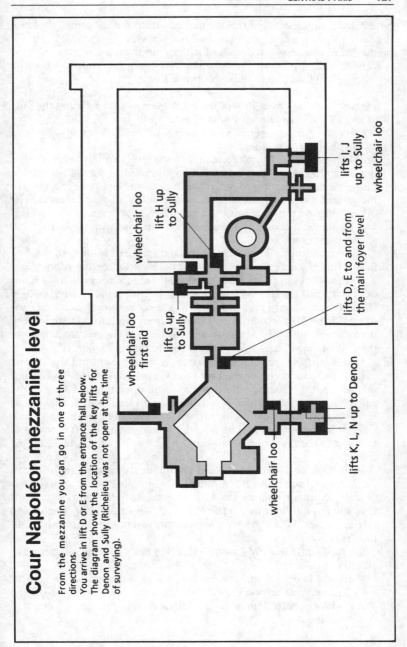

have made a detailed diagram of the mezzanine floor arrangement because this is the key to access to all parts of the Louvre. All the main lifts are marked, and you must first decide which exhibition area you are aiming for – Denon, Sully or (shortly) Richelieu. The exit you choose from the mezzanine will lead you to the appropriate lifts.

It is possible to see over 70% of the exhibits on display by using the lifts, including all the most famous works of art.

The following is a suggested tour which takes in all the main sights and avoids steps altogether:

You leave the Cour Napoléon at mezzanine level in order to get into the museum. To get up there, take lifts **D** or **E** located on the right-hand side of the escalators leading to Sully. The mezzanine level gives access into the ground floor of the main areas – currently Sully and Denon. The other things on the mezzanine are upper levels of the giftshop, restaurant, multimedia centre and more wheelchair loos with large door and sideways transfer.

Go round to the Denon entrance, and take lifts **K** or **L** to the first floor. This is where the main paintings are, including the *Mona Lisa*. There are works by Botticelli, Uccello and Titian among others. All this floor is accessible as far as Denon sector 8. Sectors 9 and 10 are via −3−6 steps. There is a huge area with paintings and you can get your best view of the *Victory of Samothrace* in Denon 3 from this floor. There is more than enough here for a long visit and the Grande Galerie alone is more than 300m long. There is a small accessible café in Denon 1.

When you have had your fill of paintings, go to the end of Denon 4 and ask for the door to be opened into the Galerie d'Apollon. This is not marked, but the guards are helpful and will open it up, as long as the gallery is not shut – which it is from time to time and commonly at lunchtimes. If you cannot get through, return to the mezzanine level, where you came from by lifts **K** or **L**, and go round to lift **G** in Sully, taking it to the first floor where you can pick up on the route described below.

In the Galerie d'Apollon you can admire the crown jewels and Suger's *Eagle Vase*. Then move on into the Sully first floor which contains art objects, Egyptian mummies and Greek vases. In Sully 8 you can take lift **C** to the ground floor to see the *Venus de Milo* and other Roman and Greek statues. When you have seen them, you must return by lift **C** to the first floor.

On the first floor move around to lift **G** in Sully 1. This gives access to all the Sully floors:

– ground floor; oriental antiquities (closed at the time of survey)
– first floor; already described, with flat access everywhere. Note the flat link back to Denon via the Galerie d'Apollon, asking a guard to open the door.

– second floor; there are some split levels on this floor, but these can be overcome using wheelchair stair-lifts. The problem with these is, as always, whether they're well maintained or not and sometimes they are not very suitable for disabled walkers. There's a wheelchair loo off room 11 (D70+ ST70+).

See what you are interested in here and then take the lift back to the mezzanine level. You can leave if you want, taking the lift back to the main Cour Napoléon floor level. If your eyes haven't glazed over, you could carry on and see the large Egyptian sculptures. Go round the 'moat' of the Mediaeval Louvre and take lifts **I** or **J** – located behind the large model of the Mediaeval Louvre and opposite some wheelchair loos – to the first floor. All the exhibits here are on the flat. To get anywhere else after this you must come back to the mezzanine. You could also take a detour to see Salle St Louis, part of the Mediaeval Louvre, by taking lift **H** located opposite lift **G**.

When the Richelieu wing is open, there will be a massive amount more to see. Judging by the care taken over access in other areas, the facilities should be good, although there may be some problems because the whole place is a historical monument. For more information get the updated leaflets and, if you need to, contact Anne-Marie Habdi.

Most of the lifts were large, with measurements as follows:

C	– (D80 W100 L120)
D and E	– (D170 W220 L270)
G	– (D110 W115 L170)
H, I and J	– (D140 W165 L135)
K and L	– (D110 W145 L165)

Wheelchair loos (D80+ ST80+) were found: off the Cour Napoléon, at the mezzanine level above the Cour, opposite lifts I, J and G; in Room 11 where there are paintings by Charles LeBrun; and there are probably others. You will have to ask the staff if you are a long way from one of the ones we discovered.

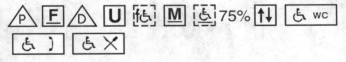

Musée de Cluny *see* Cluny, Musée de

Musée Nissim de Camondo (Nissim de Camondo Museum), 63 rue de Monceau, 75008. *Tel:* (1) 45.63.26.32 (Michelin Guide Additional Walks and Sights). Situated on the east side of the Parc Monceau this small, elegant house, built in 1910, contains an 18th century art collection furnished in the contemporary style. It was given to the nation by Count Moïse de Camondo and is particularly notable for having the oldest lift in

Paris – installed in 1911! There is some parking in rue de Monceau and a possible dropping-off point in the forecourt, about 25m from the entrance. Having crossed the gravelled forecourt, the entrance is up one step. After that it is flat to all three floors using the lift (D68 W100 L77). The lift is well hidden so you might find it necessary to ask to use it. Each floor is flat, although there may be some slightly narrow doors, the minimum being 74cm. There was no loo.

P T/C F △ ▣ E1 ↑↓

Musée D'Orsay

Musée d'Orsay (Orsay Museum), 62 rue de Lille, 75007. *Tel:* (1) 40.49.48.14 (Michelin Guide Principal Walk 11). Formerly a railway terminus and hotel, the Musée d'Orsay now houses a large and varied exhibition of paintings and sculpture. The period covered is approximately from 1850 to 1914. Photography is shown from its inception in 1839. Literature and music are included with both lectures and concerts. The Orsay provides the basis of a *recommended itinerary*.

The Orsay already had an imposing façade and the imaginative way the space and lighting inside has been used make this an exciting collection. The whole place is much more compact than the Louvre, although you will still cover between 500 and 1,000m if you want to see a great deal and seating is scarce.

Metered street parking may be available nearby, but there's not much of it. The signs send you to the underground car parks at place de la Concorde, quai du Louvre or the rue de Rivoli, all over 500m away. There's one designated parking space for disabled persons on the rue de Lille. When the Tuileries Gardens underground car park is open, for the Louvre, this may be the best place for parking. Note that the map indicates that there's parking on the port de Solférino, alongside the river, but getting from it to the Orsay is difficult as it's on the other side of the mini-motorway. Rebuilding work was going on at the time of the survey.

The taxi rank occupies the adjacent rue de Lille from which there is one step to the entrance. Alternatively there is a ramped entrance from the rue Bellechasse.

The information desk on the ground floor (level 0), to the right of the entrance, supplies a special plan of the museum in French for disabled visitors which shows the location of wheelchair loos and lifts. Wheelchairs are available on loan if you would find one helpful. There is a separate general information leaflet about the museum in English. We would suggest having a look at both these before setting out as not every lift covers all the floors and internal signposting is poor. The museum is designed so that you follow a path which covers the ground floor first, then takes you up to level 5 and finally leads you down the levels from here. The works are presented in rough chronological order, except when certain collections have been kept together.

Details of the lifts are as follows:
- lift A goes from level 0 either up to 2, or down to −1 or −2.
- lift B goes from level 0 to 2a, 2b, 3, 4 and 5.
- lift C goes from level 0 to 2, 3, 4, 5 and 6.
- lift D goes from level 0 to 1, 2, 3, 4 and 5.

Some of the lifts (D80 W105 L140) are concealed by heavy doors and only some of them have a call button at a suitable height for a chair user. On the special leaflet for visitors with disabilities they have confusingly used the same letters on the plan to mark both the lifts and some of the different exhibitions, but the lifts are marked in yellow. Note that lifts A, C and D are near the rue Bellechasse entrance while lift B is at the other end of the museum.

There are two restaurants: a smarter one on level 2 and a café on level 5. Both have movable tables and chairs. Down a tiny step from the restaurant on level 5, a terrace affords a lovely view north over the Seine, if open. Unfortunately there are very few seats other than those in the restaurant.

There are three unisex wheelchair loos (D89 ST89): on the ground floor near lift C, on the level 1 near lift D and on level 6 via the Salle de Consultation.

Musée Rodin (Rodin Museum), Hôtel Biron, 77 rue de Varenne, 75007. *Tel:* (1) 47.05.01.34 (Michelin Guide Principal Walk 4). The museum is near les Invalides and is housed in a splendid 18th century house which itself has an interesting history. The Rodin works are both inside the house and in the garden.

Parking is limited, but you will probably be able to stop in the boulevard des Invalides. There are +3 steps at the entrance, but a ramp is provided to bypass these. Wheelchairs are available for hire. There is flat access on both

Musée Rodin

ground and second floors and a lift between them. We were unable to see the lift as it was being serviced, but we were told that it is large enough for most wheelchairs. A few of the sculptures were on displays over 110cm high. The garden is flat almost everywhere. There is a step to get within 2m of *The Gates of Hell* and a small section is +11. Over 90% of the exhibition has flat access. There is a cafeteria in the gardens with flat access, but we found no adapted loos. There are some plans for redevelopment that will hopefully improve access as opposed to building new barriers and result in the provision of wheelchair accessible loos.

Musée du Vin, 5 rue des Eaux, 75016. *Tel:* (1) 45.26.63.28 or 45.25.63.26 (Michelin Guide Additional Walks and Sights). Located across the river from the Eiffel Tower just south of place de Costa Rica, this somewhat disparate museum may be worth a visit if only for its good access and free wine tasting which is actively encouraged! Parking for people with disabilities is available in the cobbled courtyard by the entrance to the museum, although a pole barrier needs to be lifted to enter the car park. Flat main entrance and mostly flat inside or gently sloped. All the displays are on the ground floor, but there are uneven flagstones throughout because it is a converted wine cellar. All the notices are in French, but an English translation is provided. There is a lunchtime café up a slight slope. Loos (D56 no ST) are on the left of the entrance hall.

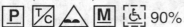

Museum of Modern Art of the City of Paris *see* Musée d'Art Moderne de la Ville de Paris

Nissim de Camondo Museum *see* Musée Nissim de Camondo

Notre Dame (Notre Dame Cathedral), pl du Parvis, 75004. *Tel:* (1) 43.26.07.39 (Michelin Guide Principal Walk 10). Situated on the Ile de la Cité, the Cathedral towers over the place du Parvis. A combination of history, architecture and a classic film make Notre Dame one of Paris' best known landmarks. It forms part of a *recommended itinerary* which also includes les Halles and the Pompidou centre. The inside is wonderfully atmospheric and there are sometimes services which are at least partly in English.

There is an underground car park beneath the place du Parvis but there are +25 steps to get out. You can obviously get out the way the cars come in and out, but be careful! There is little other parking in the vicinity and a taxi may be more convenient as there are dropping-off points nearby. The nearby RER station St Michel has a lift to street level.

The square outside is slightly cobbled. The kerb around the cathedral has been ramped at the northwest and northeast corners and then the entrance to the Cathedral is over a stone block which sticks up about 3cm. The inside is flat except for the Ambulatory which is +3. For the really adventurous, and slightly mad, the tower is +10+64+182+185. A superb view rewards those who are able to make it to the top and although there are a few perches, there are no seats.

 90%

Office de Tourisme de Paris (Tourist Office), 127 av des Champs Elysées, 75008. *Tel:* (1) 47.23.63.72 or 47.23.61.72 (in Michelin Guide Principal Walk 2 area). Situated 75m from the Arc de Triomphe before rue Galilée. There is some metered parking nearby and underground car parks down the Champs Elysées. The entrance has +1 step with two sets of swing doors. The office has booking facilities for hotels, SNCF, excursions, a bureau de change and a EuroDisney office (−3). There are no dropped counters. The office has some limited information on access in Paris though you may have to ask several times and be very insistent before they remember that they do. In 1993 they were handing out the CNFLRH guide which was published in 1987 and contains relatively little of use. Unfortunately the CNFLRH do not have the funds to undertake an update or extension of their guide. At the beginning of 1993 the Office de Tourisme were rebuilding the entrance, putting in revolving doors with no bypass. We pointed out that this wasn't a good idea for some people with disabilities, but no one appeared to take very much interest.

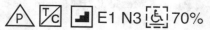 E1 N3 70%

Opéra de la Bastille *see* Entertainments/Music section

Opéra (Palais Garnier) Théâtre National, pl de l'Opéra, 75009. *Tel:* (1) 40.17.33.33 or 40.01.17.89 (Michelin Guide Principal Walk 6). The Galeries Lafayette has about the only nearby parking facilities (see *Shopping* section for details). There is no alternative to the main entrance's +10 steps to the vestibule and box office and a further +10 without handrails once inside. There is a lift (D84 W200 L100) on either side at the top of the second set of steps, going to all six floors apart from the basement. The basement can be reached by a service lift (D74 W74 L100). On the first floor there is a museum gallery which includes a split level involving −18 to the lower half and +24 to the upper half. In the basement there are +3 to a fountain statue. Guided tours are available but it is best to phone in advance as there may be rehearsals going on. Loos (D67 no ST) are on all floors. (For going to a performance see the *Entertainments* chapter).

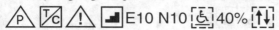

Orsay Museum *see* Musée d'Orsay

Palais de Chaillot (Chaillot Palace), pl du Trocadéro, 75016 (Michelin Guide Principal Walk 3). Just across the river from the Eiffel Tower, the Palais is a large curved building with two separate wings overlooking the Seine. When the fountains are playing, the building looks even more majestic. Limited metered parking may be available in the nearby rue de Franklin.

The east wing houses the Museum of French Monuments on the ground, first and second floors and the Henri Langois Cinema Museum in the basement. The west wing houses the Maritime Museum on the ground floor and the Museum of Man on the first and second floors. The Chaillot National Theatre is between the two wings but was closed at the time of surveying. There is a clear diagram of the lay-out of the Palais in the Michelin Guide.

East Wing
The main entrance on this side has +6 steps, but a stairlift has been installed to bypass these. This entrance leads to both the museums.

Musée National des Monuments Français *Tel:* (1) 44.05.39.10. A large, accessible and interesting collection of mediaeval sculpture, paintings and other art from many of the finest cathedrals in France. After the entrance described above the museum has flat access almost everywhere via a lift (D100 W150 L150). It is on three floors and the alternative is two flights of +35 steps, with handrails. There's a café with flat access and a **wheelchair loo (D90 ST150) beside the bar**, both on the ground floor. Wheelchairs are available for use if needed.

Musée du Cinéma (Henri Langois Cinema Museum). *Tel:* (1) 45.53.74.39. The main entrance has +6 steps as described and −25 into the Cinema Museum itself, although there is an alternative entrance found via a bumpy path through the gardens. Prior warning needs to be given to use this entrance and it is still +1+1 to enter the Palais and then a further −5+6 into the museum. On request, and with sufficient warning, the museum will provide a porter to assist you during your visit. At the time of surveying the only way to see the cinema is by guided tour in French which covers 250m with few chairs and takes 1½ hours. The museum is all on one level apart from −9 to the final room on the tour. There are no loos or restaurant. The usual exit is +10+2+11, but it is possible to use the alternative entrance route described above as an exit.

West Wing

   Musée de la Marine (Maritime Museum). *Tel:* (1) 45.53.31.70. There are +5 steps without handrails into this wing of the Palais and then flat access from here into the museum. Most exhibits are at wheelchair user eye level and there are lots of short videos. The only serious access barrier on the ground floor is a very steep ramp which doesn't have handrails all the way up it, but this can be bypassed by taking an alternative route to the left. The small basement, which contains more recent exhibitions and is not mentioned in the Michelin Guide, is −9−9−9−11−2 with handrails. There is no lift. The library, next to the ticket office, has flat access. There are plenty of seats throughout the museum. **There is a wheelchair loo (D70+ ST70+) in the foyer area on the ground floor.**

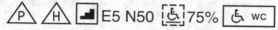

   Musée de l'Homme (Museum of Mankind). *Tel:* (1) 45.53.70.60. As with the maritime museum there are +5 steps to the west wing. There is then a small lift (D62 W105 L125) to the first and second floors where the museum is located. However, the first floor lift exit involves −5 to the museum and the second floor lift exit has −3+2. There is a fairly steep ramp on the first floor. If you don't use the lift there are +9+33+36 with handrails to the first floor and a further +22+15 with handrails to the 2nd floor. There are plenty of seats throughout the museum. Again, **a wheelchair loo (D70+ ST70+) can be found in the foyer area on the ground floor.**

   The west wing also has restaurant/bar just off the ground floor foyer area next to the loos. It offers splendid views of the Seine and Eiffel Tower from either inside or outside, and steps into this part of the building and onto the terrace are +1−1−1−2.

Palais de la Découverte (Palace of Discovery), av Franklin D Roosevelt, 75008. *Tel:* (1) 40.74.80.00 (Michelin Guide Principal Walk 2). This is the old science museum, now supplemented by the City of Science and Industry at la Villette. It has a planetarium and lots of hands-on exhibits. Staff members also do various scientific demonstrations from time to time, and it should be great for kids with an interest in these. Most, if not all, the commentaries are in French. It is in the area of the *recommended itinerary* for the Champs Elysées.

Parking is limited to a few metered spaces near the rond-point des Champs Elysées, and there's an underground car park at place de la Concorde some 300m away. The entrance has +3+13 steps without handrails to the ticket hall and then +13 without handrails to the ground floor exhibits. There is an unmarked alternative, and you must get one of the staff at the main entrance to open it up for you. It involves going about 30m to a gateway marked 'Porte B' just around the corner in avenue du Général Eisenhower. This leads to a lift (D90 W130 L108) bypassing all the steps and giving access to all the floors. Inside, each floor is flat and most exhibits are easily visible. A few exhibits are either +1 or +2.

If you want to go to the planetarium, it's best for a chair user to ring in advance, as they have to remove a seat to make space for you if you can't transfer. Alternatively you might be able to ask when you arrive so as to be able to go at the end of your visit. **Despite its being marked 'dames', the unisex wheelchair loo (D85 ST70) is on the ground floor behind the café.**

Palais de Justice (Law Courts), bd du Palais, 75001 (Michelin Guide Principal Walk 10). This is the centre of the French judiciary. It is in the same block as the Conciergerie and the Sainte Chapelle.

There is very limited metered parking in the area; alternatively there is an underground car park on the rue de Harlay. This has a lift with +1−1 step from the lower fourth to the lower first floor, from which it is possible to use the car ramp if you are adventurous and careful to get to street level, if you want to bypass the 20 or so steps.

The Palais de Justice has two entrances on the boulevard du Palais: one on the left and one on the right, if facing away from Notre Dame. The right-hand entrance has flat access and leads to an information desk from where a stair-lift may be taken to the courts. The stair-lift was broken when we visited. The left-hand entrance has +2 to a lift (D65 W101 L150), but it is quite a distance from here to the information desk. This lift goes to all floors, but you may encounter the occasional split level of +1−1 on the upper floors. The main interest and attraction is the façade outside which you can see without problems.

La Conciergerie (Prison Museum). *Tel:* (1) 43.54.30.09. A famous, or maybe infamous, building where Marie Antoinette, Danton and

Robespierre were held during the Revolution. This museum of prison life is part of the Palais de Justice. Exhibits consist of reconstructed scenes of prisoners and their guards in cells etc. The best parking is in the same underground car park as for the Palais de Justice, or the one outside Notre Dame. The entrance is off the Quai de l'Horloge with flat access to the courtyard and then +1−8 steps into the Salles des Cardes.

The main museum is up a +20 spiral staircase without handrails followed by +20 normal steps with handrails. There is no lift and the loos (D60 no ST) are to the right of the entrance. There are few seats in the building.

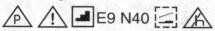

The **Sainte Chapelle** is also part of the Palais de Justice, on the Boulevard du Palais, opposite the Préfecture de la Police. The entrance has −3+1 steps to a small, but highly coloured, ground floor chapel which was used by the palace servants and has quite a low ceiling. The upper chapel is reached via +3+32+3 with handrails and has some very fine 13th century stained glass.

Palais du Luxembourg see Luxembourg, Palais et Jardin du

Palais de Tokyo see Musée d'Art Moderne de la Ville de Paris

Panthéon, pl du Panthéon, 75005. *Tel:* (1) 43.25.62.00 (Michelin Guide Principal Walk 20). This became the burial place for "great men who died in the period of French liberty". Mirabeau, Voltaire and Rousseau have their tombs in the crypt. The building has had a varied history, sometimes being used as a church; at one time it was the headquarters of the Commune, and later it became a lay temple. It has a fine exterior and impressive dome.

There is limited metered parking in the place de Panthéon. The entrance is on the rue Clotilde at the rear of the building, but it has +6+3 steps and then −26 with handrails to the crypt where the tombs are found. Those buried include Braille, Zola, Hugo and Voltaire. From the crypt it is +8 to see a display about the history of the Panthéon. The adventurous can attempt to reach the terrace which is +188 with handrails up a narrow spiral staircase from the crypt. It is a further +30 with handrails and +12+6 without handrails to view the painted ceiling of the dome. The main body of the Pantheon on the ground floor has been closed since 1985 for restoration and our survey team was unable to inspect it.

Parc de la Villette *see* La Villette

Parc Monceau (Monceau Park), bd de Courcelles, 75017. *Tel:* (1) 42.94.08.08 (Michelin Guide Additional Walks and Sights). Located below Montmartre, on the boulevard de Courcelles, this is a beautiful garden measuring about 200 by 500m. It has a simple criss-cross tarmac path running throughout. There is pay-and-display parking on the street at the east entrance with flat entrances from boulevard de Courcelles in the north and avenue Velasquez in the east. There are public squat loos (D61) which are up +3+2 steps by the north entrance. The park has a lake, refreshment kiosks and makes a pleasant escape from hectic sight-seeing. Two interesting museums, the Cernushi and Nissim de Camondo, are close by.

Petit Palais, av Winston Churchill, 75008. *Tel:* (1) 42.65.12.73 (Michelin Guide Principal Walk 2). The Petit Palais houses the **City Museum of Fine Arts** and occasional temporary exhibitions. Opposite the Grand Palais, the Petit Palais has a taxi drop-off point and metered parking outside the front and rear entrances. There are UG car parks on the Champs Elysées.

The main entrance (at the front of the building) has +23 steps. At the top of this there is a sign indicating an alternative wheelchair user entrance, although this is scarcely visible from below. Apparently the alternative entrance (at the rear of the building) has a lift, but the staff wouldn't let our survey team see it. When we last surveyed the building in 1984 this entrance was +4+2 from avenue Dutuit with a large lift (D100, W110, L120), but it may be best to check by telephone in advance if you are likely to want to use it. Once inside the building there is a further +7 (from the front entrance) to the main exhibits (although the lift may bypass these). The bookshop at the rear is reached by −7 and the pretty courtyard by −3. There are no seats available and sign-posting inside the building is poor.

Pompidou Centre (Georges Pompidou Centre, Beaubourg), rue du Renard, 75004. *Tel:* (1) 42.77.12.33 (Michelin Guide Principal Walk 13). The area around the centre is called Beaubourg after the somewhat disreputable medieval village that once stood there. Nowadays the gently sloping piazza in front of the building is a focus for a wide variety of performers trying out their songs, mime, juggling and poetry. If the weather is good it is a very animated scene. The centre is included in the *recommended itinerary* including les Halles and Notre Dame.

The centre is an ultra-modern structure which opened in 1977. It is built 'inside-out' with the services and pipework on the outside of the building, leaving a vast amount of space inside. It measures about 170m by 60m with five floors. Permanent features include the **Musée National d'Art Moderne (National Museum of Modern Art)** on the third and fourth floors, the **Centre de Création Industrielle (Industrial Design Centre)** which is a ground floor gallery, and the **Bibliothèque Publique d'Information (Public Information Library)** on the second floor with a wide range of both French and foreign books, together with slides, films and periodicals. There are frequent major exhibitions held there. Entry to the exhibitions can be covered by a day ticket or by paying for each exhibition separately. There is a large underground car park with split levels, ramps and disabled parking spaces. Entrances to and in the underground car park are well sign-posted and there is flat access via the large lift to the centre. The area around the centre is cobbled, as is rue Beaubourg where the flat main entrance is.

The building is basically flat everywhere as long as you use the lifts. The floors are carpeted and there are a number of medium-weight doors. The main method of getting between floors within the building is by escalators in transparent tubes on the outside of the structure. There are also four lifts towards the northwest of the building: one is reserved for disabled people (D102 W195 L150) and is attendant operated, whilst the other three (D97 W215 L128) are self-operated. One lift, for which you will require staff assistance, will take you as far as the first floor and from here the other three serve the higher floors.

There is a café on the fifth floor with movable tables and chairs. This has seats in the open air on the roof with splendid views over Paris. **The centre has a wheelchair loo (D90 ST85) in the main hall, next to the other loos. It may be necessary to get the key from the information centre nearby in order to use it. The loo (ST54) marked disabled in the café has less space.**

Prison Museum *see* Palais de Justice

Quatre Temps *see* La Défense

Sacré Cœur, Basilique du *see* Montmartre

Sainte Chapelle *see* Palais de Justice

St Eustache (Church), 2 rue du Jour, 75002. *Tel:* (1) 42.36.31.05 (Michelin Guide Principal Walk 13). This is a pleasant 16th century church. It has some rich decorations inside, and a remarkable façade with flying buttresses outside. Metered parking is possible in the street, or you might use the Les Halles underground car park. There is ramped access to bypass the steps at the church entrance from place René Cassin. Access inside is flat throughout, although there are some uneven flagstones. The nearest loos are in the Les Halles complex.

St Germain l'Auxerrois (Church), pl du Louvre, 75001 (Michelin Guide Principal Walk 9). In the square outside the Louvre, just off the quai du Louvre. This church has a fine porch and some interesting stained glass windows. Metered parking may be available in the square, or if not, try the underground car park of the Samaritaine department store, where lifts (D67 W97 L87) are available up to the ground floor of the store. You can then get through and go round to the rear entrance to the church which has +3 steps. The front entrance is +2+1−1 and the inside of the church is flat.

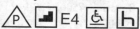

St Germain des Prés (Church), 3 pl St Germain des Prés, 75006. *Tel:* (1) 43.25.41.71 (Michelin Guide Principal Walk 18). The church is steeped in history dating back to the 8th century, having its part to play in both the Reformation and the Revolution. Parking meters can be found on both the rue de l'Abbaye and rue Jacob or you can be dropped off in the cobbled forecourt. The main entrance is across some 15m of cobbles and has +2+2 steps. Alternatively the St Margaret's entrance, half way up the side of the church on boulevard St Germain, has +1+1. The information desk inside the church is +1, whilst the chancel and displays are +2 otherwise it is flat throughout. There are two little gardens in the grounds around the church: one on the rue de l'Abbaye side has a flat entrance the other on the boulevard St Germain is +1 and has a remarkable mosaic.

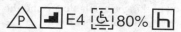

St Gervais-St Protais (Church), rue François Miron, 75004 (Michelin Guide Principal Walk 9). This is an historic 17th century church in place St Gervais next to the Hôtel de Ville. Parking may be difficult. The front entrance has +4+9 steps, whilst the rear entrance has a moderate slope then +1+6. There is flat access inside.

St Julien le Pauvre (Church), 1 rue St Julien le Pauvre, 75005. *Tel:* (1) 43.54.20.41 (Michelin Guide Principal Walk 19). Just adjacent to St Séverin is this small 13th century church with excellent views of Notre Dame. For parking see St Séverin. The main entrance has 10m of cobbles, then −2 steps. Alternatively it is possible to use the adjacent side-door entrance through the gardens which has −1. This side entrance needs opening by the staff who can be found at the information desk on the left, inside the main entrance. The inside of the church is flat. The adjacent gardens, Square R Viviani, have flat entrances and are mostly flat with numerous benches, although there are some cobbles. There are superb views of Notre Dame from the gardens.

St Louis (Church) *see* Les Invalides

St Peter's Hall *see* Musée d'Art Naïf

St Séverin (Church), 1 rue des Prêtres-St Séverin, 75005. *Tel:* (1) 48.04.98.01 (Michelin Guide Additional Walks and Sights). This 13th century church is situated on the south side of the Seine, across from Notre Dame. There is metered parking on the surrounding roads and one parking space for disabled visitors on the corner of rue de la Parchiminerie and rue St Jacques, although the facility is regularly abused. The easiest entrance on the corner of the rue St Jacques and the rue St Séverin has +1+1 very small steps. The main entrance has +3+2 and the information centre is a further +1.

St Sulpice (Church), pl St Sulpice, 75006. *Tel:* (1) 46.33.21.78 (Michelin Guide Principal Walk 21). This 17th century church is located on the place St Sulpice between rue Palatine and rue St Sulpice. It is dedicated to a 6th century archbishop St Sulpicious. Metered parking is available around the church. The easiest entrance has +4 steps with handrails from the rue Palatine. Alternative (D68) entrances have +12−1 from place St Sulpice or +5+6 from rue St Sulpice. Inside access is flat except for +2 to the altar and +2/3 to side chapels.

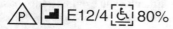

Sewers *see* Les Egouts.

Sorbonne Church *see* Eglise de la Sorbonne

Tour Eiffel (Eiffel Tower), quai Branly, 75007. *Tel:* (1) 45.55.91.11 (Michelin Principal Walk 3). The tower is probably the most famous landmark in Paris and is situated in a huge open area called the Champ de Mars. It was built for the World Exhibition in 1889, which in turn celebrated the centenary of the French Revolution. Since its opening, it claims to have had over 140 million visitors. It is included in a *recommended itinerary* together with a boat trip on the Seine.

There is parking directly under the tower, but this tends to fill up quickly and there are no reserved spaces for people with disabilities. An alternative is the car park for the Bateaux Parisiens which is at port de la Bourdonnais opposite avenue de la Bourdonnais, off the Quai Branly. This is about 200m from the tower and is ideal if you are going to take the boat trip as well, as suggested in one of the itineraries.

The tower has three floors and getting to the first and second floors poses no problems. It stands on four legs. Three of them have huge lifts giving a route up. However, there are variations in the accessibility of different legs as follows:

- Nord (north leg) is ramped directly to the ticket office, but the ramp is fairly steep. It is then flat to the main lifts.
- Est (east leg) has +7 steps which can be bypassed by a small hydraulic lift operated by staff. When things are busy it may be difficult to attract someone's attention. Again it is then flat through and you may need to get a door opened to avoid the ticket barriers.
- Sud (south leg) with +9 to the ticket desk and then access only by dozens and dozens of stairs.
- Ouest (west leg) has +13 which can be bypassed by a gently sloping ramp to the right of the stairs. You may need to remove a chain. From there it is flat to the lift, although you will need to get some doors open for a chair user to bypass the turnstile.

Our survey team were greeted by a member of staff at the north leg 'groups' entrance, despite not being a group. He ushered us into the lift ahead of the very long queue – so it can certainly be worth making yourself known. There was, however, a slight disagreement over whether the chair using member of our team could get to the third floor, as you have to buy a ticket for this at ground level. We agreed to differ and bought a ticket, which we had great pleasure in using later as the staff higher up didn't share the same reservations.

The lifts at ground level go to both the first and second floors. They are huge and have two tiers. The upper tier is reached by +18, but there is absolutely no advantage in going in the upper tier.

On the first floor, unless you go down the −7 steps to the viewing area, you can only see out on the Champ de Mars side. This is because the central part of the tower is occupied by a restaurant, conference centre, cinema (via +15), souvenir shop, café and post office. All the facilities have flat access, apart from the cinema. The viewing area down the steps is restricted because there is a balustrade all the way round at a height of 110cm and no elevated bits to help chair users. There are loos (D57 no ST) here.

To reach the second floor you either stay on the lift from ground level or take the lift from the first floor. The main section is flat and there is the

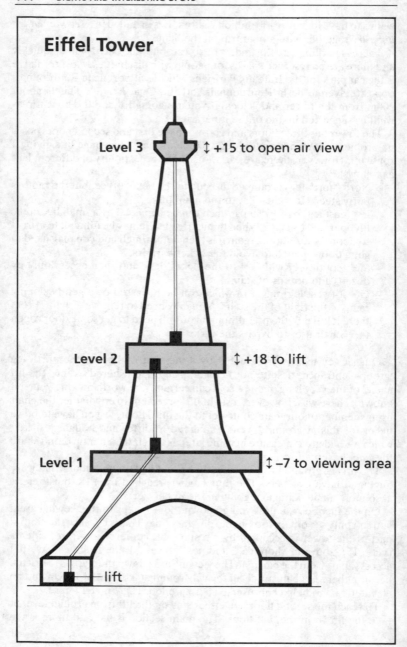

Eiffel Tower

Level 3 ↕ +15 to open air view

Level 2 ↕ +18 to lift

Level 1 ↕ −7 to viewing area

lift

possibility of viewing in all directions here. Again there is a balustrade all the way round at a height of 110cm, but there are regular gaps at a suitable height for chair users to see through. On one occasion we also managed to find a small trolley with a platform about 30cm off the ground and our chair using surveyor was able to see more from on top of this. **This floor has** an indoor area providing useful shelter, including a café, two souvenir shops and **a wheelchair loo (D80 ST92 and a hoist)**.

In the centre of both floors there are places to enable you to look back down on the car park underneath and on the second floor there are mirrors making it easier for chair users.

The second floor has an upper section which is +18. The steps are slightly spiralled, although there is a straight staircase from the covered area and we came across a stairlift in need of repair on one set of stairs. From this upper section, as well as a photo and souvenir shop, the large lifts go to the third and uppermost floor of the tower and staff can open a side gate to bypass turnstiles.

The queues for the third floor can be huge and on peak days you may face a waiting time measured in hours, however, our survey team again made their presence known and were ushered ahead of the queues. The view is unique and our chair user got up and down perfectly well, with a little help. At the very top you exit from the lift in to the lower section of the third floor which is enclosed. It offers a view through 125cm high windows with a handrail, and a labelled map helps you 'spot' the various sights on the skyline. There are seats, but they don't provide any view. To get the open-air view, there are +15 steps to the upper section where only wire mesh obstructs your view.

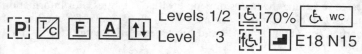

Levels 1/2 ♿ 70% ♿ wc
Level 3 ♿ ▰ E18 N15

Tour Montparnasse *see* Montparnasse

Town Hall *see* Hôtel de Ville.

UNESCO, Maison de l' (UNESCO House), 7 pl de Fontenoy, 75007. *Tel:* (1) 45.68.10.00 (Michelin Guide Principal Walk 3). This is an interesting building, especially for group visits. Informal talks, film shows and discussions can be arranged in English and individuals may like to join such activities with other groups.

There is a wide wheelchair user parking bay adjacent to the main entrance, opposite the Ecole Militaire off the place de Fontenoy. This entrance is flat. There is an alternative entrance on avenue de Suffren which has +5 steps. The ground floor is spacious and flat, housing several shops, exhibitions and a library. At the far end of the ground floor, near the avenue de Suffren entrance, there is the main conference hall which is flat/ramped except for the rostrum which is +5. There is a restaurant and café on the seventh floor. The cinema on floor −1 does not have an induction loop. Access to these public floors is flat via large lifts (D107 W195 L158). **There is a wheelchair loo (D70+ ST58 due to fixed bars) on the ground floor opposite the conference hall.**

Tourist Office *see* L'Office Tourisme de Paris

Tuileries Gardens *see* Jardin des Tuileries

La Villette, 75019. *Tel:* (1) 46.42.13.13 (Michelin Guide Principal Walk 15). This is a substantial area in northeast Paris, between porte de la Villette and porte de Panin on the boulevard Périphérique, which is being extensively re-developed. It was the site of the main cattle market and slaughter houses for a long time. The principal attraction is the City of Science and Industry with its spectacular Géode, a huge silver sphere which dominates the site. Just to the south there is la Villette Park. Further plans for development include restaurants and a hotel. The site provides the basis for one of the *recommended itineraries*.

Cité des Sciences et de l'Industrie (Centre for Science and Industry), 30 av Corentin Cariou. *Tel:* (1) 40.05.72.72 or 40.05.80.00. This is a massive structure on several floors, almost completely surrounded by an artificial lake. Inside it is spacious and a lot of thought has gone into the design regarding the needs of people with disabilities. For information for visually handicapped visitors *Tel:* (1) 40.05.75.35, for the hard of hearing *Tel:* (1) 40.05.75.19 and for general information for disabled visitors *Tel:* (1) 40.05.82.72.

The main entrance is directly above the underground car park whose entrance is on avenue Corentin Cariou. There are spaces for both cars and coaches and a taxi drop-off point before the barrier.

There is a good overall map of the complex in the Michelin Guide and diagrams of the upper levels, the 'Explora'. In addition there is an excellent hand-out available in both French and English at the information desk covering all floors. This has a sort of isometric diagram of each floor and has the lifts marked as blue tubes.

There is flat/ramped access to the lifts (D130 W150 L150). These go to both levels of the car park and up to the ground floor, level 0. **This is where you will find the information desk and ticket booths.**

It would take several hours to see everything and the entrance fee is significant, so it is not worth going there late in the afternoon. One thing to watch out for is that your cleverly computerised ticket only allows you to go through the barriers three times – these are the barriers between the 'pay' part of the complex and the public parts. Provided you know that, there is not much problem, but our surveyors crossed the boundaries too often and it caused a hassle! If you want to go to the planetarium, which costs extra, buy your ticket when you come in to ensure yourself a place, as it can get very booked up.

Basement (level −1). Entrance to this part is free. It is known as the Mediathèque, a huge multi-media library which is flat and spacious. It has audio-visual booths with videodiscs, of which four are designed for wheelchair access. The computerised catalogue of books is also at a low height. The Louis Braille room caters for the visually handicapped, including magazines, books and signs in braille. It also offers the sound of running water and plants that can be felt but it is quite small and so wheelchair user manoeuvres may be difficult. There is also a congress centre, job centre and history library, but these are only for use by prior appointment.

Main exhibition, the Explora, (levels 0, 1 and 2). You need to buy a ticket to enter this section. There is flat/ramped access to virtually all facilities which include the permanent displays called Explora. These cover themes such as the nature of the earth and universe, organic life, scientific laws and communication. Many of the exhibits have a braille description which has been put at about hand height. The exhibits include some items to do with space exploration and deep sea discoveries. There are a number of hands-on computer controlled videos and mathematical games. There are also some refreshment bars with movable chairs. The planetarium is on the second floor and has about ten wheelchair spaces but no induction loop. Across the centre of the second floor runs the Green Bridge which contains various tropical plants.

There is a super room for children on the ground floor called **l'Inventorium**, where visitors can get hands-on experience with experiments using soap bubbles, mirrors, magnets and various perspective tricks etc.

The only real problem is that to get between floors the main route is by escalator. Many people with disabilities will prefer or need to use the lifts and this involves getting a small gate opened most times by a staff member to bypass the turnstile.

La Géode. *Tel:* (1) 40.05.06.07. This projection theatre can be reached from the south side of the City of Science and Industry. Go through a revolving door or a side gate which can be opened on request. The Géode has the world's largest projection screens and looks like something from outer space. Inside there is flat access to an ice-cream parlour with movable chairs. There is a lift (D78 W85 L135) which goes up to the theatre. There are chair user spaces and headphones are available, but there is no induction loop.

Wheelchair loos (D70+ ST70+) are on virtually every floor, since wherever they have provided loos they have put in at least one huge cubicle in either the women's or men's areas.

Parc de la Villette (La Villette Park). This is located to the south of the City of Science and Industry. For parking use the same as above. Entrance is flat from avenue Corentin Cariou. Facilities in the park include a children's play area and modern sculptures. The area is flat, but there are some cobbled sections. The Canal de l'Ourcq, which divides the park into north and south, can be crossed by the west bridge via a lift on both sides (D79 W91 L200). The lifts on the east bridge were still under construction and so you must take steps at both sides +18+21+7.

The park has a number of 'follies' which vary in accessibility, but most are accessible on the ground and first floors. The follies are nine red-roofed pavilions built of enamelled iron on a concrete base. The main gallery is a raised walkway alongside the canal, giving a fine view over the park and the Géode. It can be accessed by the lift on the galerie de la Villette which goes over the canal (see Michelin Guide map).

The **Zenith concert hall** is very new, seating 6,000 and has flat access and a number of wheelchair spaces. It is used for pop and rock concerts and there is a car park alongside. The Cité de la Musique Conservatoire is for music students, while the rest of the development, as shown on the Michelin map, is not due for completion until 1994/95.

The **Cinaxe Simulator** is in the northern park about 200m to the southwest of the main entrance. This claims to be the largest simulator in the world. It is not at all good for wheelchair users as it moves quickly and has fixed seating with straps that must be moved. Unfortunately our survey team did not see inside the simulator, so it may be possible to sideways transfer, but watch out for its fairly severe jolting.

Vincennes (Michelin Guide Principal Walk 26). An enormous area just outside the southeastern section of the boulevard Périphérique. There is a large park, a partly ruined château, a zoo, a lake and floral gardens, as well as a Buddhist temple and a stadium. There is an excellent map in the Michelin Guide, detailing the location of the various sights.

The RER stations Fontenay-sous-Bois and Vincennes have large lifts, but the distances involved in the park mean that this is really best visited by car. Quieter, more relaxing and less 'disturbed' than parts of the Bois de Boulogne, it is ideal for a day with a minimum of sight-seeing. The area around the main lake is one of the more pleasant sunbathing spots in Paris, although this is probably not the place for you if you object to topless sunbathers. The park itself is pretty flat with lots of tarmac paths and there is plenty of parking on the roads which run through the park. Surveys are included of the main sights and facilities.

The Château. *Tel:* (1) 43.28.15.48. Little remains of the castle, except the 16th century Chapelle Royale (Royal Chapel), the massive Tour du Village and the impressive 14th century Donjon (Keep). It still looks quite impressive and there is a large square outside. There is a car park about 200m away or it may be possible to park closer on the road nearby. Pavements both outside and inside the grounds are mainly of gravel and/ or large cobblestones. There is flat access to the ground area around the keep, but it is +50+70+150 spiralled steps without handrails to the top. A 58cm door with a threshold hinders access to each floor. Access to the chapel is by +9. It is probably flat inside, although we didn't see it. The keep and chapel are only open to the public on a guided tour.

Parc Floral de Paris (Paris Floral Garden). The garden and special display pavilions were created for the 1969 Flower Show. It extends over 30 hectares and there is a good plan in the Michelin guide. The houses have an interesting series of small exhibitions, such as 'Paris trees', Bonsai plants, cactus, rhododendrons, tropical ferns etc. There are special exhibitions from time to time and also a children's playground. Altogether it is a nice area and quite a good place for children, as the exhibitions are small and well presented.

There is parking on some rough ground, either at the main entrance near the château, or at the Water Lily entrance down the route de la Pyramide. The garden area is fairly level. The paths are mainly metalled, but a few places are rough. About half the houses with plants or exhibitions in have flat access. There are, however, a number of houses where there are +2 or +3 steps which have not been ramped. Unfortunately no real thought has been given to access. In the Tudor garden, for example, there are unnecessary +2 steps here and there which could easily be ramped or even removed.

The **Le Bosquet restaurant** has access via a very tiny step, but the

Brasserie/Salon de Thé is up 1½ steps. The two designated adapted loos (D70+ ST40!) are marked 'WC' on the Michelin guide plan.

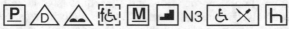

Parc Zoologique Paris (Zoological Garden), 53 av de St Maurice, 75012. *Tel:* (1) 44.75.20.10. About 2km from the château, this garden houses some 1,200 animals in natural surroundings. It is said to be the largest zoo in France. There are four entrances and parking should prove no problem. Most of the area is level, but the paths are only partly tarmacked, and there is quite a bit of rough and uneven ground. It is a big place and a thorough visit might take you between 2 and 3km. Many of the facilities were being refurbished when the survey was carried out, and for example, the large 72m high artificial rock which has a lift inside was closed. Entrance to the animal houses is via doors varying in width from 68-72cm. Sometimes there is a step and it is +2 to the lions. The walls are generally low, but the one surrounding the lions is 140cm high.

The café behind the elephant house is outside, and has movable chairs and tables. The restaurant next to the cheetah enclosure has flat access and movable chairs and tables. The souvenir shop near the elephant house is +2.

There are at least two wheelchair loos (D78 ST90) in the middle of the park which are reasonably well signed.

Centre bouddhique (Buddhist Centre). *Tel:* (1) 43.40.91.61. On route de Ceintre du Lac Daumesnil, on the south side of the lake. There is plenty of parking on the road outside the Centre. The main temple has a roof carved out of a chestnut tree and houses a 9m high statue of Buddha covered in gold leaf. It is flat through a large set of gates, with a small step up into the main temple and then flat inside. We were unable to see the smaller temple, but were told that there were many steps involved both at the entrance and once inside. There are +3 to a refreshment area which includes the loos (D69 no ST).

Lac Daumesnil (Lake Daumesnil). The name comes from a famous general who stoutly led the defenders of the Vincennes castle against invaders on several occasions early in the 19th century. The area around the lake is largely flat with plenty of paths and benches. It is possible to get to the lake's edge, but only by crossing a grassy area which drops fairly steeply into the lake. There is a restaurant to the south side of the lake with a large flat terrace and +1 step into the interior which has movable tables and chairs. Loos (D62 no ST) in the restaurant are +2. Next to the restaurant there is a crazy golf and a children's playground. Both are accessible by flat tarmac paths.

Vélodrome J Anquetil. Located south of Lake Daumesnil on the avenue de Gravelle between porte de Charenton and avenue de Maréchal. There is a large car park with flat access to the stadium, though in some places the path is gravelly and uneven. There is a large, flat area between the stadium seats and the track which we were told could be occupied by wheelchair users to watch races. The stadium seats are reached by many steps to each level. The restaurant has +1 step with movable tables and chairs. There are three loos: two are +1 (D67) squat style and the third is (D63 no ST) and +1 to the right of the restaurant as you enter the stadium and around the corner.

Wine Museum *see* Musée du Vin

World Trade Centre *see* La Défense

OUTSIDE THE CENTRE

Two of the places described here are included in the chapter with *recommended itineraries* list. St-Germain-en-Laye is particularly easy to visit if you use the RER as it is close to an accessible station. Versailles is best visited by car since you can get some superb views and see some of the gardens much more easily.

Chantilly (Michelin *Ile-de-France* Guide). Chantilly is the home of the famous racecourse. There is a large and beautiful museum – including the Petit Château and Grand Château – with extensive gardens and a nearby racing-horse museum housed in the magnificent stables. The château is surrounded by extensive artificial lakes and in mid-June each year there is a spectacular international fireworks competition called *Nights of Fire*.

If approaching from Paris on the N16 do not drive through the town, but turn right off the lower road onto the route de l'Aigle. The château has a car park about 300m from the entrance on a steepish slope. The parking area immediately by the château could be used by a solo disabled driver or others if absolutely necessary, though this is not policy and may vary depending on who is on duty. A car with a chair-using passenger can unload about 50m from the château, but it should then be parked back in the main car park.

Château et Musée (Château and Museum). The main entrance to the Petit Château is flat and is reached across a cobbled courtyard. The rooms are called the Prince's Suite and they were built by the Prince of Condé in the 17th century as part of the extensive redevelopment of the château. The Petit Château may only be viewed by a guided tour in French lasting about 50 minutes. There are plenty of places to sit down during the tour. The tour takes in the Chapel, but this is +13 steps with handrails on one side and a further +3+2 without handrails.

The museum also houses a remarkable art collection in the Grand Château which you can go and see without an organised tour. However, there are +11 without handrails to reach about two-thirds of the collection, +5 without handrails to one room and +5 +4 with handrails to a further four rooms on the east wing.

There are no adapted loos, and the loos are −7 without handrails (D64, no ST) on the left-hand side of the stairs in the courtyard opposite the main entrance.

The Park is situated to the southeast and northeast of the château. They are quite extensive, with some large artificial lakes and a Grand Canal. The monumental staircase is −16−19−9 steps from the terrace to the gardens, although much of the highly geometric layout can be seen without descending. Alternatively there is flat access to the gardens if, when approaching the château from the car park, you take a right fork before the ramp up to the château, go under the archway and into the lower level of the gardens. Once you get in, the gardens are about 80% flat with gravel paths and only the occasional step. The route recommended in the Michelin Guide is about 3km long. The visiting survey team reckoned that these gardens were not a patch on Versailles as they are not currently so well kept.

The **Grandes Ecuries (Great Stables)** are about 400m west from the château. There is car parking through the St Denis Gateway about 100m away. The **Musée Vivant du Cheval et du Poney (Horse and Pony Museum)** in the stables is up a slight slope on rough gravel. The entrance is flat with double doors and all areas are connected by ramps. You get a good layout map with your ticket. All but three rooms are on the ground floor and two-thirds of the surface is cobbled, but only slightly rough. The majority of displays are visible from a wheelchair. Many displays have English as well as French text and seats are available in display areas. The first floor is +26 steps but contains only a tiny part of the exhibits. The loos (D71 no ST) are on the ground floor near the entrance. The museum has a small café with snack foods.

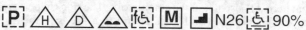

Chartres (Michelin *Ile-de-France* Guide). This beautiful town, about 70km from Paris, would make an ideal day trip. Not only does it have one of the world's most famous cathedrals, but it also has some lovely museums and easily accessible picnic spots with panoramic views. The cathedral was consecrated in 1260 and attracted huge crowds of pilgrims in the Middle Ages. It contains some 4000 carved figures and some spectacular stained glass dating from the 12th and 13th centuries and depicting as many as 5000 characters.

The cathedral square is full of restaurants, many of which have flat access. In the summer, Chartres is often much cooler and less oppressive than Paris. The easiest car park for a day trip is in the place de la Cathédrale, although it was full when we visited. **The only wheelchair loo (D111, ST65) that we found is in a souvenir shop on the south west corner of the place de la Cathédrale, next to the police station and opposite the archaeological dig. It is a pay loo in the men's.**

Chartres SNCF station, rue Nicole, 28000, Chartres. Large car park in front of the station with flat access to the ticket office, shop and a buffet with movable chairs and tables. There is flat access to all platforms via ramps which go over the tracks and are therefore quite bumpy. No ramps to the trains themselves were seen, and getting on board can be a problem because the carriage is usually up about three steep steps. The station is 600m from the cathedral, but the hill is steep. If you come by train and are without a car it would probably be best to get a taxi from outside the station where the rank has flat access. Trains to Chartres depart from the Gare Montparnasse and take less than an hour.

Office de Tourisme (Chartres Tourist Office) *Tel:* 31.21.50.00. Located in front of the west entrance to the cathedral on the corner of the rue de l'Etroit Degré, from where there are +9 steps to the entrance. There is a flat entrance via a signposted wheelchair route from the place de la Cathédrale. The staff were helpful and spoke English, although their understanding of access problems seemed fairly limited.

Chartres Cathedral is an exceptionally beautiful 11th century building with some spectacular stained glass. The easiest entrance is at the west door across a cobbled courtyard where the +5 steps can be bypassed by a ramp. Once inside, the nave and ambulatory are flat, allowing you excellent views of the stained glass. The cathedral and crypt have a flagstone floor which is uneven and rather slippery. The cathedral itself is over 100m long. There are +2 to the south arm of the transept and +4 to the north arm, but these can be by-passed from the nave near the altar. From here it is also flat to the ambulatory. The side chapels are +1 or +2 and the chancel is +3. The cathedral treasure is in the St Piat Chapel and has a very steep +6+2+23 to reach it.

Tours of the crypt begin from outside the Maison de Clerc, which is on the left if facing out from the cathedral's south door. We were unable to survey the crypt but were told that there were at least −10 at the entrance and then flat access to most of the crypt. The St Lubin crypt, however, has further steps down to it. For information on wheelchair loos and parking see the Chartres introduction above.

 80%

International Stained Glass Centre, 5 rue du Cardinal Pie, 28000, Chartres *Tel:* 37.21.65.72. This fascinating and beautiful exhibition highly rated by our surveyors, is set back from the road through large iron gates. Parking for disabled visitors is available in front of the museum on request. Flat access to the whole centre, including the auditorium. There are plenty of seats throughout. The loos (D56 no ST) are −27 steps with handrails.

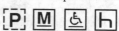

Musée des Beaux Arts (Museum of Fine Arts), 29 Cloître de Notre Dame, 2800 Chartres, *Tel:* 37.36.41.39. This museum is set back in the gardens, the entrance to which is at the end of the rue Cheval Blanc. Someone with mobility difficulties may be able to park in front of the museum on request, otherwise in the place de la Cathédrale. There is a cobbled and gravelled courtyard to the entrance which has +13+11 steps without handrails. From here it is flat to eight rooms of exhibits, but after that there are many steep staircases with many steps to the other floors. The house is a maze! There are no lifts and no loos. The gardens around the house are gravelled and have lots of benches. They also offer an excellent view of the city and surrounding countryside and would make an ideal spot to have a rest or a picnic.

 E24 40%

Fontainebleau (Michelin *Ile-de-France* Guide). One of France's major attractions, this large and impressive palace is situated some 60km south of

Paris. Used, in its time, as a hunting lodge by various aristocrats and royals, it is surrounded by a huge area of forest and it provides some attractive drives and picnic spots. The palace grew as successive kings wanted an impressive setting for displaying their art treasures as they acquired more and more of them. The buildings surrounding the Farewell Court were originally used by the servants. Later decorations, in particular the grand horse-shoe staircase, provided a dramatic setting for royal events. Most notably, it was the setting for the departure of Napoleon I on April 20th 1814 where he made a memorable farewell speech, before going into exile, giving tribute to those who had followed him. The leaflet available at the information desk has a clear plan of the principal facilities' location and marks the lift and wheelchair loo.

Even a visit to see the exterior and parts of the gardens is probably worth it; with endless possibilities for forest drives, and the Michelin Guide suggests some routes.

To get there by car take the A6 to the Fontainebleau exit and then the N7. By train, you need to go from the Gare de Lyon to Fontainebleau-Avon and then take bus A, bus B, or a taxi.

While still retaining some obstacles, Fontainebleau is one of the sights that has much improved its access since 1984. The nearest available parking is directly in front of the building itself, but there are no reserved spaces for disabled visitors and there is a time limit of two hours. There is an underground car park about 100m away which has a lift (D79 W109 L139) to ground level; alternatively you can use the car park with one space for a disabled visitor at the back of the kitchen courtyard where there is a time limit of three hours.

The entrance is on the right-hand side of the Cour de Cheval Blanc (alternatively called the Farewell Court) as you enter from the west, across cobblestones. There are two steps into the ticket hall. The staff were helpful but be careful to buy tickets for entrance into the right parts of the Palace. The main parts are:

- the Grands Appartements (Grand Apartments), Galerie de François I (François I Gallery), Salle de Bal (Ballroom) and Appartements royaux (Royal Suite) all on the first floor
- the Musée Napoléon I (Napoleon I Museum) which is entered on the first floor, but also has exhibits on the ground floor
- the Petits Appartements et Galerie des Cerfs (Small Apartments and Deer Gallery) on the ground floor
- the Musée Chinois (Chinese Museum) on the ground floor
- the various gardens, including Jardin de Diane (Diane's Garden), Jardin Anglais (Landscape Garden), the Parterre around the Basins and the Park.

For the Grand Apartments on the first floor, take the lift (D77 W130 L148) at the far end of the entrance hall, past the stairs. Turn right out of the lift, through the removable ticket barriers for the Grand Apartments.

These are flat except for −2 steps into the François I Gallery and the narrowest door width is 68cm. Turn left out of the lift and there are −6 to the Napoleon I Museum. To view the ground floor whilst avoiding stairs, take the lift back down to the ground floor and then ask for a set of adjoining doors to be unlocked. The staff seemed to be aware of this need and willing to help.

The Small Apartments can only be visited as part of a guided tour and are not always open. The Chinese Museum is a small collection which was shut when we visited. Consequently neither was surveyed.

There is a wheelchair loo (D70 ST73) +2 from the entrance hall. The key needs to be collected from the cloakroom.

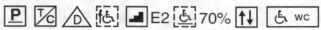

The Gardens: Parking for the gardens is signposted. You can park at the place d'Armes, place de Boishyver or a UG car park with lift underneath the place Napoléon Bonaparte. There are several entrances of which the Route des Cascades by the canal is recommended for the fine gardens and a view of the palace. Other entrances are found opposite the place Napoléon Bonaparte, the place d'Armes (though with one step) and at the main entrance to the palace. There are some cobbled areas near the buildings, otherwise the paths are made up of a combination of gravel, tarmac and sand. There are refreshments on the place Napoléon Bonaparte. The gardens are vast and benches tend to be nearer the Palace. The gardens are apparently particularly lovely in the autumn.

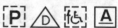

Parc Astérix, BP 8, Plailly, 60128, *Tel:* 44.60.60.00. Like its more famous successor EuroDisney, this theme and amusement park is based on cartoon characters. Asterix is a brave little Gaul who, with his roly-poly friend Obelix, always seems to get his way, whatever the odds. Sampling Asterix's Gallic charm is considerably less expensive than that of visiting his American counterpart. Parc Astérix has a combination of rides, attractions, shops, food kiosks and a great deal of cartoon memorabilia. Knowledge of the books by Goscinny and Uderzo is not vital to having a good time, although a general idea of the stories might make things clearer.

The park is about 40km northeast of Paris and is probably most easily reached by car. Take the A1 out of Paris and turn off at the prominent signpost to Parc Astérix. There is only one entrance and there are lots of disabled parking spaces which stewards will direct you to if you ask. If you don't have a car you can take the RER line B to Roissy Charles de Gaulle which has large lifts, from where a courtesy bus with stepped access will take you to the park. This bus normally runs every half an hour.

In general the park has good access and the staff were helpful and expressed a keen interest in minimising access barriers. The rides are similar to those in fairgrounds, although far larger in size, and you cannot get on whilst remaining in your chair. On the other hand the staff were very willing to help people with transferring out of chairs. If you get to a ride and decide not to go on it there is no problem about using the exit gates, and you may consider getting in through these gates as well, as our survey team did. This will get the attention of the staff who will often let you in without queuing. This may sound a bit sneaky, but in general the staff seemed very willing to bend the rules and to give wheelchair users and other disabled visitors priority.

It must be stressed that there is a great deal more on offer than just 'rides'. Our survey team included a chair user who was unable to transfer but had a very enjoyable day. There's a whole load of shows and happenings, and the various venues for these are all wheelchair accessible. Our advice would be to check out when the 'shows' are and plan your day around them. You might wish to check at the main information point at the entrance whether certain things are functioning to save traipsing a long way unnecessarily. There are many wheelchair loos throughout the park, details of which are below.

The main entrance to the park is flat and gates at the ticket office can be opened if necessary. Although it is not cheap, Parc Astérix is competitively priced. In 1992 adults paid 150Fr, while children who are less than 140cm high paid 105Fr. Under 3's (regardless of height!) go free. Children are prohibited from some rides for safety reasons.

Detailed maps are given with the tickets and show where all the main attractions are. However, the park is constantly undergoing change and, as we found, the maps may not be completely accurate. Information points are marked on the map, but they did not all seem to exist, so if you have any questions, ask before you leave the entrance area. We were assured that the map would not be altered for quite some time which is useful as we have referred to numbered attractions below.

The park covers 16 hectares and a full visit could probably involve travelling about 3km. You can borrow a wheelchair at the information desk which is on the right after the main entrance. There are lots of benches throughout the park. The cost of food in the park is not exorbitant, and there is no problem with bringing a picnic. There are a number of nice areas to sit and eat it. Most restaurants in the park are accessible and have movable tables and chairs.

Unless stated otherwise it can be assumed that any ride mentioned has access that is flat and wide enough for a wheelchair user to get to a place for transferring.

The following attractions, listed with their name and number, may present access problems:

- (8) *La Descente du Styx*: Entrance for wheelchair user is through a special gate by the exit. There are −9−9 steps with handrails down to the platform, although the staff will help anyone down and will stop the moving platform so that you can transfer.

- (15) *Le Tapis Volant*: No wheelchair access for safety reasons.
- (33) *La Balade d'Astérix*: Similar to the Descente du Styx - see number (8) above.
- (37) *La Trans'Averne*: The entrance is too narrow for a chair user so the exit must be used, which is −9 without handrails.

The following venues have convenient wheelchair spaces, and wheelchair access, so they are easily accessible to other people with disabilities:

- (6) *L'Arène des Gladiateurs*: Using the flat main entrance there are ground level spaces.
- (18) *La Delphinarium*: Access via the main entrance for the ground level view. Our intrepid survey team went up the long ramped exits from the top of the arena which gave a far better view. The gate is quite a way round to the left from the main entrance and requires someone to reach over and push the locking-bar down.
- (19) *La Place du Moyen Age*: There is a special raised level/stage for actors allowing wheelchair users to see the events.
- (25) *La Troisième Dimension*: Flat access and special wheelchair spaces in the back row.
- (32) *Le Théâtre du Barde*: Flat access and two rows of wheelchair spaces – one at the back and one in the middle.

There are seven sets of wheelchair loos of varying quality. We have listed them in relation to their 'region' and number on the plan of the park handed out at the entrance.

In *Via Antiqua* (5), women's +1 step (D70+ ST130), men's (D70+ ST70+) but inward opening door.

In *Cité Romaine* (12), women's (not surveyed), men's (D83 inward opening ST115)

In *Le Grand Lac* (17), women's (not surveyed), men's (D80 ST100). (16) in Arcimboldo restaurant, women's and men's (D82 inward opening ST182).

In *Le Village d'Astérix* (35), women's (not surveyed), men's (D100 ST100).

In *La Rue de Paris* (21), women's (D85 ST95), men's (D85 ST105).

In *La Place de Gergovie*, there is a unisex loo at either end of Relais Gaulois. One is in Chez Selfservix (39) with (D89 ST145).

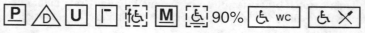

Parc St Cloud (St Cloud Park) (Michelin *Ile-de-France* Guide). A huge area of over 450ha of woodland just west of Paris on a hillside overlooking the Seine across the river from Boulogne-Billancourt. The main entrance is from the park's eastern end and it is possible to drive everywhere in the park stopping wherever you want. Some of the laid-out gardens are terraced with splendid flights of steps, but without ramps or handrails. There are benches, but the size of the park makes long distances likely. Internal signposting to facilities in the park, such as loos and restaurants, is non-existent. There are four restaurants in the park, but all the loos are narrow with +4 or −4 steps at least and usually a lot more. All the restaurants have parking, flat access and movable chairs.

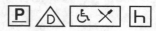

Rambouillet (Michelin *Ile-de-France* Guide). Southwest of Paris on the D150 about halfway between Versailles and Chartres. The château may only be viewed by guided tour and is closed on Tuesdays as well as from October to March.

Rambouillet is a delightful town and the château is often used as a summer residence for the President. The château is just off the place de la Libération, on the corner of rue de Général de Gaulle and rue de la Motte. Behind it are some substantial artificial lakes and extensive gardens. The tourist office is also on this corner with +4 steps to enter, as is the Hôtel de Ville with +6 and a car park which has two double spaces reserved for people with disabilities.

The entrance to the château is 150m away over cobbles. For a smoother entry go 500m north up rue de la Motte and enter the château grounds through Grille de l'Hôpital and there is a small car park, from where the château is 300m away along a tarmac road. There is more parking on the rue de Général de Gaulle.

For security reasons the survey team was unable to measure anything inside the château and some were about 60cm. The entrance has +5+8+12 steps and the ground floor has the magnificent Marble Hall. There are three sections where it is necessary to negotiate +15 leading to the reception rooms and, although the survey team were told that there was a lift, they could not see it.

In the grounds is the Chaumière des Coquillages (Sea Shell Cottage) which forms part of the tour. A semi-circle of rocks and +4 form an odd and difficult barrier. The gardens have flat gravelled paths and the roads into the forest offer areas of great beauty for picnics or just relaxing round the lakes.

The place du Roi de Rome also has an interesting garden with a fountain. There are +2 to a stone picnic table.

There is a public loo (automatic cubicle with D46 and no ST) round the side of the tourist office. The restaurants and cafés do not have any adapted loos, but the Restaurant Bisson, opposite the tourist office car park, has +2+2 at the entrance and a loo with D57 and no ST.

St Denis (Michelin *Ile-de-France* Guide) is a suburb to the north of Paris with a number of interesting sights. You might visit it because of your interest in French history, because of the cathedral or because of an interest in the history of flying.

Cathedral, pl de la Légion d'Honneur, St Denis, 93200, *Tel:* (1) 48.20.15.57. Built in the 12th and 13th centuries, St Denis has long been a centre of pilgrimage and most of the kings of France were buried here. You can see the steady development of funeral and monumental art. After the 14th century, it was usual for the heart to be removed from the king's body before embalming and for it to be buried elsewhere. Although the bodies were originally buried at St Denis, the tombs were emptied at the time of the Revolution.

Located in the centre of town, parking near the cathedral is limited. The main entrance has one step through a wooden gate and then +3 into the cathedral. The nave is −3, although a ramp is available on request. Many of the statues and points of interest can be seen at this level.

The crypt, housing the tombs of Marie Antoinette and Louis VIII among others, is −15 without handrails. The chancel and ambulatory is +20 with handrails where you will find more royal tombs and monuments. An audio guide to the cathedral in the form of headsets is available in English.

Musée de l'Air et de l'Espace (Museum of Air and Space), le Bourget Airport. Located just north of St Denis, this museum forms part of a small airfield in which hangers have been converted to exhibition halls. Le Bourget was the main airport for Paris for half a century, until Charles de Gaulle became operational quite recently.

There is ample parking directly outside the museum. The main entrance is flat. An English guide sheet is available. Most of the displays are on the ground floor with low level information boards. There is flat access to the permanent exhibition and to Halls C (military), D (early planes), E and F (space craft). There is a viewing platform which is +25, but you don't need to get up there as you can see everything from the floor. The café across the tarmac has one step at the entrance and movable tables and chairs. **The men's wheelchair loo (D78 ST105) is in**

Hall C, whilst the women's (D78 but no ST because of fixed handrails) is in Hall F.

P T/c M ⌊&⌋ 90% | & wc | | & X |

Musée d'Art et d'Histoire (Art and History Museum), 22 bis, rue Gabriel Péri, 93200 St Denis. The museum is set back from the road just south of the cathedral, but is well signposted. It is a small museum in a former Carmelite Convent which has been partly restored and has a wide range of exhibits including paintings, archaeological remains, modern art and collections of modern posters.

Parking is available on the main road. The museum is approached up a 20m path, part of which is cobbled. Because it is located in a convent, most of the displays are in rooms off the ground floor, although a few are upstairs. Most have a small step. We were told that other steps on the ground floor can be avoided by using an alternative route, but locked doors prevented this when our survey team visited. There is no lift and it is +21 to the first floor and a further +21 to the second, with a handrail. The loos (D57 no ST) on the ground and first floors are +1.

P △ ▟ E1 N21 ⌊&⌋ 40%

Parc de la Courneuve (Courneuve Park). This 400 hectare park is located on the RN301/D114 off the A1 autoroute north of Paris near St Denis. There are two car parks off the RN301 and one off the D114. Entrances into the park are flat or ramped and it is flat/ramped throughout.

It is a beautiful park with a boating lake, stables, gardens and seasonal attractions throughout the year. There are some steep slopes on the north side of the lake and to the Vallée des Fleurs. In addition to numerous refreshment kiosks there is a restaurant/bar, with ramp and one step at the entrance, on the east side of the central green. There are four public loos (D56 no ST) shown on free maps. The maps are good and signposting is adequate. Long distances could be involved.

P △D ⌐ | & X | ⊓

St-Germain-en-Laye Château (Michelin *Ile-de-France* Guide). This small (100m by 50m) Renaissance château with its adjacent gardens are an attractive and highly accessible site. It has a varied history, several associations with the British Royal Family and contains the Musée des Antiquités Nationales (National Museum of Antiquities). A visit forms the basis of one of the *recommended itineraries*.

Located to the west of Paris, it is served by an RER station just across the road with a large lift operated by the RER staff which leads to a ramp 50m down the road from the château entrance. There is parking on adjacent roads although it's a somewhat busy and congested area. The entrance to the site has 30m of cobbles and leads either to the gardens or the château.

Château. Flat entrance. The museum is spread over three floors with a lift (D90 W135 L200) connecting each floor, and flat or ramped access everywhere. The lift is used with staff assistance and is on the left through the souvenir shop. There are spare wheelchairs in the wheelchair loo if needed although there is seating throughout the museum and the exhibits are all at wheelchair eye level. On the ground floor there is a facsimile of the Bull's Hall in the Cave of Lascaux. The cave has been closed to the public to prevent deterioration of the paintings. On the mezzanine there are other exhibits from prehistoric times. The first floor contains many antiquities from Greek, Roman and Egyptian times.

   The wheelchair loo (D90 ST100) to the left of the souvenir shop exit is unisex, despite being in the men's. It is kept locked but the staff will provide a key. It should be noted that strenuous efforts have been made to make this building accessible and staff were helpful.

Jardin Anglais (English Garden). Running north from the château, the garden offers panoramic views of the Paris basin, particularly from the rond-point du Rosarium which is 500m from the entrance. Like the château the entrance is across 30m of cobbles. Access is generally good although the surfaces are rough. The garden is about 500m square and has three kiosks with seating and an expensive restaurant with a flat entrance in the southeast corner of the gardens. Loos in this restaurant have flat access through narrow doors.

The town of St-Germain-en-Laye starts just across the road from the château. It's quite attractive and has some pedestrianised areas. In general the pavements are narrow, and many of the small shops are congested and have a step at the entrance.

Vaux-le-Vicomte (Michelin *Ile-de-France* Guide), 77950 Nancy, *Tel:* (1) 60.66.97.09. The château, 40km southeast of Paris, is only a short drive from Melun on the N36. Alternatively you can get by train from the Gare de Lyon to Melun in 40 minutes. There is plenty of parking on the road opposite the house. The entrance is down a gravelled ramp and then has −3+1−16 steps to the narrow ticket barriers. The staff were unhelpful and would not allow us to survey. The house looks to be an access nightmare with about +15 to the front doors across a moat. Separate tickets can be bought for the gardens but you still have to make it to and through the ticket booths. Once inside, the gardens are pretty flat and so this may be the best option. The house is supposed to be lovely and it certainly was from the outside. From April to October there are afternoon fountain displays on the second and fourth Saturdays of the month. No loos were seen.

 E35

Versailles (Michelin *Ile-de-France* Guide), *Tel:* (1) 30.84.74.00 or 30.84.76.76. Versailles is the largest and possibly the most magnificent royal palace, built on a truly monumental scale. It has spectacular gardens which are beautifully kept. The town grew up as a result of the presence of the palace, to house the people who served the court, together with civil servants, gardeners and domestic servants. The palace provided the government headquarters for about a century, prior to the Revolution in 1789. The Michelin *Ile-de-France* Guide has some excellent plans and maps. Versailles provides the basis for one of the *recommended itineraries*.

On various Saturdays and Sundays through the summer, there are musical and aquatic entertainments, sometimes with fireworks. These can be spectacular, in the setting of the gardens and artificial lakes. Information on these can be obtained from the Tourist Office, 7 rue de Réservoir, 78000 Versailles, *Tel:* (1) 39.50.36.22.

The palace and gardens are unbelievably huge and it is important not to try to see too much. For this reason, we would advise some planning. You must first decide whether you want to go inside the palace. This is possible as there's a lift inside to the first floor. However, as you will read in the survey, long distances are involved. The staff we spoke to recommended late afternoon as the least crowded time for visiting the palace, as most people have gone home to Paris for dinner. During peak times people with disabilities will have problems manoeuvring amidst the crowds inside. If you have particular interests the staff also suggested ringing to check what parts of the building are open, as renovation regularly results in the closure of certain sections.

If you decide to concentrate principally on the grounds, the gardens and on outside views of the facade, there is a suggested route in the chapter on *Recommended itineraries*.

If you go by road, take the N185 from porte St Cloud on the boulevard Périphérique.

To get there by train, go by SNCF from Gare St Lazare to Versailles' Gare Rive Droite, rue du Maréchal Foch. You need to buy a ticket from the 'Banlieue' ticket booths (24-29), which are opposite the international service desk, roughly in the middle of the station concourse. A regular service leaves from the Banlieue platforms (1-6) and it is a small step with a 20cm gap. Although ramps are meant to be available, there was a distinct absence of station staff to provide you with one. The journey takes about 30

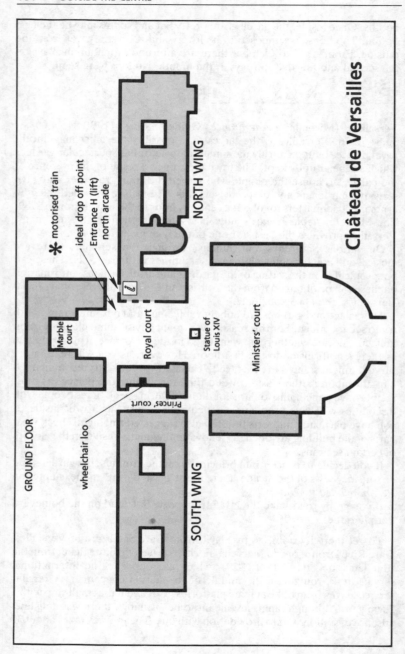

Château de Versailles

* motorised train

ideal drop off point

Entrance H (lift)
north arcade

NORTH WING

Marble
court

Royal court

Statue of
Louis XIV

Ministers' court

GROUND FLOOR

Princes' court

wheelchair loo

SOUTH WING

minutes. At Versailles, after a similar −1 from the train, there is a lift (D95 W95 L105) from the end of platforms 3 and 4 down to the ticket hall and street level. From here it is about 1km to the palace itself. Although RER line C also takes you to Versailles, in this case Gare Rive Gauche, it presents serious access problems (see RER write up).

We found two wheelchair loos in the town, both in McDonalds. One is in the branch in rue du Maréchal Foch, on the right-hand side of the counter. It is signed and unisex (D88 ST110). The other is in the branch opposite Versailles-Rive-Gauche RER line C station, rue Royale (D70+, ST70+).

Parking for the château is outside the main gates, immediately in front of the palace. From the parking area there is some 400m to go, much of it over a rough cobbled surface. The car park is shown on the diagram; car parking is on the left side and coach parking on the right. With a little gentle persuasion we were allowed to park our minibus in the Cour des Princes (Princes' Court), which would be our recommended spot for disabled drivers to use too. There is a real problem with the public parking areas since the car park on the left has a strict 2.1m height restriction with bars over the gates. This means that if you're in a minibus or a car with an elevated roof, you can't get into this space at all. The coach park on the right is strictly (and bureaucratically) for coaches only. As you can see, we managed to get permission to park our minibus inside the grounds, but the 'formal' arrangements are not good.

If there are disabled passengers or if the driver is disabled, you are allowed to drive right into the palace courtyard, and get quite close to where you go into the building or through the arches into the gardens. In view of the distances involved, this is a valuable facility. To get there, go up the road between the car and coach parking areas which is initially marked 'no entry'. Just before the main gate there are two information points. A gendarme at the gate will undoubtedly want to know what you are doing. However, we found them to be most helpful, and when we explained that we were going to drop off two disabled passengers, they radioed for someone to meet us further up.

To get into the palace, go to entrance H which is off the archway to the right just before the raised part of the courtyard on the right, *see* diagram. Note that the entire 150m long area in front of the palace is cobbled. **There's a wheelchair loo just off Princes' court (D80 ST76)**, *see* diagram.

The Palace. At entrance H we found that the staff were helpful and some of them spoke good English. There are wheelchairs available for use. If you require tickets, go next door and join the queue. The only lift (D137 W185 L77) is at entrance H and from here it goes to the first floor.

Because there is only one lift and certain areas are inaccessible for wheelchair users, the choice of exhibits is slightly limited. However, there is an enormous amount to see, especially the more impressive and beautiful exhibits such as the Hall of Mirrors and State Appartments.

Parking at Versailles

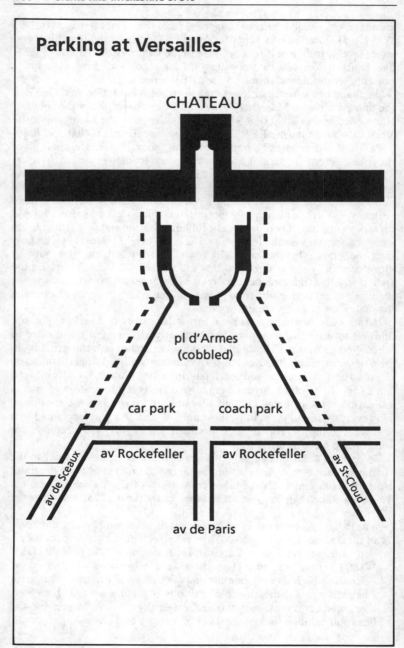

Certain areas are visited only on a guided tour. Chair users are not normally allowed on these, but we got the impression that with some arm twisting this rule could be bent. Other areas are simply not on public display from time to time. The guided tours and closed areas change from year to year.

Most of the ground and first floors can be reached without steps, but the second is reached only by those with plenty of energy for stair-walking. Fortunately the second floor doesn't offer a great deal to see. Beware the slippery marble staircases, 80% of which have handrails on at least one side.

For food there is a café/restaurant outside the main entrance, which is +1−18−4 with handrails for part of the way. The nearest café in town is a good 500m away. The bookshop with 68cm door is in the Princes' Court near the wheelchair loo.

Gardens. These are magnificent, especially at certain times of the year, and are free to get into. You can get an idea of their size from the Michelin *Ile-de-France* Guide which allows three hours for a 'quick' tour. The paths throughout are gravelled and only occasionally uneven. If steps exist, ramps tend to have been provided, although your initiative may be stretched finding some of them. One notable area which isn't ramped is the Orangerie, boasting 'great' staircases of one hundred steps. There is a very steep slope from the Water Gardens by the palace to the Apollo Basin by the Grand Canal which may be inaccessible for many chair users, but the atmosphere and view from the upper section surrounding the palace's rear will leave a lasting impression.

A **motorised train** leaves from the gardens area just through the arch from entrance H and circumnavigates the entire gardens, canal and trianons. There is not enough space to put a wheelchair on to the train but sideways transfer is possible and staff will safeguard your wheelchair until you return. *The 'train' is highly recommended.*

Grand Trianon. This pavilion is located some 1½km away from the palace whilst still remaining within the confines of the gardens. It has its own small car park and an entrance of +3 steps without handrails. The ground floor is flat, but tiled and rather slippery. Seating and wheel-chairs are available. It is −7 to the gardens. **There is a wheelchair loo (D70+ ST90) in the men's 150m from the main gates**.

Petit Trianon. 300m from the Grand Trianon, this pavilion has an entrance with one step and all the exhibits are on the first floor which is +4+28 with handrails most of the way.

Boats can be hired from the landing stage in the Petite Venise (Little Venice), on the nearest end of the Grand Canal to the palace. You have a choice of rowing boats which are boarded via −2−1 steps without handrails or a trip by motor boat which has −2+1+2+1 with handrails onto the boat and then −3 once on the boat. **The Petite Venise** area has a snackbar, open grass areas and **wheelchair loos (D72 ST76).**

EURO DISNEY THEME PARK

Euro Disney Resort, BP 105, Marne-la-Vallée, 77777, France *Tel:* (1) 49.41.49.10, *Tel from the UK:* (071) 753 2900, *Tel from the US:* (407) W-DISNEY.

You can make reservations for accommodation using *Fax:* (1) 49.30.71.00 or 49.30.71.70. For special assistance or information on special event schedules, *Tel:* (1) 64.74.30.00 for the Guest Relations Desk.

Euro Disney is located some 32km east of Paris off the A4 in Marne-la-Vallée. It is well signposted from the road and is also on the RER Line A at Chessy. As well as the theme park with all its rides and attractions, the site also has six hotels each with its own theme, a Davy Crocket campsite, a lake and a golf course. What is there now is only the beginning of a development which has a planned expansion right through to the year 2017. Another theme park will be built around the Disney MGM Studios, adjacent to the existing site and there will be more hotels and a water-sports facility.

The brochures describe it as "the most spectacular entertainment experience in the world". While this is obviously part of the hype, a visit is thoroughly recommended, particularly for families with children, and for any groups of people who want to have a fun time. It is smaller than its American counterparts and the main theme park is about $^2/_3$km (or half a mile) across. It can provide enough variety and entertainment for a mini-holiday on its own, certainly for two or three days.

We recommend the *Mainstream unofficial guide to Euro Disney* by Tania Alexander published by Mainstream Publishing, Edinburgh. There is also *Euro Disney Resort Paris – The Guide* published by Disney Hachette which gives practical advice and 'gets you in the mood' for the fantasy. There are lots of others, including a *Michelin* guide.

It's quite expensive to get in, so if you do go, make the most of it. Sort out when and where the entertainments are, and remember that there's sometimes a fireworks display *Fantasia in the Sky* and the *Main Street Electrical Parade* in the evenings. So be prepared to pace yourself and do a little planning.

The hotels and campground offer various two or three-day "all-inclusive" holidays and you can book these direct with Euro Disney. Prices vary according to the time of year.

There are a number of organisations selling packages, including British Airways and P & O European Ferries. In addition, there are (among others):

Cresta, Cresta House, 32 Victoria St, Altringham, Cheshire WA14 1ET, *Tel:* (0345) 056511

Eurocamp, 28 Princes St, Knutsford, Cheshire WA16 8BN, *Tel:* (0565) 633844

Paris Travel Service, Bridge House, Ware, Herts, *Tel:* (0920) 461000

Wallace Arnold, Gelderd Rd, Leeds LS12 6DH, *Tel:* (0532) 636456

Your local travel agent will doubtless be able to put you in touch with many more and there are dozens of tour operators who can include entrance tickets to Euro Disney as part of their package. However, some words of warning are appropriate since only a limited number of tour operators have much experience of making bookings for people with disabilities. If your needs in relation to travelling and accommodation are fairly specific, then make sure that your operator knows what you need and has a reasonable chance of delivering it. Eurocamp does not have pitched tents at Camp Davy Crockett as it does at other sites, but uses the cabins whose access limitations are described in the section on camping. Wallace Arnold came across in their brochure as being more clued up than the others; they at least mention travellers with disabilities and say that they have particular staff to deal with those bookings.

A company who specialises in organising trips for families and groups with disabled members is **ATS Travel,** 1 Tank Hill Rd, Purfleet, Essex RM16 1SX, *Tel:* (0708) 863198 *Fax:* (0708) 860514, or in the US, PO Box 2718, Winter Haven, Florida 33883, *Tel:* (813) 324 5994 *Fax:* (813) 324 0537. From the UK they organise holidays using air travel at between £250 and 350, while transport to and from the airport costs over £100 more for wheelchair accessible transport. They can offer other less expensive packages using wheelchair accessible coach transport from the UK.

John Grooms Freeway, 10 Gloucester Drive, London, N4 2LP, *Tel:* (081) 802 7272 *Fax:* (081) 809 1754, is a travel service which gives advice about accessible accommodation and travelling, as well as organising specific trips. They have a fully accessible coach and arrange holidays to a number of destinations, including Euro Disney. They are happy to help, even if Euro Disney is only one of the places you want to visit in France.

Mobility Ambulance Services VIC Industrial Park, West St, Erith, Kent DA8 1AA, *Tel:* (0322) 441155 *Fax:* (0322) 441011, organise occasional group holidays to Euro Disney.

If you're travelling independently, the 1992 rates for entrance to Euro Disney were 225Fr (150Fr for under 12s), two days 425Fr (285Fr under 12) and a three day pass 505Fr (375Fr under 12). The entrance fee allows you free and unlimited use of all the rides, except the Rustler Roundup Shootin' Gallery, as well as the shows and parades. What you will have to pay for is food, and the things you're tempted to buy as souvenirs. You should note that the official 'picnic' area is outside the main entrance.

One of the cheapest ways of 'doing' Euro Disney, particularly if your visit is part of a more general holiday, is to book your own accommodation off-site and then buy a one, two or three day pass. Several of the hotels we have listed outside Paris with adapted rooms are quite close by. However, *this will mean missing out on the themed hotels in the evening*.

The Euro Disney hotels

These nearly all have rooms to sleep four people, usually with two double beds, or one double and two bunk beds. They are therefore more economical for families than for couples or single people. They all have adapted rooms for people with disabilities.

We surveyed three hotels in some detail and found the access to be generally good. Two had wheelchair loos in 'public' areas. All had adapted bedrooms with adequately spacious bathrooms for side transfer, but they all had conventional baths with a shower fitting and handrail. This clearly does not suit everyone and we hope that in the future some rooms will be available with a wheel-in shower and a suitable seat and rails for those who prefer that. Prices vary. At the Cheyenne and the Santa Fe a room was around 600Fr, while at the five star Disneyland Hotel it was 1200Fr. Prices also depend on the time of year.

Hotel Cheyenne, BP 115, 77777, Marne-la-Vallée, Cedex 4, *Tel:* (1) 60.45.62.00 *Fax:* (1) 60.45.62.33.

The hotel is built in the style of a Wild West town, with a sheriff's office, saloon etc. There are a number of hotel bedroom blocks including dozens of ground floor rooms. Car park outside. There is flat access to reception and to all facilities, including the kids' cartoon area, games room, bar, restaurant, laundry, dance hall and outside seating area. There is also flat access to the bedroom blocks.

There are about twenty adapted rooms for disabled guests. The one we saw (room 1739) had low level light switches and a bathroom door (D75 ST83), so there was plenty of room. There was a conventional bath with appropriate handrail. There was apparently no provision if you preferred a wheel-in shower with a seat to a bath. Also there was no adapted loo with ST near the public areas such as the saloon.

Hotel Santa Fe, BP 116, 77777, Marne-la-Vallée, Cedex 4 *Tel:* (1) 60.45.78.00 *Fax:* (1) 60.45.78.33. The hotel is built in the style of a New

Mexico town. It aims to reflect the earthy architecture together with the desert setting. As you approach the hotel there is a towering drive-in movie screen with an image of Clint Eastwood. A yellow highway centrestripe aims towards the horizon, suggesting the infinity of the American West.

Car parking is immediately outside. Flat access to the reception, to all ground floor facilities and to adapted bedrooms. On the ground floor you will find the information desk, bar, restaurant, games room and shop.

There are about thirty adapted bedrooms. The one we saw (room 20014) was some 200m from reception. It had a 70cm door, and an adapted bathroom (D77 ST96) and a bath with handrails. It was adequately spacious.

There was a wheelchair loo (D77 ST120) near reception.

Disneyland Hotel, 77777, Marne-la-Vallée, Cedex 4, *Tel:* (1) 60.45.65.00. This is right outside the theme park main entrance. There is parking some 50m away. Flat entrance, but there are some heavy doors. The rotating doors can be by-passed. There are three lifts (D120 W160 L160) and these go to all four floors. The restaurant is on the second floor with movable chairs and tables. Facilities such as the swimming pool, sauna, and children's games room are reached by going up to the second floor and then to the west wing and back to ground level by lift.

The eight adapted rooms have huge doors and bathrooms. The one we saw had a bathroom (D80 ST190). It had a conventional bath/shower with handrail. There is a wheelchair loo (D86 ST190) near the information desk. The hotel has a wheel-in shower in the Health Club.

Camp Davy Crockett is included in the chapter on *Accommodation*, and there are regular shuttle buses running to and from the theme park. There is an indoor heated swimming pool in the campsite village, and good washing facilities, with generally good access. There is a maximum of one step here and there, the equivalent of a kerb.

Getting there

We are told that Euro Disney have an accessible minibus to take you from your resort hotel to the theme park, if you cannot use the normal shuttle buses. We are not sure how readily available this facility is.

If you are coming by car from the centre of Paris, leave via porte de Bercy and continue along the A4 in the direction of Metz-Strasbourg. The complex is off exit 14, while Camp Davy Crockett is off exit 13 (Serris). The main visitors' car park is some way from the main entrance to the theme park but there is a special car park assigned for "non-ambulatory" guests close to the Disneyland Hotel and about 200m from the entrance. Follow signs for "les Hôtels du Parc" and "Disneyland Hotel". Signposting to this car park is quite good, although there is no indication that you have actually reached the correct car park except for the fact that you can't go any further. There may be staff along the route trying to direct you somewhere else so it is wise to ensure that before you follow their directions they know you are a wheelchair user or disabled walker. Otherwise they may direct you to the wrong car park. When we visited, the attendant failed to see the wheelchair user members of the survey team and so initially we were sent in the wrong direction. The main car park is a long way from the main entrance. Even using the moving pavements which run alongside the parking area you could easily walk up to 700m to the entrance. We recommend that disabled walkers also use the alternative car park by the Disneyland hotel.

By RER, Line A has been extended to Marne-la-Vallée, Chessy, and the station has flat access, bringing you to within about 250m of the main entrance. Several central Paris stations can give flat/lift access to RER stations (see the chapter on *Travelling in Paris)*.

When the Channel Tunnel opens, high speed trains are scheduled to stop at the Euro Disney resort, but you won't be able to travel directly from London. You will either have to change in Lille, or go to the gare du Nord and take the RER.

Getting in

Directions to the ticket barriers are clearly marked from the special car park. Entrance to the park is through turnstiles but alongside each turnstile there is a 91cm gate which can be opened for access. There are attendants at each gate. Our survey team arrived in the morning and the queue to get in was enormous. We were able to bypass it, however, by going to the Guest Relations Kiosk which has a counter height of 115cm. This is located by the readmissions point which is actually closer to the car park than the main entrance. We explained we were there to survey and were allowed to buy tickets without queueing. However, a family including a chair user also bought tickets at the kiosk. Officially the guest relations kiosk is only a ticket purchase point for hotel and camping ground guests, but the staff were clearly reasonably accommodating. This may vary from day to day and from one member of staff to another, but it is certainly worth a try to avoid the lengthy queues for the main entrance especially if standing is a problem. The queueing aspect highlights the value of pre-booking, but you may be stuck with coming on a day when the weather isn't so good. Having obtained our tickets (a "passport" which gives you access to every ride and show for the whole day) we were able to enter the park via the readmissions point.

Inside the Euro Disneyland park

The theme park and the cast (staff members are all regarded as members of the cast) aim to bring the Disney stories to life, hence Mickey Mouse, Peter Pan, Snow White and the seven dwarfs, Alice in Wonderland and many others. The futuristic Discoveryland is unique to Euro Disney, and was inspired by the likes of Jules Verne, Leonardo da Vinci and H G Wells.

All the cast members are supposed to speak English and French and you can easily tell what languages they do speak as they have the appropriate national flags on their jackets.

Throughout the park our survey teams reported that the cast (staff) were helpful and gave assistance wherever they could. They seemed very knowledgeable and are worth asking for directions and help with rides. They are, however, under instruction not to give physical help to anyone. It is a regrettable knock on from the position where the company is frightened of being sued in connection with some kind of accident. American fears of litigation are well known, but the official position is a nonsense in our view, because it takes no account of common sense and ordinary human behaviour in the effort to 'protect' the owners against all eventualities.

The main attractions are the **parades** and **entertainments**, both of which are generally wheelchair accessible, the **rides**, where there are some restrictions, and the **ambience or atmosphere**. Details of the times of the parades and of various entertainments can be obtained from City Hall on Main Street, near the main entrance. Basically you will either love it or hate it! If you come with kids you will almost certainly love it.

Remember that the park is quite big and there are long distances to wheel or walk to see things. There are likely to be long queues at weekends and during holiday periods for major attractions.

On the diagram you will see that you can use the railway to get to or from the other end of the theme park. A visit minimising the distance you go could take you down Main Street to the Central Plaza. This is about 300m. A detour into Frontierland would take you some 200m and back, if you want to get close to Big Thunder Mountain. You may also want to get a glimpse of Adventureland, and if you add in the bits nearest to the Central Plaza, it might add a further 300 to 400m to your trip. Going on into Fantasyland it is only another 300m to the station at the far end. You could then make your way back through Discoveryland, probably taking you some 700m via Videopolis or Cinémagique. This will take you a total of around 2km, possibly a fraction more. Over a whole day that is not a huge distance, and taking suitable breaks for eating and just sitting and watching could make it relatively easy.

There has obviously been much thought put into the design of the park and it is a shame that the rides and some internal transport could not be designed to accommodate chair users without having to transfer. In particu-

Euro Disney theme park

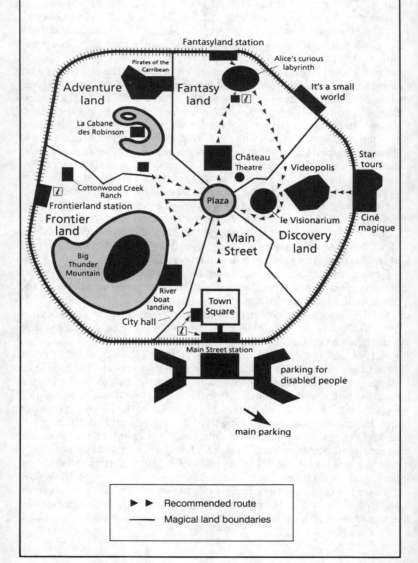

lar, the lack of portable ramps at the three stations to help get from the platform into the carriage is a serious omission. It is advisable for a chair user to bring along a couple of friends to help where necessary. The parades and various entertainments all seem pretty accessible, although with the parades there can be a problem with the crowds of people. You may have to be a little pushy if your eyeline is only just over 1m above the ground!

Wheelchairs are available for hire at the Town Square end of Main Street for people who can't walk very far. The chairs are manual ones but with high wheels so it is possible to push yourself if you can. However, the assistance of an able-bodied friend is almost certainly necessary as, if you are not a regular user, your arms will tire!

The *Guest Special Services Guide*, available from the Guest Relations window at the main entrance and from City Hall on Main Street, mentions problems at the different attractions. These include boarding restrictions where the ride is jerky or violent (such as in the runaway mine train on Big Thunder Mountain) and advice for parents that some young children might be disturbed by some of the tableaux. Those using wheelchairs are given priority on all the rides, so *if you think you might have problems with the distances or with the standing around in queues, we would strongly advise you to use a chair*.

Guide dogs are allowed in most of the park, although this is not relevant to people from the UK because of quarantine rules. Portable tape players and audio cassettes are available from City Hall for sight-impaired visitors.

Most of the restaurants have wheelchair accessible loos.

The park is divided into five magical lands, all with architecture, landscaping, entertainment and characters in a distinctive theme. They are:

i)   Main Street, USA,
ii) Frontierland,
iii) Adventureland,
iv) Fantasyland,
v)   Discoveryland.

The write-up here should be used alongside the Euro Disney Guest Guide and the Special Services Guide which contains a map of the park and descriptions of all the attractions. There were so many rides that it was impossible to survey them all, but the ones that we did try are mentioned below, with some additional comments on some of the others.

An old-fashioned steam train runs around the perimeter of the park, stopping at the end of Main Street, Frontierland and Fantasyland. A fourth station in Discoveryland is expected to open during 1993. It's an excellent way of getting an overview of the park and includes a trip through the Grand Canyon diorama complete with wild cats and a howling wolf. You're not allowed to shoot the buffalo!

The train can be very useful in reducing the distances you need to walk or wheel. Coming from the main entrance and entering the arches underneath

Main Street station, there is flat access to the platform via a lift (D116 W138 L128) on your right in the second alcove. The train stops at Fantasyland and Frontierland but there are two steps to the coaches through a gap of 70cm in the side of the carriage. The sides of the train are open, so going on board is possible for some chair users. There is no ramp available. At the other two stations there is at least one ramped access to the platform.

Travelling around the Park

There is flat access (sometimes involving a lift) to most parts of the park. Anywhere you come across steps or a pavement there is a ramp or alternative flat route close by.

There are guided tours which are usually four hours long and these can be adapted to cater for specific needs. It is advisable to telephone beforehand, *Tel:* (1) 64.74.21.41. Otherwise, go to City Hall, the information point on the left of Main Street as you pass underneath the railroad station from the main entrance.

A point worth noting is the problem of crowds especially during the school holidays. With so many people around, it is sometimes hard to spot where the ramps are and you may have to be prepared to shout "Excuse me!" quite frequently in order to move about freely.

Beware of being caught close to one of the Disney characters who make appearances every now and then. Within seconds the crowds will be swarming with loads of young children wanting autographs and movement may become difficult. Wheelchair users are also quite likely to be kissed by one of these furry creatures if they happen to spot you so avoid them at all costs if you feel the whole experience might be rather patronising. It is one of those things over which Disney can't win. Smaller children may love to meet and cuddle some of their fantasy characters. Teenage children and older disabled people may have very different feelings: some will welcome it, some won't. All we would suggest is that you don't get too uptight about it either way!

Most of the rides have accessibility problems in that there is flat access to the edge but chair users will then have to transfer to a seat. The survey team did not find any ride where it was possible to wheel straight on. When we visited the park, company policy did not allow members of the cast to help visitors with disabilities onto the rides although rarely did members of the cast stick to this rule and there was some talk of it being changed. However, it is advisable to have some able-bodied friends along to help. Transfer to seats depends on the ride. Sometimes it will involve a couple of steps up or down. On one occasion it involved getting into a boat. You will have to decide for yourself whether transferring from your chair is practical or not.

The flat access route may be difficult to spot and may require being accompanied by a member of staff to the edge of the ride along a route separate to the usual queue. If in doubt, ask a cast member. There are normally plenty about. It is most probable that, providing you can transfer to the seats, wheelchair users and their party will be able to avoid queueing for rides as long as there aren't too many at one time. You'll find that the flat access route usually bypasses the long wait. This can be of considerable benefit. On one occasion, our team was able to bypass a queue 45 minutes long in order to go on a ride that lasted only 5 minutes. Some of the rides may throw you about quite a bit. For each ride it is worth asking a member of the cast about what is involved.

Loos

The loos are marked on the map given in the guest guide and, although it is not to scale and rather simplistic, all the toilet facilities indicated do exist. They vary in that some are unisex and others are separate cubicles in the men's and women's loos. The design is roughly uniform (D79, ST100). The dimensions are not the same throughout the park but are never smaller than the figures given. The doors are occasionally large and heavy and you may require help. Likewise, the flush mechanism was occasionally in an awkward spot and difficult to reach. However, there is flat access to all the loo facilities and there are at least twelve at the various spots marked on the map.

Main Street USA

The Main Street station for the Euro Disneyland Railroad is overhead as you enter the park. Access has already been described.

The Main Street consists of arcades of shops and restaurants, all of which have flat access entrances. There is an array of Disney memorabilia available, as well as "old-style" barber shops, sweet shops, gift shops and the like. It is also possible to hire a camera or video-camera for the day if you happen to have forgotten your own. The restaurants are all American style as one would expect with movable tables and chairs, although quite cramped in places. If it happens to be raining on the day you visit then the indoor arcades will become very crowded. It was in the Main Street that we encountered Mickey and Roger Rabbit and other characters during our visit.

There are plenty of places to sit down if you just want to enjoy the atmosphere.

In the various "lands" the following rides and attractions were visited by the survey teams and all have access problems as mentioned earlier except when it states otherwise.

Frontierland

Frontierland has a range of attractions and rides. There are nine main attractions, five restaurants and half a dozen shops.

The **Big Thunder Mountain runaway train** ride is rated as probably the best thrill ride in Euro Disney, but it is not suitable for pregnant women, anyone with back or neck problems, or anyone with weak muscles. Those who cannot walk are not normally allowed on, since in case of breakdown people have to get out using a considerable number of steps.

In the **Phantom Manor** you have to transfer into a 'doom buggy', which is a carriage for two which swivels around through 180' as you go round the haunted manor. It says in the Guest Special Services Guide that you can transfer and put your chair in the buggy in front of you.

The **Cottonwood Creek Ranch** and **Cowboy Cookout Barbecue** restaurant have flat access, and movable tables and chairs.

The **Rustler Roundup Shootin' Gallery** has flat access and two shooting positions to accommodate wheelchair users.

Adventureland

There are three main attractions, together with five restaurants and some eight shops or shopping areas. It is a world recreating the adventures associated with pirates, with the Swiss Family Robinson castaways and the stories of the Arabian Nights.

Adventure Isle is set in the middle of a lake. Access involves two rope bridges and there is a winding staircase up to "La Cabane De Robinson". Most of the paths are wheelchair accessible and cast members will advise on what is possible.

Pirates of the Caribbean is a boat ride with two drops. It is a bit rough and those who cannot walk down steps in the event of a malfunction are not encouraged to try it. Nor are people who might be hurt by the jerky movements.

The **Adventureland Bazaar** is an authentic 'Arabian Nights' casbah with market stalls and shops, all with flat access. It is backed by stone walls crowned with multicoloured onion-shaped domes. There are many stalls with produce in front of them lying on the ground, so take care! There is a giraffe in the corner of the Bazaar who pops out occasionally.

Café de la Brousse has flat access, with movable tables and chairs. It serves a variety of food cooked in African style.

The **Restaurant Aux Epices Enchantées** also has flat access, with movable tables and chairs. This one serves African, Indian and other exotic specialities.

Fantasyland

Fantasyland takes you into the world of Peter Pan, Alice, Snow White, Pinocchio and Dumbo the Flying Elephant. It has fourteen main attractions, seven restaurants and nine shops. It has two major entertainments venues, the Fantasy Festival Stage and Le Théâtre du Château. Details of performances can be obtained from City Hall. Both are fully wheelchair accessible. The theatre which is located next to the castle and close to the central Plaza has up to five performances a day during the summer.

A centrepiece is **Le Château de la Belle au Bois Dormant** (or Sleeping Beauty's Castle). Its style is derived from illuminated manuscripts and the 1959 film 'Sleeping Beauty'. It has two floors and is listed as being fully wheelchair accessible. There is a gradual slope up to the entrance and the ground floor is flat everywhere. There is a lift up to the first floor but it wasn't working when the survey team visited. The only alternative is a flight of stairs. Upstairs is a small gallery with various hand-woven tapestries depicting scenes from Sleeping Beauty. The dragon is in the underground level also wheelchair accessible. Look for signs for 'La Tanière du Dragon'.

Alice's Curious Labyrinth is a maze, designed for wheelchair users accompanied by a friend. It thus has flat access. The disabled persons' entrance follows a special route through doors which avoid awkward obstructions. The maze is accessible except for the castle. You can easily lose yourself in Alice's extraordinary looking glass world.

It's A Small World is a boat ride through a miniature world peopled with colourful children in their native costumes. Transfer to the boat is necessary and there's a ramp and +3 to the exit.

Discoveryland

Discoveryland has six main attractions, including two entertainment venues which are fully chair accessible. One is **Videopolis**, which presents live entertainment on stage. There is a raised seating area with movable tables and chairs and a sloped auditorium. There is a ramp to a dance floor down one side. The other is **CinéMagique** where you can see a three-dimensional film called *Captain EO*, starring Michael Jackson. There are a couple of restaurants and also a couple of shops.

Autopia is a small car racing track. Wheelchair users would have to transfer and people need to be able to take a few strong bumps.

Star Tours has flat access (well signposted) up to the ride via lift (D110 W135 L167). Then wheelchair users have to transfer. It goes off into the *Star Wars* galaxy. Described as a "turbulent thrill ride through space", a chair user will need to be accompanied and it is not suitable for anyone with a weak back. There is a souvenir shop with flat access.

Constellations is a large souvenir shop with flat access throughout but it can get very crowded.

Swimming pools

Paris can be hot and humid, especially in the summer, and there are times when the idea of a swim can be really appealing. There are a number of accessible pools which you will find marked on the Michelin *Paris Plan*.

Piscine de Champeret, 36 boulevard de Reims, 75017. *Tel:* (1) 47.66.49.99 or 47.66.99.98. If you travel south on the boulevard de Reims you will find the pool between the exterior boulevards and the boulevard Périphérique. Parking may be possible on the boulevard de Reims or the avenue Brunetière. The entrance has +2 very small steps and then there is flat access to the changing rooms. We were told that the pool has two wheelchair user changing rooms with shower and loo. Although we measured the door (D80), we were unable to check the facilities inside. There is one large pool, with a slide and a diving board, and one small children's pool. Access to the large pool is by a ladder with a drop of about 30cm to water level.

Piscine Emile-Antoine, 9 rue Jean Rey, 75015. *Tel:* (1) 45.67.10.20. This pool is centrally located and close to the Eiffel Tower. There is metered parking on rue Jean Rey. For other parking see the Eiffel Tower recommended itinerary. Access to the main entrance from street level is via a steep ramp. There is flat access to the changing rooms which have some cubicles (D80+). Loos in the changing rooms could not be fully surveyed, but some had 70 or 80cm doors. The pool is on the first floor and there is flat access via a lift (D80). Otherwise it involves +3+15+18 steps with handrails. From the lift there is a door (D76) to the pools: one children's pool and one full-size pool. Access to the pools is via ladders and the water level is about 30cm below the pool side. There is a shelf around the pool at water level. There is a sun terrace reached by going through the footbath and then it's −5.

Piscine Georges Vallerey, 148 av Gambetta, 75020. *Tel:* (1) 40.31.15.20. The pool is on the corner of avenue Gambetta and boulevard Mortier and the only nearby parking is on the surrounding roads and is metered. Flat main entrance and it is flat to the changing rooms via a lift (D80). Otherwise it is +9+4+21 steps. Both men's and women's changing rooms have a separate disabled person's changing area (D80) with loo (D84 ST76) and a flat access shower. From here it is flat to the poolside. Access to the pools – one 50m pool from 2.1m to 3.8m deep and a children's pool – is via ladders and the water level is about 25cm below the side, with a shelf at water level for holding on to. The pool has a sliding roof making it possible to be both indoors and outdoors and the complex is often used for races. Poolside seating is at least +13+3 with subsequent levels from −10 to +30.

Piscine Jean Taris, 16 rue Thouin, 75005. *Tel:* (1) 43.25.54.03. This was unfortunately closed for refurbishment when we visited. The nearest parking is metered and is about 100m away around the Panthéon. The main entrance is flat via a lift from street level, otherwise it is via −14 steps. We were told that there was soon to be an adapted disabled person's changing room with a loo, flat access shower and flat access to the pools. There is a chair hoist to help anyone get into the large pool. The small one has wide steps for getting in.

Piscine Suzanne-Berioux, 10 pl de la Rotonde, Forum des Halles, 75001. *Tel:* (1) 42.36.98.44. The pool is on level −3 of les Halles and is situated at the opposite end of the Grande Galerie from place Carrée, next to the cinemas in place de la Rotonde. Car parking and access in les Halles is thoroughly explained in the *Sights* chapter. There is flat access to the pool entrance, and an adapted disabled person's changing room (D89) with loo (D86 ST76), flat access shower and flat access to the pool. Ask for the key at the ticket office. The pool is 50 by 20m in size, and from 0.8m to 2m deep. The water level is 25cm below poolside and access to the water is via ladders.

Sports stadia
•••••••••••••••••••••••

Parc Omnisports de Paris-Bercy, bd de Bercy, 75012. *Tel:* (1) 43.46.12.21.
Located on the corner of boulevard de Bercy and quai de Bercy, you cannot
miss this stadium because its enormous steel and glass structure towers over
the road. It is about 600m from the Gare de Lyon and it's on a site of about
300m square. This means that walking round it to find the right entrance
involves over 1km.

If you're going to something, it might be worth 'casing the joint' first by
car if you can, and then you will at least know exactly where you are going.
The stadium has its own car park on ground level which is well signposted
and has spaces for people with disabilities. There is then flat access to the
main entrance via an access ramp for the fire services, which avoids
+24+18 steps without handrails. Our survey team was told of lift access
within the building as well as adapted loos for disabled people, but we were
unfortunately not allowed in to survey them. We were also told that it is
possible for spectators to stay in their chairs for events if they wish.

Parc des Princes, 24 rue du Cdt Guilbaud, 75016. *Tel:* (1) 42.88.02.76. This
is the major stadium in Paris where international rugby matches and
important football games are played. It is just outside the boulevard
Périphérique near porte de St Cloud.

All the audience are accommodated in seats and, although it is a modern
building, no thought at all has been given to the needs of people with
disabilities. Sadly the management do not seem very interested in doing
anything to improve things and absolutely nothing has been done in this
regard since we last surveyed it in 1985. We made some suggestions then
and we made them again in 1992!

Access is possible, after a fashion, and with some difficulties. It is easy to
get into the area around the stadium and priority parking may be given to
disabled spectators if requested in advance. Each entrance to the lower tier
of seats has +9 steps and there is a central handrail. The steps are wide.
There are two official places for chair users, approached through entrance
F1 and up the +9. For those that can transfer to a seat, Row N, right round
the stadium, is the easiest one to get to. Each seat is behind a gangway, thus
giving relatively easy access. The seats are rather small – they are rounded
bucket seats and not very good for someone needing support. The loos
(D58 no ST) are −9−11. Only one cubicle in the men's has a pedestal. The
restaurant is −21+1 with movable chairs.

Roland Garros, 2 av Gordon Bennett, 75016. *Tel*: (1) 47.43.00.47. This
stadium is home to the world famous French Tennis Open Tournament.
Like Wimbledon it is a sort of tennis village containing a centre court, a

number 1 court and 14 others, as well as restaurants and shops. It is just outside the boulevard Périphérique near porte d'Auteuil. There is parking inside the grounds if you get prior permission via the Porte Suzanne Lenglen Sud entrance which is about 50m from the centre court. All main entrances are flat or ramped and have spaces for wheelchairs right by the edge of the court, except numbers 3 and 9.

Part of the number 1 court spectating area has flat access. Follow the sign at gate 3. The main stadium surrounding the centre court is not easily accessible. Perhaps the easiest entrance is at the west side which has only −10 steps then +4+4 without handrails to the court's ground level. There are no lifts to the upper tiers. We were told that staff will help lift chair users into the stadium. Between rows of seats there are a few spaces for wheelchairs.

The main restaurant is called the 'Buffet de Roland Garros' and has a ramped entrance to avoid a +10 with handrails. The first floor is +20. We saw the standard loos (D64 no ST), but were not allowed to survey those marked as **wheelchair loos**.

Other facilities surrounding the centre court include a post office and banks. Generally this is a large area, approximately 200m square, but access around the tennis village as a whole is flat. The area is well signposted and with plenty of plans of the complex. A leaflet on access, only in French, is available from the office of the Fédération Française du Tennis just outside the centre court.

Hippodrome de Longchamp (Longchamp Race Course), route des Tribunes, bois de Boulogne, 75016. *Tel:* (1) 42.24.13.29. This is the world's longest track and supposedly the most difficult. It is in the bois be Boulogne by the Seine. The normal visitors' car park is in the middle of the track and visitors reach the stands via an underground passage involving two flights of steps. Consequently disabled spectators are advised to negotiate a parking space near the main entrance. From the main entrance, the best way is to bear left and go between towers 3 and 4 where there is a ramp to the bottom storey of the grandstand and to the flat terrace leading to the track. There are large lifts in towers 3 and 4, and a ground floor restaurant is +1 step. No loos have been adapted. Please note that, because the racecourse was completely closed when we visited recently, **this information is from a survey made several years ago**. On a side note, the French system of betting appears to be extremely complicated and if not careful you may find you have backed the wrong horse! For racing information consult the sporting journal *Paris-Turf*.

Entertainments

CINEMAS

It would be impossible to list all the cinemas in Paris. It is worth noting that apart from some major American releases, the soundtracks are likely to be in French. We have only listed a few of the larger and more accessible cinemas which appear in the CNFLRH 1987 handbook. We managed to visit most of these. Note that films are listed in *Pariscope* which comes out on Wednesdays. If the film is listed as v.o. it means that it is in the original language with French subtitles. If listed as v.f. then it has been dubbed into French. *Pariscope* also lists whether cinemas are "accessible aux handicapés", and while this listing is by no means reliable, it gives you a certain moral advantage when you want to get in.

On the Champs Elysées

Parking in the Champs Elysées is not easy, but we managed to find an underground car park next to George V métro station with a lift (D80 W138 L108) which serves all six floors including ground level. In terms of wheelchair loos, the only one we found was in the Gaumont Ambassade cinema which is listed below.

Gaumont Marignan, 27 av des Champs Elysées, 75008. *Tel:* (1) 43.59.92.82. There is metered parking on the Champs Elysées within 50m and nearby underground car parks. There is one step at the entrance. Only some of the six screens are on the ground floor and they still involve +8 with handrails. The men's loos (D62 no ST) are +3 with handrails. We were told that you cannot stay in your chair for the film.

Gaumont Ambassade, 50 av des Champs Elysées, 75008. *Tel:* (1) 43.59.19.08. There is some metered parking on the Champs Elysées within 60m outside the Virgin Megastore. In addition a taxi rank is situated in the central island of the Champs Elysées. The entrance is flat but of the seven screens only number 3 has a relatively minor barrier consisting of −3 steps. The CNFLRH guide says that screen 2 can be entered from rue du Colisée. Other screens are reached via 20 or more steps. There is a **wheelchair loo** (D83 ST72). You can stay in your chair at the back of auditorium number three and soundtracks are in the language of the original version.

UGC Champs Elysées, 65 av des Champs Elysées, 75008. *Tel:* (1)

45.62.20.40. Metered parking nearby, and underground car parks. The entrance has a small step. There is one large auditorium on the ground floor with flat access. The loos (D59 no ST) are +3+2 steps with handrails. You can stay in your wheelchair during the film and films are shown in the original version's soundtrack.

Triomphe, 92 av des Champs Elysées, 75008. *Tel:* (1) 45.62.45.76 or 36.65.70.76. There is metered parking but it is over 200m away. The entrance has one step, and of the four screens only number one has flat access. Other screens are −23 steps with handrails. The loos (D57 no ST) are on the ground floor and are +1. We were told that you cannot stay in your wheelchair during the performance, although the CNFLRH entertainments handbook suggests that you can.

Café, 3rd arrondissement

Elsewhere in Paris

Gaumont Parnasse, 82 bd du Montparnasse, 75014. *Tel:* (1) 43.35.30.40. No metered parking is available on the boulevard du Montparnasse within

200m, but there is some on the rue du Montparnasse opposite the cinema. The entrance is flat and of the five screens, numbers 1,4 and 5 all have flat access. Screens 2 and 3 have +3 and −22 steps respectively with handrails. The loos (D61 no ST) near screen 1 have flat access. You can stay in your wheelchair according to CNFLRH. Soundtracks are in the language of their original version.

Grand Rex (see *Concert hall* section for this multi-purpose site).

Paramount Opéra, 2 bd des Capucines, 75009. *Tel:* (1) 47.42.56.31 or 36.65.70.18. There is an underground car park on the rue de la Chaussée d'Antin nearby. The entrance is flat and of the seven screens numbers 2 and 4 have flat access. There is a **wheelchair loo** (D70+ ST70+). According to staff you can apparently stay in your chair. Films are shown with the original soundtrack.

Studio de la Harpe, 13 rue St Séverin, 75005. *Tel:* (1) 46.34.25.52. Nearest métro is St Michel which has an accessible RER station. There are two auditoria, the first of which has wheelchair access and **wheelchair loos**. You can stay in your chair during performances. There are normally sub-titles in the original film language for those with hearing difficulties. **This information is based on the CNFLRH listing**.

Music venues

Music is a universal language, and it's always interesting to see how other people present it. We have only included a fraction of the possible venues, but hope to have highlighted some of the more interesting and accessible. We have also tried to cover a range of tastes and interests. Please don't feel limited as there may be countless venues that we didn't have the time to look at which you may want to try.

Concert halls and rock venues

Auditorium des Halles (Auditorium Châtelet), Forum des Halles, 5 porte St Eustache, 75001. *Tel:* (1) 42.36.13.90 or 42.33.00.00. Linked to the west side of the underground shopping complex, the Auditorium is on level −2 and can be reached by a lift (see les Halles in *Sights*). There is RER access and underground car parking. The entrance is flat and there is place for chairs in the left and right back corners. There is a **wheelchair loo** (D70+ ST70+) on level −3 and several others in and around the les Halles area. Again, see the main write-up.

Auditorium du Louvre. *Tel:* (1) 40.20.51.51. Off the Cour Napoléon under the pyramid. It is used for concerts, 'colloques' (teach-ins), conferences and films. The entrance is flat, but with heavy doors. There is plenty of space at the top of the sloped seating for chair users. See the Louvre in *Sights* for lift access and wheelchair loo details.

Le Bataclan, 50 bd Voltaire, 75011. *Tel:* (1) 47.00.30.12. A modern music/ rock venue and one of the best, although it is certainly not plush! There is metered parking on the boulevard Voltaire itself and drop-off points within 20m of the building. The main entrance has flat access. The large auditorium is mostly flat but does contain some split levels for example the bar is +3 steps. The women's loos are −6 whilst the men's have flat access (D56 no ST). You can stay in your wheelchair during performances.

Café de la Danse, 5 passage Louis-Philippe, 75011. *Tel:* (1) 39.56.12.85 or 48.05.57.22. A small concert hall/theatre which may prove difficult to find. The passage Louis-Philippe runs from 21 rue de Lappe. The streets are narrow, but it may be possible to park in rue de Lappe. The entrance has one step with flat access from there into the auditorium on the ground floor where you can remain in your wheelchair. There are wheelchair loos (the men's was D86 ST94). The only steps are to get to the bar on the balcony level which is +19 with a handrail on one side.

Centre Culturel Algérien, 171 rue de la Croix Nivert, 75015. *Tel:* (1) 45.54.95.31. We did not survey here, but according to the CNFLRH the exhibition hall is wheelchair accessible, there are 'adapted' loos and assistance is provided. People who are partially sighted are welcome.

La Cigale, 120 bd de Rochechouart, 75018. *Tel:* (1) 42.23.38.00. A modern/ popular music venue within an all-seater auditorium. There is metered parking on the boulevard de Rochechouart within 50m. The entrance has a small step and a further +3+7+7 with handrails leads to the auditorium. The staff will provide assistance if needed. The bar and cloakroom are on the ground floor and have flat access. Once in the auditorium there are spaces for wheelchairs. If you want to get to the balcony level it is +19. The loos (D57 no ST) are on the auditorium level.

Elysée Montmartre, 72 bd de Rochechouart, 75018. *Tel:* (1) 45.52.25.15. Younger and more excitable crowds gather at this traditional, though inexpensive, venue for 'alternative' bands. There is metered parking nearby. The entrance has +3 steps and then there are +7+25 with handrails into the auditorium itself. We were not allowed to survey the loos.

Espace Cardin, 1 av Gabriel, 75008. *Tel:* (1) 42.66.17.81. The building contains a theatre, cinema, restaurant, exhibition gallery and conference rooms. Metered parking on avenue Gabriel within 50m of the entrance, and a taxi rank by place de la Concorde, also within 50m. The main entrance has two steps.

The entrance to the **theatre** is +1 from street level, but there is a flat way in at the rear of the building. The restaurant, with access from the main entrance, is flat, spacious and has movable tables and chairs. There is flat access to the balcony level of the theatre, where there are wheelchair spaces.

The **exhibition gallery** is reached via −21−3 steps with handrails. The loos (D69 no ST) are also on this level. The cinema is at the opposite end of the building and has −21. There are no lifts.

Grand Rex, 1 bd Poissonnière, 75002. *Tel:* (1) 45.08.93.89 is a large venue for rock and jazz gigs which also has a cinema. There is metered parking outside on the boulevard Poissonnière. The entrance has a small step and there is flat access to the ground floor via 'porte 1'. A few spaces exist for wheelchair users to remain in their chairs. There is flat access to cinema no 5, but chair users would find it hard to get further than the back of the auditorium as there are a series of −4 steps leading down to each of the lower levels. There are **wheelchair loos** (D90 ST92) near this screen with flat access.

Olympia, 28 bd des Capucines (on corner with rue de Caumartin), 75009. *Tel:* (1) 47.42.25.49. We were unable to see beyond the box office, but were told that there is 'good' access and lots of wheelchair users frequent the place.

Rex Club, 5 bd Poissonnière, 75002. *Tel:* (1) 42.36.83.98. Just next door to the 'Grand Rex' but far less accessible. It is predominantly used for disco functions. The entrance has one step, followed by −8−8−17 steps with handrails down to the band area and bar. If you find yourself in a really 'get up and go' mood you'll have to invite a friend to help! The loos (D59 no ST) are an additional −9−18.

Salle Favart, 5 rue Favart, 75002. *Tel:* (1) 42.96.12.20. This is an old music hall which now plays classical music and is the home to the 'Opéra Comique'. The main entrance is at the rear, on place Boieldieu, and has +6+5−13 steps. These can be avoided by using a side entrance on rue de Marivaux, which has flat access and leads immediately to the lift. Rue de Marivaux also has metered parking, taxi ranks and dropping off points. Access to the concert hall is either via +25 with handrails, or by the rather small lift (D66 W114 L76). We were told that they have a special wheelchair available for use which will fit into the lift. Once you get to the 'Orchestre' level there is flat access to the circle or to some of the stalls. You can stay in your chair during the performance. The loos (D57 no ST) are on the ground floor.

Salle Gaveau, rue La Boétie, 75008. *Tel:* (1) 49.53.05.07 for box office or 45.62.69.71 for management. This concert hall for classical music is located on the junction of avenue Delcassé and rue La Boétie. There is a side entrance to a car park in avenue Delcassé and some metered parking in the street. The main entrance has one step, but a side entrance is ramped. There is a lift (D89 W169 L109) to all floors apart from the third. There is space for three chair users to stay in their chairs on the second floor. Loos (D65 no ST) are +4 on the fourth floor. There is also a large and accessible piano exhibition, including a piano used by Chopin.

Salle Pleyel, 252 rue du Faubourg-St-Honoré, 75008. *Tel:* (1) 45.63.88.73 for box office or 45.61.06.30 for management. Located 50m from the junction of avenue Hoche and rue du Faubourg-St-Honoré, this hall is used for classical and modern concerts. There is a public underground car park 80m from the junction in avenue Hoche, which is accessible by lift (D80 W87 L150). The entrance to the hall has one step. There are three lifts: one (D67) has flat access, the piano lift (D100) is +1, and the third (D67) is +3. There is space for wheelchairs in the auditorium. We were not allowed to see the loos.

Opera

Inside Paris

Opéra de la Bastille, 120 rue de Lyon, 75012. *Tel:* (1) 44.73.13.00. Disabled people needing special seating, and particularly for wheelchair spaces, should *Tel:* (1) 44.73.13.73. The Opéra Bastille is one of the prestigious buildings of the 1980s, built to commemorate the bicentenary of the fall of the Bastille in 1789. Drop off point outside the front entrance. Underground car parking can be found in 'Parking Opéra-Bastille' at 34 rue de Lyon. There are some reserved spaces for people with disabilities and lift access (D110 W140 L140) to street level or to the Grande Salle de l'Opéra. However, from the car park it is at least 150m to the theatre foyer. The spacious foyer has a flat entrance, with lifts from either end of the main hall. Chair users are asked to contact the Opéra at least two weeks in advance if possible to improve the chances of reserving a space. The best chair spaces are on the Parterre where you can watch without having to transfer. This is reached by lift (D110 W140 L140) and there is a **wheelchair loo** (D80 ST95) nearby.

Opéra (Palais Garnier), pl de l'Opéra, 8 rue Scribe, 75009. *Tel:* (1) 47.42.57.50. Since the opening of the Opéra Bastille, the programmes here at the original Opéra now include more ballet and contemporary dance. Parking is difficult in this central location, but for a matinée it would be possible to use the underground car park at Galeries Lafayette. **There is no alternative to the +10 steps without handrails at the main entrance to the vestibule and box office, followed by a further +10 without handrails once inside.** Take one of the two main lifts (D84 W200 L100), on either side of the second set of steps, to the first floor. From here there is flat access to the front side of the stalls. Although vision may not be brilliant from here, this very old theatre was not designed with wheelchairs in mind, and space is almost non-existant. Alternatively you can try the boxes (D67) on the second, third and fourth floors which are +1, but we would encourage you to check the details with box office staff in advance. Loos (D67 no ST) are on all floors.

Outside Paris

Opéra Bobigny, 1 bd Lenine, Bobigny, 93000. *Tel:* (1) 48.30.60.56 is a large prestigious opera house in the suburbs. It is also the end of the accessible tramway from St Denis. We gathered the following **information by questionnaire**, but is sounds so good that we thought it worth a mention. The kerbs are dropped outside, the auditoria are accessible by lift and wheelchair users can stay in their chairs to the side of the front row or transfer to a seat. **Wheelchair loos** (D70+ ST70+) are on the first floor which is served by the lift.

NIGHTCLUBS

Crazy Horse Saloon, 12 av George V, 75008. *Tel:* (1) 47.23.32.32. This expensive 'French' style evening's entertainment includes a welcoming bouncer dressed in Canadian Mountie uniform. There is a drop-off point directly outside the main doors and parking is no problem according to the manager. The entrance is flat and a lift (D80) takes you down to the bar and 'performance' area on the lower ground floor. The manager assured us that disabled guests would receive the same high level of hospitality and showed us an exquisite **wheelchair loo** (D70+ ST70+) to prove his point! There is space for wheelchairs in its small auditorium. It is often used as a stop-off point for the rich and famous – and our surveyors bumped into a member of the Home and Away television series cast, just to illustrate this!

Le Lido, 116 av des Champs Elysées, 75008. *Tel:* (1) 40.76.56.10 or 45.63.11.61. This glizty and expensive show includes an evening meal –

which is fair enough for around £50 per person! There is metered parking nearby and an underground car park by George V métro with lift (D80 W138 L108) access from ground level to all six floors. The entrance has +2 steps followed by a 30m corridor up to the reception desk. From here there is flat access to the back row of the auditorium's outer circle, then −4 to each sucessive lower level. Tables and chairs are movable whilst loos (D59 no ST) are on the ground floor.

The **Moulin Rouge**, pl Blanche, 82 bd de Clichy, 75018. *Tel:* (1) 46.06.00.19. Possibly the most famous venue, and it is similarly expensive. Access when we surveyed in 1985 was via −30 steps and we were told that this has not changed.

THEATRES AND MARIONNETTES

If you want to try to include a theatrical evening or matinée in your visit we would suggest that you book in advance, confirming the venue's accessibility, particularly if you wish to remain in a wheelchair. Spaces tend to be scarce, and you never know who else might be in town. You will probably want to book additional seats next to the allocated chair spaces anyway.

Theatre is a more difficult medium than music, as it is more dependent on language. One thing we have included is a number of marionnette (puppet) theatres which may be of particular interest to families with children and which should provide entertainment even if your French is limited.

Unfortunately, surveying theatres was not an easy task since they tend to be locked up outside performance times. We were nevertheless able to see how entrance into the stalls could be achieved, and were shown wheelchair spaces on seating plans by box office staff.

Café de la Danse (see *Concert Halls* section for this dual purpose venue).

Théâtre Antoine-Simone Berriau, 14 bd de Strasbourg, 75010. *Tel:* (1) 42.08.77.71. Parking is difficult and the nearest car park we found was in rue d'Hauteville over 500m away. The car park had a lift (D70) followed by a steeply ramped exit. The obvious alternative is to use a taxi. It's about 1km from the Gare du Nord. The theatre has a flat entrance to the box office and apparently flat access into the stalls where there is wheelchair space in the centre aisle. None of the loos were big enough for chair users.

Théâtre de l'Atelier, pl Charles Dullin, 75018. *Tel:* (1) 46.06.49.24. There is public car parking just down the rue Dancourt towards boulevard de Clichy, but it should be pointed out that the area is particularly hilly. The theatre's entrance is across 30m of cobbles on the place Charles Dullin. You can avoid the two large steps on to this small square by using the ramp in the northwest corner by the Café du Théâtre. The entrance has one step to the box office. From here were assured that it was flat into the auditorium. They have wheelchair spaces in the centre aisle of the stalls.

Casino de Paris, 16 rue de Clichy, 75009. *Tel:* (1) 48.74.15.80. There is a small step to the box office and a further +3 into the stalls. The seating plan allows for four wheelchair spaces at the back of the stalls. We were told of loos in the basement, but with no lift.

Théâtre Champs Elysées (Comédie des Champs Elysées), 15 av Montaigne, 75008. *Tel:* (1) 47.20.08.24 or 47.20.36.37. There are +2 or +3 steps, depending on which door you use, to the box office. This is followed by a further +5 into the stalls. Although the CNFLRH says that there is a lift, this was news to staff in the box office on our visit. The stalls contain space for wheelchairs but there was no wheelchair loo.

Théâtre de la Huchette, 23 rue de la Huchette, 75005. *Tel:* (1) 43.26.38.99. The street outside is very narrow. The tiny theatre has a small step at the entrance. Space exists down the aisle for wheelchair users but there is no accessible loo.

Marionnette (puppet) shows

On most Wednesday, Saturday and Sunday afternoons, Guignol, the French equivalent of Punch and Judy, can be enjoyed in a number of parks around Paris.

Marionnettes du Champ-de-Mars, rue du Champ-de-Mars, 75007. *Tel:* (1) 45.74.69.75 or 46.37.07.87. This show takes place in the southeast part of the Champ de Mars and is about 500m from the Eiffel Tower. There is a car park at place de l'École Militaire. Otherwise metered parking can be found much nearer on avenue de la Bourdonnais. Access to the park and to the show is flat and you can enter from rue Marinoni. The show is indoors and a chair user can either stay in their chair, or transfer to a bench.

Marionnettes des Champs Elysées, rond-point des Champs Elysées, 75008. *Tel:* (1) 42.57.43.34. On the north side of rond-point des Champs Elysées, there is an underground car park within 30m, but without a lift to ground level it involves +23 steps with handrails. Metered parking can be found on avenue Matignon nearby. The performances are open air so access at the entrance and inside is flat, although the surface is a little rough. There are benches but you can stay in your chair. It is not a big viewing space, so get there early. This show claims to be the oldest marionnette show in Paris.

Marionnettes du Luxembourg, Jardin du Luxembourg, 75006. *Tel:* (1) 43.26.46.47 or 43.50.25.00. There is metered parking in the streets around the Luxembourg gardens. A flat entrance to the gardens exists in the corner of rue Guynemer and rue d'Assas. It is then approximately 100m to the theatre entrance which has +3 steps without handrails. The show is indoors. The staff said that it is unlikely that a wheelchair user can remain in their chair when it is busy, so be prepared to transfer to a seat. Public loos are within 100m of the marionnettes including a **wheelchair loo** (see Luxembourg gardens in *Sights* chapter).

Marionnettes de Montsouris, parc Montsouris, 75014. *Tel:* (1) 46.65.45.95. We did not manage to see this ourselves, but it is listed by the CNFLRH as being wheelchair accessible. They say that you can stay in your chair during performances.

Marionnettes du Parc des Buttes-Chaumont Guignol de Paris, av Simon Bolivar and rue Botzaris, 75019. *Tel:* (1) 46.36.32.01. Again listed by the CNFLRH as being wheelchair accessible.

Marionnettes de Paris, Lac Orée, bois de Vincennes, 75012. *Tel:* (1) 42.57.37.13. Another theatre listed by the CNFLRH as being wheelchair accessible.

Théâtre Musical de Paris (Châtelet TMP), 22 rue Edouard Colonne, 75004. *Tel:* (1) 40.28.28.28 or 40.28.28.40. This was a major opera centre before the Opéra Bastille opened. It is likely to change in function in coming years. **The information here was gathered by post.** The main entrance is in the place du Châtelet, but there are steps. We were told that there is ramped access at 17 avenue Victoria. Wheelchair users can stay in their chairs at the 'orchestre' circle level, where there are also adapted loos. There is a lift and an induction loop system.

Théâtre National de l'Odéon (Odéon Théâtre National), 1 pl Paul Claudel, 75006. *Tel:* (1) 43.25.70.32. This is a companion of the Comédie Française, presenting a wide range of plays. There are two auditoria: one presenting mainly contemporary plays, and the other a range of plays in various languages. Metered parking is available in place de l'Odéon. The entrance has +8 steps from place de l'Odéon and to reach the 'orchestre' or circle level and the large auditorium there is another +5 with handrails but there are no lifts. Information from the CNFLRH indicated that there is a flat way in, but we didn't find it. Two wheelchair spaces are located in the back row of the main auditorium, but this is some 50m from the stage. The loos (D56 no ST) are on the ground floor.

Petit Casino – Café Théâtre, 17 rue Chapon, 75003. *Tel:* (1) 42.78.52.51 or 42.78.36.50. There is very little parking in the tiny nearby streets. The entrance has one step. Inside there is flat access (although the corridor is only about 80cm wide) to the restaurant and theatre areas. The chairs and tables are movable and loos (D57 no ST) are through the kitchen. It has a cosy atmosphere and at the time of our visit seemed to be showing a French equivalent of 'Run for your Wife'!

Théâtre du Rond-Point (Companie Renaud-Barrault), 2 av Franklin D Roosevelt, 75008. *Tel:* (1) 44.95.09.09 or 42.56.60.70. A traditional concert hall just off the Champs Elysées which sponsors a well-known series of Sunday morning concerts. Many young performers make their debut here. Outside the building on avenue Franklin D Roosevelt there is metered parking, as well as taxi/car dropping off point, all within 50m. The main entrance is flat and there is flat access to the ground floor auditorium which has wheelchair spaces. A lift (D77 W110 L130) leads to a gallery on the first floor and a restaurant with movable tables and chairs in the basement. The

Théâtre Montparnasse

small auditorium in the basement can accommodate a few chairs. The basement also has **wheelchair loos** (D80 ST100). A shop is +4 steps from the ground floor, but this modern building is otherwise very accessible.

Théâtre de la Ville, pl du Châtelet, 75004. *Tel:* (1) 42.74.22.77. It is possible to take the RER line B to St Michel. Parking in the area is difficult, and the

Hôtel de Ville underground car park does not have a lift to street level. One step to the box office. Access to the auditorium is by a lift through a flat administration entrance on quai de Gesvres. Unfortunately this was locked when we surveyed, but we were told that chair users regularly came to performances without any trouble. Allocated wheelchair space is in the front row of the stalls. It is listed as being wheelchair accessible by the CNFLRH.

Rue de la Gaîté is just to the east of the Gare Montparnasse and offers a wide range of French theatre for the connoisseur. Parking, followed by a short walk, is possible in the Gare Montparnasse car park (see *Getting around* chapter). There was no wheelchair loo in any of the theatres and we were told that the nearest was in the Gare Montparnasse. There's also one in the Meridian hotel nearby. There are lots of restaurants around for pre- or post-performance eating. The following theatres were surveyed:

Grand Edgar, 6 rue de la Gaîté, 75014. *Tel:* (1) 43.20.90.09. The entrance has one step and we were told that there is flat access into the auditorium with plenty of space for wheelchair users to remain in their chairs.

Comédie Italienne, 17 rue de la Gaîté, 75014. *Tel:* (1) 43.21.22.22. The entrance has one step, and although the staff of this tiny theatre were welcoming they said that wheelchair users are required to transfer into seats 'for security reasons'.

Théâtre de la Gaîté Montparnasse, 26 rue de la Gaîté, 75014. *Tel:* (1) 43.22.16.18. A flat entrance gives you trouble free access to the two designated wheelchair spaces on the right-hand side of the stalls.

Théâtre Montparnasse, 31 rue de la Gaîté, 75014. *Tel:* (1) 43.22.77.74. There is a flat entrance to the box office, but then +3 steps into the auditorium where we were assured there is plenty of space for you to remain in your wheelchair.

Le Petit Montparnasse, 31 rue de la Gaîté, 75014. *Tel:* (1) 43.22.77.74. This small theatre is around to the side of its parent body so there is flat access to the Théâtre Montparnasse's box office. The entrance to 'Le Petit' is apparently ramped.

Just off the end of rue de la Gaîté we also came across the following:

Edgar comprising the **Café d'Edgar** and **Théâtre d'Edgar**, 58 bd Edgar Quinet, 75014. *Tel:* (1) 42.79.97.97. These are two more tiny auditoria, the former having one step at the entrance, whilst the latter is flat. Both have room for a couple of wheelchairs in the aisle and you are not required to transfer.

Shopping
·················

Paris shops have a unique style and tend to have a flair for presentation, so much so that some of the displays become works of art. Although a lot of attention is paid to clothes and fashion, any visitor should take time to experience and taste the delights of their food markets and shops. Food is especially well presented, decorated and packaged. The French have managed to maintain their 'local' traders which have largely been lost in Britain due to pressure from the large department stores and supermarkets. Although this allows for a wonderful variety of stores, many with specialist products, Paris has a good number of department stores as well.

Although shopping enthusiasts will probably just want to let their spirits run free and a great deal will depend on where you are staying, we have made some notes on a few areas where there are lots of shops close together. These are basically around:
- les Halles and the Samaritaine end of the rue de Rivoli
- the big department stores in the boulevard Haussmann, place de la Madeleine, place Vendôme and the other end of the rue de Rivoli
- the Champs Elysées
- some accessible markets in various parts of the city

The shopping itinerary outlined in the chapter on *recommended itineraries* is centred on the second area, stretching from boulevard Haussmann to the Louvre end of the rue de Rivoli.

Les Halles and east end of the rue de Rivoli

The area including the Forum des Halles and the Montorgueil market seems to be a trendy place. The diversity of shops and restaurants attracts a wide range of people. There are **wheelchair loos** around les Halles and in Samaritaine 2.

Forum des Halles, 75001 (Michelin Guide Principal Walk 13), is built around a sunken plaza. The shops here sell a huge range of goods, including clothes by current top French designers. The Forum has been thoroughly surveyed and there's a detailed description in the chapter on *Sights*. If you are looking for shops selling particular items, the computerised information points in the Forum will probably be helpful.

Montorgueil Market, rue Montorgueil, 75001, is north of the Forum running up from the St Eustache church into rue des Petits Carreaux to the junction with rue Réaumur. It happens every day with a whole variety of shops sprawling out onto a beautifully made pedestrian precinct. You will find everything here including a supermarket. The wide precinct is flat apart from extremely high kerbs which can usually be bypassed using the occasional ramps.

The **rue de Rivoli** is the Paris equivalent of Oxford Street and is certainly as long. It contains many department stores and reputedly France's largest, La Samaritaine. Some at the east end are only a short walk from the Forum des Halles.

La Samaritaine, 75 rue de Rivoli (on the corner of rue du Pont Neuf), 75001. It spreads itself across intervening roads into four separate buildings. Some entrances have two or three steps, but all the buildings have unsigned flat or ramped entrances as well. Each building has large lifts which serve all floors. Samaritaine 4 can be reached by a first floor bridge across rue du Pont Neuf from Samaritaine 2, and vice-versa. Inside access is fairly good, although some areas are congested. There are ramps inside to get around most of the split levels. At the time of surveying, Samaritaine 3 appeared to have misplaced its wooden ramp, so part of it was +4.

Despite numerous attempts to convince us otherwise, **we found a wheelchair loo (D100 ST100) on the first floor of Samaritaine 2**. Because there's no signposting, and the staff we asked were unaware of its existence, we're describing its location in some detail. There are three red lifts in the centre of the building: one is long and narrow, whilst the other two are more typically square in shape. If you turn left out of the square ones on the first floor, go 10m then turn right, go another 10m then turn left, you should find a fire exit and stairwell. The wheelchair loo is on the right-hand side of the stairs, unmarked.

Boulevard Haussmann area, down to the west end of the rue de Rivoli

Boulevard Haussmann is the home of the department store, and even has a Marks and Spencer. The main stores are Printemps, Galeries Lafayette and Monoprix. There are some notable food shops around the Madeleine and some famous fashion shops like Gucci near the place Vendôme. At the west end of the rue de Rivoli is a WH Smith bookshop.

Au Printemps, 64 bd Haussmann, 75009. *Tel:* (1) 42.82.50.00. This vast department store sells literally everything, or so it seems. The only parking nearby is in the Galeries Lafayette underground car park with flat access via a large lift (D120 W140 L150), except from the first level down. There is a taxi or car dropping off point outside. Entrances are flat and there are eleven floors, of which ten are accessible by lift (D130 W170 L170). The top floor which includes the terrace and restaurant can

Shopping from the bd Haussmann to the rue de Rivoli

only be reached by escalator. Most of the floors are tiled or carpeted, but the ground floor is marbled and can be quite slippery. Men's and women's loos (D53 no ST) exist on alternate floors. The roof restaurant with movable tables and chairs offers a panoramic view, but has access problems as mentioned earlier. In general the store is well laid out and signposted.

Galeries Lafayette, 40 bd Haussmann, 75009. *Tel:* (1) 42.82.34.56. This is another big department store. An underground car park with lift (D120 W140 L150) has flat access except from the first level down. Note that there are ten underground levels of parking, so it's important to remember your floor and colour location. Because of its central location the car park is often crowded, but is probably less so during July and August. Entrances are flat and access inside is good with large lifts serving all nine floors. The sixth floor restaurant is accessible and there is a **wheelchair loo** (D85 ST120) opposite the restaurant entrance. Although it is by far the best department store in terms of access, signposting is not particularly good.

Monoprix is effectively part of the ground floor of Galeries Lafayette. Parking is the same as for the Galeries. There is flat access to the shopping area.

There is a **Marks & Spencer** in its traditional form opposite the Printemps. Again we would suggest you use the Lafayette parking. The entrances are flat and large lifts go to all floors. There is a **wheelchair loo** (D134 ST81) on the third floor, although it is not designated as such.

In **place de la Madeleine** there is Hédiard, Fauchon and a number of food shops with exceptionally mouth-watering things on display.

Hédiard, 21 pl de la Madeleine (in the northwest corner), 75008. *Tel:* (1) 42.66.44.36. Parking is possible in the public car park across rue Chauveau Lagarde from the shop. We spoke to the car park's director who assured us that disabled people would be welcomed – we suggest you ask at the entrance for assistance. The shop itself is all on the ground floor and has a small step at the entrance. The interior is very spacious.

Fauchon, 26 pl de la Madeleine (in the northeast corner), 75008. *Tel:* (1) 47.42.60.11. This store is split into three sections on both sides of rue de Sèze in the northeast corner of the place de la Madeleine. For parking see Hédiard. The wine and perishable food section is on the south side of the rue de Sèze with one step at the entrance. Food to take away is on the ground floor and the wine cellar is, perhaps not surprisingly, downstairs (−20 steps with handrails). The café on the first floor is reached only by escalators, as unfortunately the lift in this building is only for staff going up to the second floor. Across the road, the left-hand section, with one step at the entrance, mostly sells non-perishables and the basement bar and first floor restaurant can both be reached by a lift (D80).

Next door, again with one step, you can sample the cakes. It's an ideal spot for buying special presents to take back home provided you can carry them! After an entrance with one step the shop is spacious. Part of the shop is upstairs, +7+18 with a handrail on one side, for ordering items and the staff said that they would be happy to talk on the ground floor if access is a problem.

Marché de la Madeleine, is a small covered food market at the bottom of rue Tronchet. If you're hungry, but couldn't afford anything in either of the above shops, your answer is just around the corner. Flat entrance from rue de Castellane, or a small step from rue Tronchet.

Place de la Madeleine also has a small outdoor market for **flowers and plants** on the east side of its central square from Tuesday to Sunday. The only problem is getting through the heavy traffic.

There are several smart shops like **Gucci** and **Hermés** around the **place Vendôme** and, if you can afford it or like to think you might one day, most entrances are flat or +1.

Fauchon

At the west end of the rue de Rivoli is **WH Smith**, 248 rue de Rivoli (on the corner with rue Cambon), 75001. *Tel:* (1) 42.60.37.97. It is a typical English branch of this chain selling today's English newspapers as well as magazines and books. Unfortunately there is very little room to manouvre in. The rue de Rivoli entrance has one step. The first floor, for books only, is +7+7+12 steps with one handrail.

Galignani, 224 rue de Rivoli (between rue Castiglione and rue d'Alger), 75001, *Tel:* (1) 42.60.76.07. This traditional bookshop has an English section at the back. The entrance has one step and there is more space inside than in WH Smith.

Avenue des Champs Elysées

The Champs Elysées is long and wide, so we have offered suggestions for a visit in the *Recommended itineraries* chapter. It has several relatively small shopping galleries, and a Virgin Megastore. There are also company offices including those of many of the major airlines. There is some metered parking and also underground car parks, of which the one near George V métro has a large lift. However, the whole area is very busy and parking is not easy.

Galerie des Champs Elysées, 84 av des Champs Elysées (on the corner with rue de Berri), 75008. The shopping arcade itself has a flat entrance. It includes a wide variety of shops and most have flat access or a small step. More stores exist in the basement, accessible by escalator or −25 steps with handrails. The loos (D55 no ST) are on this lower level.

Galerie du Claridge, 72 av des Champs Elysées, 75008. Metered parking is on the main road. This rather expensive arcade specialises in clothes and jewellery. The floor surface is marble and may be slippery. All of the thirty or so ground floor shops have flat access and more shops in the basement can be reached by escalator or −7−7−7−5 steps with handrails.

Virgin Megastore, 52 av des Champs Elysées, 75008. *Tel:* (1) 40.74.06.48. The biggest music store in France stays open to midnight seven days a week. The entrance has one step, but inside everything is flat or ramped and a large lift serves all other floors. We were disappointed not to find a wheelchair loo here.

Centrally located food markets

These are a few **food markets** located towards the centre of the city which are likely to tempt and tantalise you the most. There are three types:
- the 'covered' market (marked on the Michelin *Paris Plan*) which opens daily
- the open air market which tends not to take place so often and is usually packing up by early afternoon
- the street market which consists of shops sprawling over into the street and tends to sell just about everything

Marché Buci (street; open Tues-Sun), rue de Buci and rue de Seine, 75006. It takes over pretty much all of the pavement space and so you'll have to watch out for the odd vehicle attempting to pass through. It is not as large as marché Mouffetard, the other street market, but access is far easier. Road space defuses any overcrowding and this picturesque spot just south of the Seine has a pleasant atmosphere. Traders' ramps assist in providing almost perfect access, although not intended for such a purpose. There's a handy supermarket in rue de Seine.

Marché Carmès (open air; open Tues, Thurs & Sat), place Maubert, 75005. This has a fairly small offering of food and clothes. You may have to fight with the odd kerb or narrow gangway, but there should be no problems otherwise.

Marché Enfants Rouges (covered; open Tues-Sat 08.00-13.00 and 16.00-19.30, Sun 08.00-13.00), 39 rue de Bretagne, 75003. It sells food and flowers, has a flat entrance and is flat throughout.

Marché Monge (open air; open Wed, Fri & Sun), place Monge, 75005. Although we didn't get a chance to see this one 'in action', the central pavemented area of the square is flat and up an average kerb.

Marché Mouffetard (street; open daily), rue Mouffetard, 75005. This again offers a wide variety of goods for sale including a stunning range of food. The street is fairly narrow, and the combination of a slope running down to St Médard's church along with cobbled stones make it quite a challenge for chair users. There is good underground car parking in place Bernard Halpern off rue Daubenton with a lift (D80). This car park also contains a loo (D77 ST100+) on the first level down next to the office, although you may have to get the key from the next door office which has one step.

Marché Porte St Martin (covered; open Tues to Sat 08.00 to 13.00 and 16.00 to 19.30, Sun 08.00 to 13.00), rue du Château d'Eau (on corner with rue Bouchardon), 75010. It sells mostly food. The entrance is flat, as is the spacious inside.

Marché Saint Germain (covered; open Tues to Sat 08.00 to 13.00 and 16.00 to 19.30, Sun 08.00 to 13.00), rue Mabillon, 75006. This has a split level which can be overcome using different entrances; for the lower level enter with one step from rue Mabillon, whilst for the larger upper section there is one step or a steep ramp from rue Clément and a flat service entrance in rue Lobineau signposted as the wheelchair entrance, but you may encounter difficulties with parked cars.

Flea market

The **Marché aux puces (Flea market)** (Michelin Guide Additional Walks and Sights) is just north of the boulevard Périphérique by the porte de Clignancourt. It lies on either side of the rue des Rosiers, and to the northeast of the rue R J Valles. Back in the 19th century the market grew up on the city boundary and it became an established trading centre in the 1920s. It is well signed with particular areas having groups of stalls and shops. The areas have names such as Vernaison, Rosières, Malik, Biron and Malaisse. Most of these are marked on the Michelin Guide diagram.

There is a car park in avenue de la porte de Clignancourt, just on the south side of the Périphérique. Some streets nearby have metered parking and there's an underground car park at Malaisse on rue des Rosiers with a lift (D130 W140 L230), near the junction with rue J H Fabre. Malaisse also has **wheelchair loos** (D90 ST130) between numbers 41 and 42 at the top of the U-shaped street. Malaisse is not on the Michelin Guide diagram, but it is across the road from Vernaison where it says rue Marceau.

Good loo guide

A major problem for people with disabilities, and particularly for chair users, is to find suitable and accessible loos.

In Paris there are still some 'squat' loos – best described as being simply a 'hole in the ground' – and these get more common in Europe the further south you go. There are not many properly accessible toilets anywhere in the city. Many of the public loos are in cafés and restaurants and can by no stretch of the imagination be described as accessible. A few of the entertainments venues now have wheelchair accessible loos, but are not listed here as they're not open throughout the day (see *Entertainments* chapter for details).

Regrettably the brand new roadside wheelchair loos which you will see cannot be used by visitors. You need a special card to gain entry, and although we tried to negotiate with those responsible in the town hall, they were adamant that the cards would only be issued to local people. We were told that these would be available as part of a European-wide system, but since a realistic date for implementing such a scheme is probably 2010, we are disappointed that nothing else is being done in the meantime. From where we sit, it seems a mad piece of bureaucracy, and is particularly infuriating in that these loos are often in places where the nearest other wheelchair loo is half a kilometre away.

The main places which are likely to have a wheelchair loo with the possibility of sideways transfer are some larger or newer hotels, the main railway stations and some of the larger museums. There are wheelchair loos at half a dozen of the most famous and important tourist sites such as the Louvre, Eiffel Tower, Orsay Museum, the Pompidou Centre, La Villette and at la Grande Arche de la Défense. Unlike London, only a small number of the big shops and department stores have wheelchair loos.

The loos in our list all have large cubicles, and most have adequate space (over 70 cm) for side transfer to the WC. Wherever possible we have measured the distance for side transfer. It appears as ST55 if there is a 55cm gap alongside the WC. We have used abbreviations for repetitive data: door widths are indicated by D85 for a width of 85cm or D70+ for a width of more than 70cm; sideways transfer appears as ST100+ for more than 100cm.

The provision of rails and other facilities like lever taps was highly variable, and it has not been possible to describe these with sufficient accuracy to be helpful. Even in new facilities the standard of design was poor; we came across several real howlers where fixed rails impeded sideways transfer, whilst many that had plenty of space had been arranged to cause maximum problems for the disabled user.

We should point out that sometimes you will come across a loo where there's a charge for its use, but this is usually only 2Fr.

The general location of each wheelchair loo is given on the map. This should help you to see quickly which one you are nearest to. You can then use the information here together with a street plan to find it. If you want to use the 'semi-public' ones in hotels, these are usually somewhere near the reception desk, and you can always say that you're "thinking of having a drink in the bar", or something to that effect, if challenged by staff. We've tried to say **exactly** where they are, so that you don't have to ask, and can walk or wheel in with a degree of confidence.

Arrondissement 1

Jardin des Tuileries (The Tuileries Gardens), (Michelin Guide Principal Walk 2). The gardens are between the Louvre and place de la Concorde, and the Museé d'Orangerie is at the western end. Its main entrance has +4 steps without handrails, but there is an alternative side entrance with a lift. A unisex wheelchair loo (D79 ST89) is on the ground floor.

Les Halles (Forum des Halles), (Michelin Guide Principal Walk 13). There are four wheelchair loos inside the les Halles complex, all on level −3, and two close by outside:

inside – level −3, place Carrée, just inside the entrance to the clearly signed unisex loos (D70+ ST70+).
– level −3, unisex loos (D70+ ST70+) are by the entrance/exit to parking Sud.
– inside the Videoteque de Paris entrance, (see level −3 in *Sights*).
– level −3, in McDonalds, on the corner of rue l'Arc en Ciel and rue Basse; unmarked loos (D70+ ST70+) are left past the counter and through the restaurant.

outside – in the Kentucky Fried Chicken at the junction of rue Berger and boulevard de Sébastopol. Turn left at the counter and zig-zag through the restaurant following the sign to the unisex 'toilettes' (D70+ ST70+).
– in the Novotel hotel in place Marguerite de Navarre, opposite 19 rue des Halles. The main entrance is just off the junction between rue du Pont Neuf and rue Berger. Access is flat through the main doors, turning left past reception, following the signs to the restaurant/bar and the unisex loos (D86 ST70) are on the left before you reach the bar.

The Louvre, 34–36 quai du Louvre, (Michelin Guide Principal Walk 1). The Pyramid is the main entrance and is flat and wide. There is a lift down to the Cour Napoléon. There are several wheelchair loos (D80+ ST80+) at

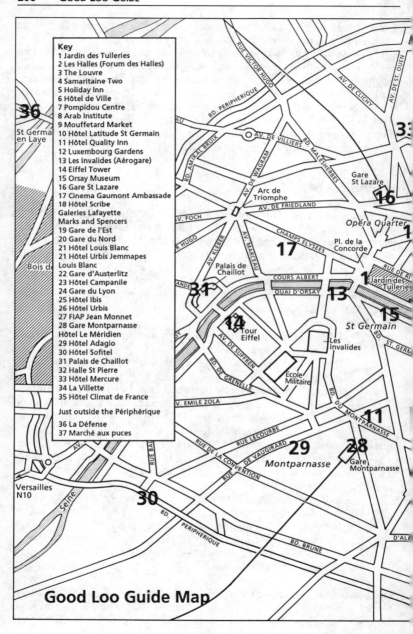

Key
1 Jardin des Tuileries
2 Les Halles (Forum des Halles)
3 The Louvre
4 Samaritaine Two
5 Holiday Inn
6 Hôtel de Ville
7 Pompidou Centre
8 Arab Institute
9 Mouffetard Market
10 Hôtel Latitude St Germain
11 Hôtel Quality Inn
12 Luxembourg Gardens
13 Les Invalides (Aérogare)
14 Eiffel Tower
15 Orsay Museum
16 Gare St Lazare
17 Cinema Gaumont Ambassade
18 Hôtel Scribe
Galeries Lafayette
Marks and Spencers
19 Gare de l'Est
20 Gare du Nord
21 Hôtel Louis Blanc
21 Hôtel Urbis Jemmapes
Louis Blanc
22 Gare d'Austerlitz
23 Hôtel Campanile
24 Gare du Lyon
25 Hôtel Ibis
26 Hôtel Urbis
27 FIAP Jean Monnet
28 Gare Montparnasse
Hôtel Le Méridien
29 Hôtel Adagio
30 Hôtel Sofitel
31 Palais de Chaillot
32 Halle St Pierre
33 Hôtel Mercure
34 La Villette
35 Hôtel Climat de France

Just outside the Périphérique
36 La Défense
37 Marché aux puces

Good Loo Guide Map

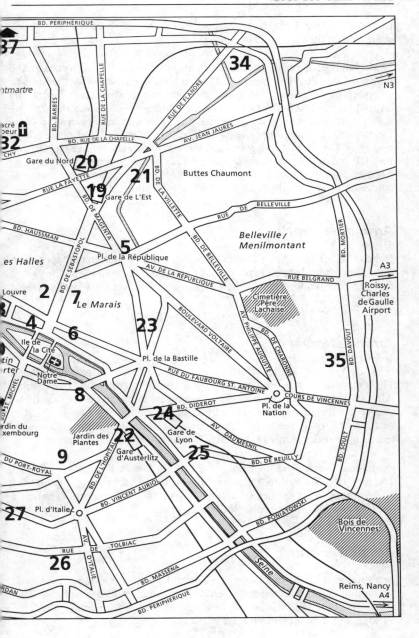

this level and some on the mezzanine just above. There are other wheel-chair loos in the Louvre (see *Sights*).

Samaritaine 2, 75 rue de Rivoli. This part of the department store is on the corner of rue du Pont Neuf. Despite numerous attempts by the staff to convince us otherwise, we found that there is a wheelchair loo (D100 ST100) on the first floor. Because there's no signposting, and the staff we asked were unaware of its existence, here is a detailed description of its location. There are three red lifts in the centre of the building. One is long and narrow, whilst the other two are more typically square in shape. If you turn left out of the square ones on the first floor, go 10m then turn right, go another 10m then turn left, you should find a fire exit and stairwell. The wheelchair loo is on the right-hand side of the stairs, unmarked.

Arrondissement 3

Holiday Inn, 10 pl de la République. Go through the main entrance, turn right after about 10m and take one of the large lifts down to the lower first floor. In the corridor both the men's and women's loos have wheelchair loos (D83 ST70+).

Arrondissement 4

Hôtel de Ville, pl de l'Hôtel de Ville (Michelin Guide Principal Walk 9). The entrance to the building is on the rue de Rivoli and is +4 steps. Alternatively there is flat access via a side gate and a steep 1:4 ramp, and you will have to get this specially opened. There are two designated wheelchair loos on the ground floor, one in Exhibition Centre and one off the main corridor. Only one (D80 ST61) was seen by surveyors.

Pompidou Centre, rue du Renard, (Michelin Guide Principal Walk 13). The loo (D90 ST85) is in the main hall next to the other toilets, and it may be necessary to get the key from the nearby information centre. There is a loo (D70 ST54) marked 'disabled' in the café.

Arrondissement 5

Arab Institute, 1 rue des Fossés-St-Bernard, (Michelin Guide Additional Walks and Sights). At the river Seine end the main entrance is flat and six glass lifts (D80 W125 L130) serve all the floors. A wheelchair loo (D85 ST90) is in the basement on level −2.

Mouffetard Market, rue Mouffetard. The underground car park in place Bernard-Halpern off rue Daubenton has a lift (D80) to a loo (D77 ST100+) on the first level down next to the office. You may find, as we did, that you have to get the key from the office, which has one step.

Arrondissement 6

Hôtel Latitude St Germain, 7–11 rue St Benoît. The hotel is just northwest of the St-Germain-des-Prés church. After one step at the entrance, turn left to the lift. Go down to the lower first floor, through the door opposite and slightly to the right and the next door at the end is a unisex wheelchair loo (D74 ST108).

Hôtel Quality Inn, 92 rue de Vaugirard. We have been told there is a wheelchair loo on the ground floor.

Luxembourg Gardens, rue de Vaugirard, (Michelin Guide Principal Walk 21). The public loos and one unmarked unisex wheelchair pay loo (D70+ ST150) are 100m inside the park from the place André Honnorat entrance on the south side. Although we were not allowed to measure it, we judged its size visually.

Arrondissement 7

Les Invalides, (Michelin Guide Principal Walk 4). In the **Aérogare des Invalides** southeast of pont Alexandre III, you will find a unisex wheelchair loo (D70+ ST86) on the right through a security door between the Bureau de Change and Eurocar Rental. The number for the security door can be obtained from the information desk at Air France Ticket Sales.

Eiffel Tower, quai Branly, (Michelin Guide Principal Walk 3). There are no access problems in getting to the unisex wheelchair loo (D80 ST92) in the indoor area on the second level. (See Tour Eiffel in *Sights*).

Orsay Museum, 62 rue de Lille, (Michelin Guide Principal Walk 11). The information desk on the ground floor, to the right of the entrance, supplies a special plan of the museum in French for disabled visitors which shows the location of wheelchair loos and lifts. Some of the lifts (D80 W105 L140) are concealed by heavy doors. Note that lifts A, C and D are near the rue de Bellechasse entrance, while lift B is at the other end of the museum. There are three unisex wheelchair loos (D89 ST89): on the ground floor near lift C, on level 1 near lift D and on level 6 via the Salle de Consultation.

Arrondissement 8

Gare St Lazare, 13 rue d'Amsterdam. A unisex wheelchair loo (D75 ST86) is on the first floor opposite quai 19. If you enter through the flat access entrance on rue d'Amsterdam, it is about halfway down the platform.

Cinéma Gaumont Ambassade, 50 av Champs Elysées, within 60m of the Virgin Megastore. This loo (D83 ST72) has been included as it is the only one we found in this area, although access to it will be restricted to the opening times of the cinema.

Arrondissement 9

Hôtel Scribe, 1 rue Scribe, on the junction with boulevard des Capucines. The main entrance on rue Scribe has one step. If you pass the information desk on the left of the main foyer with the reception on the right, the unisex wheelchair loos (D86 ST90) are in an alcove to the left of reception.

Galeries Lafayette department store, 40 bd Haussmann. Entrances are flat and access inside is good with large lifts serving all nine floors. The sixth floor restaurant is accessible and there is a wheelchair loo (D85 ST120) opposite the restaurant entrance.

Marks and Spencers, bd Haussmann, on the corner with rue de Caumartin. It has flat entrances and lifts to all floors. Although not designated as a wheelchair loo, the third floor has a loo (inward opening D134 ST81).

Arrondissement 10

Gare de l'Est, pl de 11 Nov 1918. A unisex wheelchair loo (D70+ ST175) can be found by the flat rue d'Alsace entrance.

Gare du Nord, 18 rue de Dunkerque. A unisex wheelchair loo (D80 ST90) is at the eastern end of the station, on the right if you enter from rue de Dunkerque.

Hôtel Louis Blanc, 232 rue du Faubourg St Martin, at the junction with rue Louis Blanc, has one step at the entrance. If you pass reception and the lift on your left, a unisex wheelchair loo (D70+ ST100) is on the right. It has a plastic removable seat.

Hôtel Urbis Jemmapes Louis Blanc, 12 rue Louis Blanc, just southeast of the St Martin canal. Go through the flat entrance, turn left into the open plan lounge area and the loos, with a women's loo (D70+ ST75), are clearly signposted.

Arrondissement 11

Gare d'Austerlitz, 55 quai d'Austerlitz. There is flat access to a unisex 'wheelchair' loo (D76 ST52) in the women's loos behind the ticket offices, on the left-hand side when entering from quai d'Austerlitz.

Hôtel Campanile, 9 rue du Chemin Vert. If you go through the front entrance and turn left past reception a unisex wheelchair loo (D70 ST70) is inside the door on the right marked 'toilets'.

Arrondissement 12

Gare du Lyon, pl Louis Armand. A unisex wheelchair loo (D70+ ST105) is in front of the entrance to platforms 5-19 on the upper level, which is flat from rue de Chalon.

Hôtel Ibis, 77 rue de Bercy, just east of Palais Omnisports de Paris-Bercy, opposite rue Corbineau. The entrance is flat and a wheelchair loo (D77 ST84) is in the men's loos on the restaurant/bar level with +8 steps which can be avoided by a stair-lift.

Arrondissement 13

Hôtel Urbis, 177 rue de Tolbiac. The main entrance to the hotel has −4 steps, but it is flat from passage Foubert. Wheelchair loos (D76 ST114) are in the men's and women's loos along the corridor to the left.

Arrondissement 14

FIAP Jean Monnet, 30 rue Cabanis, has a large entrance foyer with flat access. A wheelchair loo (D70+ ST70+) is on the left of reception.

Hôtel Le Méridien. 19 rue du Cdt René Mouchotte, opposite Gare Montparnasse. The entrance is flat and if you keep reception on your right, a unisex wheelchair loo (D96 ST90) is to the left of the lifts.

Arrondissement 15

Gare Montparnasse, 17 bd de Vaugirard. The entrance on boulevard de Vaugirard is flat to level C and the wheelchair loo (D70+ ST70+) is on the same side of the building.

Hôtel Adagio, 257 rue de Vaugirard, near Vaugirard métro. The main entrance has +2 steps. At reception turn right and take the lifts to floor −2 where there is a unisex wheelchair loo (D81 ST87).

Hôtel Sofitel, 8–12 rue Louis Armand. If you go through the main doors, turn left then right and go past reception on your left, a unisex wheelchair loo (D85 ST68) is directly in front of you.

Arrondissement 16

Palais de Chaillot, pl du Trocadéro, (Michelin Guide Principal Walk 3). Just across the river from the Eiffel Tower. Into the east wing there are +6 steps with a stairlift to bypass them. There is a unisex wheelchair loo (D90 ST190) in the Musée National des Monuments Français on the ground floor. There are +5 without handrails into the west wing of the Palais and a unisex wheelchair loo (D70+ ST70+) is in the far right-hand corner of the foyer by the restaurant/bar.

Arrondissement 18

Halle St Pierre, 2 rue Ronsard (Michelin Guide Principal Walk 7). This building includes the Musée d'Art Naïf Max Fourny and Musée en Herbe. The main entrance is flat and a unisex wheelchair loo is on the first floor via a lift (D79 W97 L190).

Hôtel Mercure, 1-3 rue Caulaincourt. The entrance is flat and a unisex wheelchair loo (D70 ST80) is on the first floor, directly opposite the lifts. The loo door was locked when the survey team visited, but staff quickly found the key and said that it was usually unlocked.

Arrondissement 19

La Villette, (Michelin Guide Principal Walk 15). **Cité des Sciences et de l'Industrie**, 30 av Corentin-Cariou. There are wheelchair loos (D70+ ST82) on virtually every floor, since wherever they have provided loos they have put in at least one huge cubicle. They are all in either the women's or men's areas as we didn't find any unisex loos.

Arrondissement 20

Hôtel Climat de France, 2 av du Professeur André Lemierre. Take the lift to the first floor and the wheelchair loo (D70+ ST200+) is clearly signposted.

Just outside the Périphérique

La Défense (Michelin Guide Principal Walk 27) has four wheelchair loos:

- **Grande Arche de la Défense.** Behind the lifts are +6 steps with a wheelchair stairlift to bypass them to the unisex wheelchair loo (D70+ ST70+) about 50m to your right at the end of the corridor.

- **Quatre Temps** is a huge shopping mall over a massive car park. The only wheelchair user loo we found was off the Patinoire area on level 2 right at the far end of the building (see our map of La Défense). The loo has a large cubicle, but included some bars on either side of the WC helpful to anyone with arthritis, but which make side transfer difficult.

- **World Trade Centre (CNIT).** There is an unsigned wheelchair loo on the ground floor, half-right as you come into the building from the Parvis. It is in the 'general' loos which are signed and, as you go in, the men's is on the left and the women's on the right. The wheelchair loo door (D70+ ST70+) is straight ahead, but it had a very low seat and looked as though it needed an attachment to raise it to a conventional height.

- **Hôtel Sofitel** which is part of the CNIT complex; you need to go through the Trade Centre, as otherwise access is only via revolving doors, leave by the Soprite Esplanade, which is half-left from the main entrance, then turn left and the hotel entrance is about 50m. Take the lift to the first floor, turn left and the unisex loo (D75 ST90+) is almost immediately on your left before you get to the reception desk.

The **Marché aux puces (Flea market)** (Michelin Guide Additional Walks and Sights) is just north of the boulevard Périphérique by the porte de Clignancourt. It lies on either side of the rue des Rosiers, and to the northeast of the rue R J Valles. Both a men's and women's wheelchair loo (D90 ST130) can be found in the Malaisse area, between numbers 41 and 42 at the top of the U-shaped street. Malaisse is not mentioned on the Michelin Guide diagram, but it is across the road from Vernaison where it says rue Marceau.

Recommended itineraries

When you are visiting a strange city and struggling with working things out from guidebooks, it's sometimes difficult to identify the easiest and most interesting areas to visit. We are therefore making a few preliminary suggestions which may help, especially if you are only making a brief visit. *What we have done is to identify ten varied 'itineraries' or groups of sights which should involve minimum distances, and which are linked to the limited accessible transport.* For some you would have to go by car or taxi, but several can be reached on the RER. One thing you need to watch out for is opening times, as some major museums and buildings are closed one day a week, particularly on Mondays and Tuesdays. You will find details about this in the Michelin Guide.

We have given them an 'order of priority', but we appreciate that this is based on personal preference. What you want to do will depend on your particular interests, how long you've got, what transport you have and what the weather is like.

The itineraries are:

> The Eiffel Tower and a boat trip on the Seine
> Les Halles and Notre Dame
> La Défense
> Versailles
> The Louvre or the Orsay
> St-Germain-en-Laye
> Montmartre
> La Villette
> Shopping
> The Champs Elysées

The Eiffel tower and a boat trip on the Seine

This particular itinerary is an ideal way to see a lot of Paris with a minimum of effort and much of it can be done from the comfort of a glass-covered boat! It would be a good thing to do early on during a visit, as you will get a good idea of the layout of the city and of the major sights. It's best to do it on a nice sunny day if you can, or possibly to do the boat trip in the evening when things are floodlit.

Unfortunately it's not near an accessible RER station, and chair users should consider using the accessible mini-buses for this one (see *Getting around in Paris*), if not coming by car or taxi. The best place for parking is the Bateaux Parisiens car park at the port de la Bourdonnais off quai Branly and opposite avenue de la Bourdonnais. It is on the riverside, only about

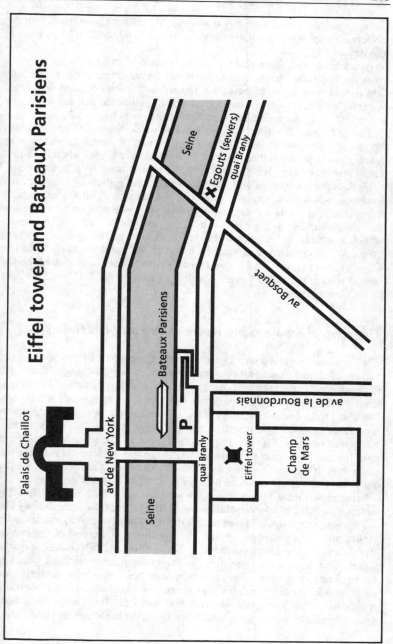

Eiffel tower and Bateaux Parisiens

Palais de Chaillot

Seine

av de New York

quai Branly

Bateaux Parisiens

P

Seine

Egouts (sewers)

quai Branly

av Bosquet

av de la Bourdonnais

Eiffel tower

Champ de Mars

200m from the tower (see the diagram). Alternatively there is parking underneath the tower itself, but this is congested and tends to fill up early in the day.

Apart from the Champ de Mars behind the tower, the fountains and view from the Palais de Chaillot across the river, the other thing you could easily add to your visit is les Égouts (the Sewers) at the end of pont de l'Alma some 400m away. Note that there is a marionnette (puppet) theatre in the corner of the Champ de Mars (see *Entertainments* chapter).

The order you do things is up to you. If you do the tower first you may appreciate the relaxation of the boat trip afterwards, which takes about an hour. The only snag is that the view from the tower is best when the sun is fairly low in the sky, either early in the morning or in the late afternoon.

Each of the places involved – the Tour Eiffel, les Égouts and the Bateaux Parisiens – is written up in some detail elsewhere and all are reasonably accessible. The boats do vary slightly and if you have your own vehicle you can consider using the *Bateaux Mouches* which are slightly more wheelchair-friendly. They are on the other side of the river about 1km away. Additionally you can see the Champ de Mars and the whole Palais de Chaillot area to good advantage. **The only wheelchair loo en route is on the second level of the Eiffel Tower.** There is another in the Palais de Chaillot, but it's +5 steps.

The central area around Notre Dame and Les Halles

The diagram covers a compact area right in the centre of Paris with a wide variety of things to do and see, many of which are accessible. There are underground car parks at both les Halles and the Georges Pompidou Centre. The Pompidou car park has facilities for coaches and minibuses. We also found one with *valet parking* in rue Bailleul near the corner with the rue du Louvre. You just drive up, get out at street level, and someone else parks your car for you. Parking in the Notre Dame underground car park has poor access as the only alternative to the 20 steps out is to use the car ramps. It's alright to drop a disabled passenger off before entering the car park, but a chair-bound driver would certainly have a problem.

Most importantly if you are using this method of getting around, **the RER stations at both Châtelet-les-Halles and St Michel are fully accessible by lift**.

Points of interest with good access include the new developments at les Halles and the Pompidou Centre, the big shops at the end of the rue de Rivoli and Notre Dame cathedral. The Hôtel de Ville has a splendid façade, and there is a flat way in to the exhibition rooms which will take you a little time to negotiate. The various historic buildings on the Ile de la Cité also have interesting façades and there are excellent views from both riverbanks. Past the river you run into the Left Bank with its unique atmosphere and numerous cafés. There are other buildings and interesting

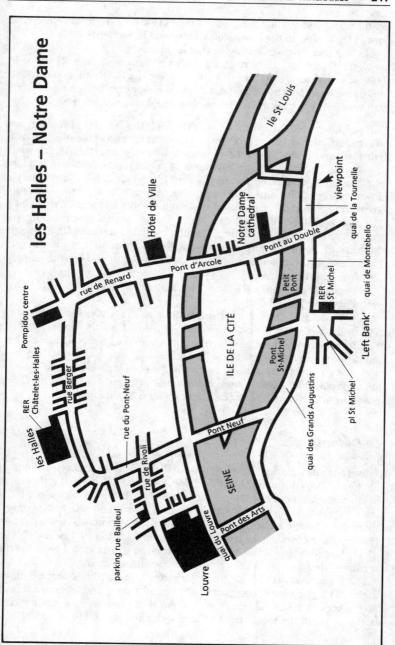

les Halles – Notre Dame

Ile St Louis

viewpoint

Notre Dame cathedral

Hôtel de Ville

Pont au Double

quai de la Tournelle

Pont d'Arcole

quai de Montebello

rue de Renard

Pompidou centre

Petit Pont

RER St Michel

'Left Bank'

RER Châtelet-les-Halles

rue Berger

ILE DE LA CITÉ

Pont St-Michel

les Halles

pl St Michel

rue du Pont-Neuf

quai des Grands Augustins

Pont Neuf

rue de Rivoli

parking rue Bailleul

SEINE

Pont des Arts

Louvre

quai du Louvre

features and you will find details elsewhere in the text. **There are wheelchair loos at les Halles, in the Pompidou Centre and in Samaritaine 2.**

The distance involved, if you start at les Halles, go round the route as far as Notre Dame, a little way along the river bank and then return to les Halles, would be about 3km. If you are using the RER you could reduce this to less than 2km by using the stations at either end of the route. Even if you have left your car at les Halles, you could take the train back.

If you have used the car park in rue Bailleul, the first things you will pass are the large department stores on your right at the end of the rue de Rivoli. Turn left up the rue de Pont Neuf to get to les Halles. Rue Berger which leads to the Pompidou centre has numerous restaurants, cafés and fast food joints, most of which have flat access. After Pompidou, the route takes you down the rue de Renard to the magnificent façade of the Hôtel de Ville. There are detailed descriptions of all the main sights elsewhere in the guide. The itinerary then leads you to Notre Dame, which is something you shouldn't miss. Across the pont au Double, with the statue of Charlemagne on the right, it's worth turning left along the riverside so that you can get a good view of the cathedral from nearer the east end, and see the magnificent flying buttresses.

It is possible to take the RER back to Châtelet-les-Halles from St Michel, in the place St Michel.

If you are still feeling adventurous, there are dozens of interesting restaurants in the left bank area around St Michel. Equally you may want to walk or wheel back alongside the river, then over the Pont Neuf and back to the car park in rue Bailleul or to les Halles.

As there's a lot to see and do, you could split this itinerary into two; tackle the les Halles/Pompidou Centre end on one day, and take in Notre Dame with a wander round the left bank and St Germain on another.

La Défense

This is the ultra-modern development with the Grande Arche at the end of the Grand Axis through the Arc de Triomphe and Concorde. It is described in considerable detail in the chapter on Sights. It has an accessible RER station on line A and good underground parking with lift access. Not only is there the Arche, which is fully accessible and affords superb views, but also Quatre Temps, one of the largest indoor shopping malls in Europe. It's an ideal place for a day of sunshine and showers, so you can see the view in the sunshine, and get out of the rain while shopping or eating.

It's not necessary to repeat the description of the facilities which is under *Sights*. This reasonably compact site has good access, and **there are at least four wheelchair loos**, although with somewhat variable accessibility. The best two are at the top of the Grande Arche and in the Hôtel Sofitel.

Versailles

While the palace and gardens at Versailles are huge, it's a unique place and it is possible to see quite a lot if you plan your visit. If you can't walk very far it would be preferable to come by car, or to do some sightseeing by taxi. Train travel is possible using the direct line from Gare St Lazare to Versailles; there is flat access at both stations, provided you can handle getting on and off the trains. However, the station is almost 1km from the palace. If you prefer to use the accessible minibus service, this might be a visit on which to splash out, and make a half-day or even a whole day booking.

The normal distance from the car parks in front of the palace is about 400m across a bumpy forecourt. Disabled visitors are allowed to drive right up to the archway leading to the gardens to unload. The car has to be taken back to the car park (although see the full write-up for further details). If you unload near the arch, go through it to the gardens and take the little 'train' described below; you would walk or wheel only about 100/200m.

Ornamental Lake, Versailles

Itinerary Around Versailles

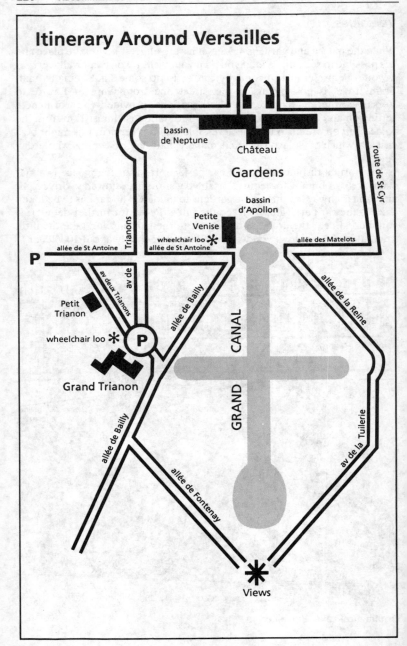

If you want to go inside the palace, we've described (under *Sights*) how being dropped off by the same archway leaves you next to the visitors' enquiry desk and lift. You will have to go quite a long way inside the palace to see much of it, probably over 500m. Part of this will be against the flow of other visitors, since there's only the one lift. Some parts of it are spectacular, particularly the Hall of Mirrors.

To see the gardens and the palace's façade, it is probably best either to go through the archways from the Royal Court and into the gardens behind, going as far as you want. From the parking in place d'Armes in front of the palace, you should expect to cover about 1km to see a reasonable amount. Just past the archway on the right side, there's a regular motorised 'train' which takes visitors for an extensive tour of the gardens. It is slightly awkward to get into, but most disabled walkers would find it possible. For chair users there's the possibility of sideways transfer, which is again a bit awkward as you are transferring upwards through a rather narrow gap. If you can get on board, it's an ideal way to see the gardens.

Alternatively you can drive down the sides of the gardens, possibly stopping for a bit by the Neptune Gate, and going in from there. Another car park can be found in allée St Antoine for stopping and seeing the gardens round the Trianons. You can also drive south along the allée St Antoine to see the Apollo Basin and the huge artificial lakes including the Grand Canal. The diagram shows a drive right around the Versailles site. Some parking places are marked. You should get good views of both the palace and gardens. Probably the best thing is to drive around the indicated route, getting a feel for what is there. Then you can decide where to stop and spend some time when going around a second time. The best places for stopping and looking at particular things may depend on the time of year. We've shown this in the diagram, and called it the grand circuit.

We found five wheelchair loos:
- off the Princes Court, to the left of the Royal Court of the main palace
- 150m from the Grand Trianon
- near the boat hire place on the Grand Canal
- in town inside McDonalds, rue du Maréchal Foch, on the right-hand side of the counter. It is signed and unisex,
- and in McDonalds opposite Versailles-rive-gauche RER line C station, rue Royale.

The Louvre or the Orsay

Either of these make an itinerary on their own. They are thoroughly described in their respective write-ups. Neither is near an accessible RER station, so it would be best to come by car or taxi. Both have cafés and restaurants, and **a number of wheelchair loos**. Although the Orsay is large, it doesn't begin to compare with the vastness of the Louvre and, unless you specifically want to see certain art treasures, we would recommend the Orsay museum as being interesting and more manageable. Having said that, just seeing the new Louvre entrance and riding down on 'le Tube' is quite an experience, and a visit to the Louvre is perfectly practicable provided you plan to see a sensibly limited group of exhibits.

St-Germain-en-Laye

An ideal place for a visit to a small château, just outside Paris. The town alongside is crowded with narrow pavements, but there are lots of cafés and small shops.

The RER station on line A is fully accessible with a service lift, and the château is only some 200m away across the road. If you come by car, the underground car park has steps up from the final level. If you are going to have problems getting out of the car park, it's probably best to be patient, and wait for a space in the metered parking at street level; there's a limited amount, but some of it is quite close to the château.

The château itself is almost fully accessible, see the detailed write-up. It is probably the most compact château (with some interesting exhibits) that you can get into in the Paris area. **It has a good wheelchair loo**.

Montmartre

Because this is a hilly area with cobbled streets and pavements at the top of a hill, it poses special problems. On the other hand it's an interesting and atmospheric place, offering splendid views over the city.

There are various ways of approaching it.

If you can get on to the Promotrain on which you need to transfer into a seat in little coaches which are up 2 steps, then you can see a lot of it. There are details in the Montmartre write-up. It goes from place Blanche.

There's a very limited amount of metered parking near the top, so you will have to be patient and/or lucky to find a space. A car park can be found in the place d'Anvers, with its entrance off the boulevard de Rochechouart. This has four levels of underground parking, but the lift is tiny (D75 W80 L80) for getting up to level −1, from which are 20 steps to street level. Consequently the only practical way for disabled drivers or those unable to be dropped off before entering the car park is to use the car ramp out, taking appropriate care.

Place d'Anvers is about 200m from the funicular railway which has been modernised, and has entirely flat access both in and out of the cable-car. At the top a call button and intercom will allow you to get the gate opened if the ticket office is not staffed.

At the top of the railway there are good views. The place du Tertre, where the painters are, is a further 200m of cobbles uphill from here. An alternative approach is to take a taxi up to the Église St Pierre just by the square, and then you can either walk or wheel down. Église St Pierre has +2 at the entrance, and contains some fine gold and red stained glass.

Although the Sacré Cœur is +25 steps from the road near the top of the funicular, if you can possibly get help to make it up and down, it's well worth it. It is one of Paris' great sights, and dominates the northern skyline. The inside is flat, and there are some amazing mosaics and stained glass. It also retains the atmosphere of being a house of prayer, and not just a place where tourists come to gawp. From the terrace just below the Sacré Cœur, the views are superb on a clear day.

You can get back down to the place d'Anvers using the funicular.

There's a wheelchair loo in the Halle St Pierre at the bottom of the hill (see Musée d'Art Naïf in *Sights*), but note that it has a 20Fr entrance fee. Additional wheelchair loos are located in the hotel Mercure at the end of rue Caulaincourt which is nearby; they are commonly kept locked, and you might have to buy a drink in order to use one of them.

La Villette

This includes the Science and Technology Museum, and the amazing reflective Géode behind it. The site is compact and accessible. Outside an extensive park includes some themed play-areas for children, and part of the canal which passes through the centre. It is quite possible to spend a whole day here.

Not being near any of the accessible RER stations, you would do best to come by car or taxi. The underground car park provides lift access to the main hall of the museum. The entrance to the car park is from avenue Corentin.

A thorough description of the facilities appear in the chapter on *Sights* under la Villette. There are more wheelchair loos in the Cité des Sciences than anywhere else in Paris!

Shopping

The best grouping of shops, apart from the indoor complexes at les Halles and Quatre Temps appears to be the one described in the section on shopping. This starts at boulevard Haussmann, goes past the Madeleine as far as the west end of the rue de Rivoli.

Underground car parking is possible at Galeries Lafayette. The area is not near an accessible RER station. **There are wheelchair loos in Galeries Lafayette and at the Hôtel Scribe near the Opéra.**

The Champs Elysées

The avenue itself is broad and long and slopes very gently. Everyone has heard of it, with the Arc de Triomphe at one end and place de la Concorde at the other. In the middle are the Grand and Petit Palais, surrounded by flat accessible gardens. There are a lot of expensive shops, together with airline offices, banks, travel agents, cafés and cinemas. At the top end, near the Arc, is the main Tourist Office which is written up elsewhere.

The snag with it is that it's a wide straight street and, although it doesn't look it, it's about 2km long. *What we recommend or suggest is that it's best seen by driving in a car or taxi along it, going round the Arc and crossing place de la Concorde.*

If you want to spend a little time there absorbing the atmosphere, there's underground car parking in avenue George V off the Champs Elysées. At the time of writing, much of the car parking along the road was being rebuilt and hopefully enlarged. In the avenue George V car park a lift (D80 W138 L108) goes to all six floors including the ground floor, and spaces for disabled people were near the lift. Parking near the place de la Concorde is more difficult, but a huge underground car park is being built under the Jardin des Tuileries which will be open soon and hopefully have good access for pedestrians.

You can come on the RER line A, but Étoile station has no lifts. There are, however, escalators from platform to street level in both directions, if you take the Champs Elysées exit, and follow the same route back down. If you take other exits/entrances you may encounter steps.

Access to the Arc de Triomphe is not easy, as described under *Sights*. It's about 1.5km to the Palais de Chaillot, and just across the river you could 'do' the suggested Eiffel tower and boat trip itinerary. Depending on how long you've got, and whether or not you want to while away the hours at an expensive Champs Elysées café, you could easily combine both into one day. We didn't manage to find any loos for wheelchairs users in this area, even in the Virgin Megastore – shame on them.

What to do if it's wet

Few cities look at their best when it decides to rain. Additional hazards are created by the traffic slowing down and the difficulty of finding a taxi.

However, there are things that you can do, and several places you might want to go to, where it doesn't really matter whether it rains or not. If you are visiting when the weather is a bit changeable, you might want to save these up for a possible rainy day.

In particular we would recommend the **City of Science and Industry** at **la Villette**. It offers plenty of variety indoors, and lots of things that will appeal to most children. Access is good and it includes exhibits, films, a planetarium and the unique Géode with its special presentations.

If you are into art, you have a variety of places, with the **Louvre** and the **Musée d'Orsay** top of your list already no doubt. The Orsay is more manageable in terms of size, and has a good ambience, good access and well-presented exhibits. However, if you must 'do' the Louvre, it too has magnificent art and unique historical treasures.

The **Beaubourg** or **Georges Pompidou Centre** has a variety of things going on. It has an underground car park, and the permanent Museum of Modern Art on the fourth floor. Not far away is the les Halles centre with a wide variety of both shops and eating places.

Another idea is to do some **shopping**, and the group of large department stores on the **boulevard Haussmann** near the Opéra might be a good place to start. You might like to 'take' tea in one of the expensive hotels around there if you want a bit of class and a rest in the afternoon. Alternatively, in terms of shopping, the huge complex at **Quatre Temps** in La Défense is all under cover.

We've mentioned quite a number of **marionnette theatres** which would appeal to most children – who are the ones who tend to get most frustrated if it rains a lot – and these might provide at least an hour or so's entertainment in the dry.

An out-of-town sight with good access and quite a lot to see indoors is Fontainebleau. Obviously it would be more enjoyable to see it on a good day and to enjoy the grounds and the surrounding forest; nonetheless it is still possible to have a very interesting time indoors.

Useful phrases and vocabulary

A phrasebook can be useful for travellers who have only distant memories of schoolday French. We also recommend carrying a pocket dictionary so that if necessary you can point at words to supplement your vocabulary.

There are certain basic phrases and questions to do with access which you may need, and we thought that it was worth collecting a few of these. This may enable you to find things more quickly, or remind you of some of the necessary vocabulary. Making the effort to speak a little French almost invariably produces a positive response.

General

Could you help me please?
Pourriez-vous m'aider, s'il vous plaît?

I cannot walk very far.
Je ne peux pas marcher beaucoup.

I can only get up a few steps.
Je ne peux monter que quelques marches.

I am disabled and cannot climb steps.
Je suis handicapé et je ne peux pas monter les escaliers.

I find escalators very difficult.
Je trouve les escaliers roulants très difficiles.

I cannot carry anything heavy.
Je ne peux rien porter de lourd.

Although I do not use a wheelchair, I would like to use the lift please.
Bien que je ne sois pas dans un fauteuil roulant, je voudrais utiliser l'ascenseur s'il vous plaît.

Can I sit down somewhere?
Puis-je m'asseoir quelque part?

Is there a reduction in price for a disabled person?
Est-ce qu'il y a un tarif réduit pour les personnes handicapées?

Can I remain in my wheelchair?
Puis-je rester dans mon fauteuil roulant?

Do you have an induction loop?
Avez-vous une boucle magnétique?

About access

Is there an entrance without steps?
Est-ce qu'il y a une entrée sans marches?

Is there a route which avoids the steps?
Est-ce qu'il y a un passage qui contourne les marches?

Do you have a ramp for those steps?
Est-ce qu'il y a une rampe pour ces marches?

How many steps are there?
Combien des marches y a-t-il ici?

Do the stairs have handrails?
Est-ce qu'il y a une main courante placée dans l'escalier?

Where is the lift?
Où se trouve l'ascenseur?

Are the doors over 75cm wide?
Est-ce que les portes sont suffisamment larges pour 75cm?

Is there an adapted toilet here for a wheelchair user?
Est-ce qu'il y a des toilettes adaptées pour les handicapés près d'ici?

Where can I park near here?
Où se trouve le parking près d'ici?

Facing problems

Call the hospital.
Appellez l'hôpital.

I need some more medicines.
J'ai besoin d'autres médicaments.

Where is the nearest pharmacist?
Où se trouve la pharmacie la plus proche?

I need to find a doctor who speaks English.
J'ai besoin d'un médecin qui parle anglais.

Help!
Au secours!

My wheelchair is broken.
Mon fauteuil roulant est cassé.

I've damaged my crutches.
J'ai cassé mes béquilles.

I've lost my crutches. Where can I buy some?
J'ai perdu mes béquilles. D'où puis-je en acheter?

I need another cushion.
J'ai besoin d'un autre coussin.

I need another footplate.
J'ai besoin d'un autre pose-pieds.

My tyre is flat.
Mon pneu est crevé.

Travelling by car

Do you have a vehicle adapted for a disabled person? With hand controls?
Avez-vous une voiture adaptée pour un conducteur handicapé? Avec des commandes à la main?

I have a disabled passenger in the car.
J'ai un passager handicapé dans la voiture.

I am a disabled driver.
Je suis un conducteur handicapé.

Would you put my wheelchair in the boot?
Pourriez-vous mettre mon fauteuil roulant dans le coffre?

Do you have taxis adapted for disabled people?
Avez-vous des taxis adaptés pour les personnes handicapées?

Can I drop someone off near the entrance please?
Puis-je déposer quelqu'un près de l'entrée s'il vous plaît?

Can I park near the entrance?
Puis-je me garer près de l'entrée?

Windscreen notes

Vehicle with a disabled passenger
Véhicule transportant un handicapé

Passenger is a wheelchair user
Le passager utilise un fauteuil roulant

Driver is a wheelchair user
Le conducteur utilise un fauteuil roulant

Only parking for.... minutes
Garé pour.... minutes

Travelling by train

I want to catch a train to....
Je voudrais prendre le train pour....

I want to go to....
Je voudrais aller à....

I would like to use the lift please.
Je voudrais utiliser l'ascenseur s'il vous plaît.

Can I get on the train in my wheelchair?
Puis-je monter dans le train avec mon fauteuil roulant?

It tells me in this guide that you do have access for a disabled person.
On me dit dans ce guide que vous avez un accès pour les personnes handicapées.

I am on the platform and I am in a wheelchair.
Je suis sur le quai et je suis dans un fauteuil roulant.

Where is the exit I can use to avoid the barriers?
Où est la sortie je peux utiliser pour éviter les barrières?

Can you show me please?
Pouvez-vous me montrer s'il vous plaît?

Can you confirm that the lift is working today?
Pouvez-vous m'assurer que l'ascenseur marche aujourd'hui?

I cannot get up into the carriage.
Je ne peux pas monter dans le compartiment.

Travelling by bus

Would you help me get on the bus?
Pourriez-vous m'aider à monter dans le bus?

Would you help me get off the bus?
Pourriez-vous m'aider à descendre du bus?

Can you arrange for someone to meet me please?
Pourriez-vous faire en sorte qu'on vienne me chercher?

Would you call me when we reach Montparnasse?
Pourriez-vous me faire signe quand nous arrivons à Montparnasse?

At the hotel

Do you have any adapted rooms for disabled guests?
Avez-vous des chambres adaptées pour la clientèle handicapée?

Do you have any ground floor bedrooms?
Avez-vous des chambres au rez-de-chaussée?

Are there steps to get to the restaurant?
Y-a-t-il des marches pour accéder au restaurant?

Could you move the bed to make more space?
Pouvez-vous bouger le lit pour faire plus de place?

Do you have a board to put under my mattress?
Avez-vous une planche pour placer sous mon matelas?

Can you bring my breakfast to my room?
Pouvez-vous apporter le petit déjeuner dans ma chambre?

Useful words

brakes	freins (m)
crutches	béquilles (f)
chest	poitrine (f)
cushion or pillow	coussin (m) ou oreiller (m)
disabled	handicapé
folding	pliant
handle	poignée (f)
handrail	main courante (f)
hard of hearing	mal-entendant
heart	coeur (m)
induction loop	boucle magnétique (f)
lift	ascenseur (m)
painkiller	coupe douleur (f), anesthésiant (m)
partially sighted	mal-voyant
ramp	rampe (f)
seat	siège (m)
steps	marches (f)
wheelchair	fauteuil roulant (m)

Symbols
• • • • • • • • • • • • • •

Although the guidebook is written in English, much of the information about accommodation and about the main sights is summarised in the form of symbols. It is intended that this will enable you to use much of the information, as the symbols have clear criteria. Their precise meaning is described in the list which follows.

The symbols define the information which you may need before you reach a building or area, followed by details of the entrance, and then of access inside the building. The existence of a lift, of steps and of accessible toilets and eating facilities is defined. Where appropriate, any special facilities for visually handicapped people or those who are hard of hearing is noted.

In the vast majority of situations, facilities which are suitable for the wheelchair user will also be OK for those with other disabilities or access problems.

The information that a building has a flat entrance and is 60% wheelchair accessible is represented by:

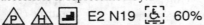 E2 N19 ⌊&⌉ 60%

The information that parking is difficult and that the area is hilly; that there are two steps at the entrance; that the ground floor representing 60% of the whole has no split levels but that there are −19 steps to the basement is represented by:

Symbols key:

☐P☐	Parking with flat, lift or ramped access, normally attached to, or part of the building.
⌊P⌋	Parking normally possible within 100m.
⟋P⟍	Parking may well be difficult.
T/C	Taxi/car dropping-off point outside, within 20m of the entrance.
⟋H⟍	Hilly area.
☐F☐	Flat area.
⟋D⟍	Long distances may be involved.
◢◣	Bumpy surfaces in getting to the building.
☐U☐	Wheelchairs available for use.

A friend or escort for a chair user is advised eg. because of the size or surface.

Access is particularly difficult.

Good signposting.

Poor/non-existent signposting.

Special exhibitions/facilities for people who are partially sighted.

M Flat main entrance.

A There is a flat way in or flat approach. Normally open.

[A] There is a flat way in. Opened on request.

Steps.

E Entrance E3 or E1+1 etc indicate the steps at the main entrance. Alternatives are indicated thus: E12/2.

N Inside. Where numbers are added, they indicate the steps up or from the GF. If you can go either way it is indicated thus: N+25/−14 (25 steps up or 14 steps down).

Handrails on both sides throughout.

Handrails on both sides in parts of the building.

Flat/ramped/lift access everywhere, after any steps at the entrance.

Flat/ramped/lift access to part of the building (after any steps at the entrance).

Lift, larger than D70 W90 L110. Flat from the foyer or equivalent.

Lift, but there are possible problems eg. stepped access or small size.

Narrow doors or gaps eg. between displays. Cannot be by-passed <75cm.

Narrow doors or gaps but can be by-passed or avoided <75cm.

Special loo facility for a wheelchair user, with side transfer >80cm.

Loos with flat access.

Telephone at suitable height for a wheelchair user.

Café/restaurant facilities accessible to a wheelchair user.

Seats available.

Few/no seats available.

Equipment provided for deaf people eg. an induction loop or special hearing aids.

 Hotel with flat/lift access to the main facilities (reception, bedrooms and restaurant) and with specially adapted rooms for disabled guests, and a disabled person's toilet with space for side transfer.

 Hotel with adapted room.

 Hotel with at least one ground floor bedroom.

 Hotel with a maximum of 5 steps to negotiate between the main facilities (reception, bedrooms and restaurant). The number in brackets indicates the number of steps.

FRENCH

Bien que ce guide soit publié en anglais, la plupart des renseignements concernant le logement et les sites principaux á visiter sont représentés sous forme de symboles. Cette méthode a été choisie afin de rendre l'emploi de ce guide aisé. Chaque symbole est expliqué de façon précise dans la liste qui suit.

Ces symboles définissent les informations dont vous pourrez avoir besoin avant de visiter certains endroits ou bâtiments, suivies par les détails concernant l'entrée et les facilités d'accès à l'intérieur même du bâtiment. La présence d'ascenseurs, d'escaliers, de toilettes et de cafétérias est également indiquée. Les aménagements spéciaux pour les non-voyants et les mal-entendants sont également spécifiés.

Dans la majeure partie des cas, les aménagements convenant aux utilisateurs de fauteuils roulants seront aussi très pratiques pour ceux qui souffrent d'autres handicaps ou de difficultés d'accès.

Les cas pour lesquels un bâtiment dispose d'une entrée de plain pied et étant accessible à 60% par fauteuil roulant sont représentés par:

  E2 N19 60%

Les cas pour lesquels le parking est difficile d'accès ou le sol est accidenté; pour lesquels il y a deux marches à l'entrée; pour lesquels le rez-de-chaussée représentant 60% de l'ensemble ne s'étend que sur un seul niveau mais pour lesquels il y a −19 marches jusqu'au sous-sol sont représentés par:

Symboles clefs:

 Parking avec accès plat, par rampe ou par ascenseur; le plus souvent inclus ou attaché à l'ensemble.

 Parking normalement disponible à moins de 100 mètres.

 Parking pouvant être difficile.

 Arrêt pour voitures/taxis, à moins de 20 mètres en face de l'entrée.

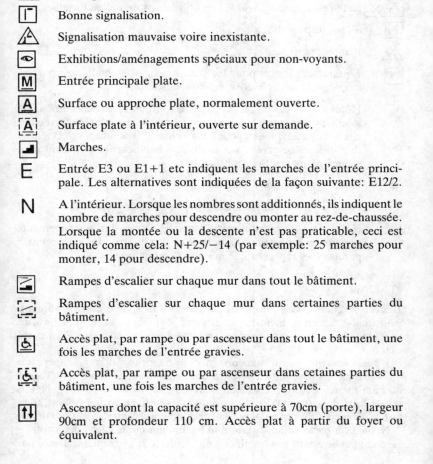

H Aire accidentée.

F Surface plate.

D Longues distances possibles.

△ Surfaces bosselées lors de l'accès au bâtiment.

U Fauteuils roulants disponibles.

Personne ou ami conseillé à cause de la longueur ou de la surface de l'ensemble.

△! Accès particulièrement difficile.

Bonne signalisation.

Signalisation mauvaise voire inexistante.

Exhibitions/aménagements spéciaux pour non-voyants.

M Entrée principale plate.

A Surface ou approche plate, normalement ouverte.

[A] Surface plate à l'intérieur, ouverte sur demande.

Marches.

E Entrée E3 ou E1+1 etc indiquent les marches de l'entrée principale. Les alternatives sont indiquées de la façon suivante: E12/2.

N A l'intérieur. Lorsque les nombres sont additionnés, ils indiquent le nombre de marches pour descendre ou monter au rez-de-chaussée. Lorsque la montée ou la descente n'est pas praticable, ceci est indiqué comme cela: N+25/−14 (par exemple: 25 marches pour monter, 14 pour descendre).

Rampes d'escalier sur chaque mur dans tout le bâtiment.

Rampes d'escalier sur chaque mur dans certaines parties du bâtiment.

Accès plat, par rampe ou par ascenseur dans tout le bâtiment, une fois les marches de l'entrée gravies.

Accès plat, par rampe ou par ascenseur dans cetaines parties du bâtiment, une fois les marches de l'entrée gravies.

Ascenseur dont la capacité est supérieure à 70cm (porte), largeur 90cm et profondeur 110 cm. Accès plat à partir du foyer ou équivalent.

Ascenseur pouvant présenter quelques difficultés, par exemple: marches à gravir ou capacité réduite.

 Portes ou espaces étroits ne pouvant être contournés <75cm.

 Portes ou espaces étroits pouvant être contournés ou évités <75 cm.

 Sanitaires spéciaux pour utilisateur de fauteuil roulant, avec transfert latéral >80 cm.

 Sanitaires accessibles par surface plate.

 Téléphone à hauteur accessible aux utilisateurs de fauteuil roulant.

 Café/restaurant accessible aux utilisateurs de fauteuil roulant.

 Sièges disponibles.

 Peu ou pas de sièges.

 Equipement fourni pour les personnes mal-entendantes; par exemple: séance explicative ou équipements spéciaux.

 Hôtel avec accès de plein pied; accès par ascenseur aux aménagements principaux (réception, chambres et restaurant) et avec des chambres adaptées pour les clients handicapés, et avec des toilettes réservées aux personnes handicapées disposant d'un espace permettant un transfert latéral.

 Hôtel avec chambres adaptées.

 Hôtel ayant au moins une chambre au rez-de-chaussée.

 Hôtel avec un maximum de 5 marches entre les aménagements principaux (réception, chambres et restaurant). Le chiffre entre parenthèses représente le nombre de marches.

ITALIAN

Benchè la guida è dell'informazione relativa all'allogio e ai monumenti principali e'riassunta in forma di simboli. I simboli, descritt nella lista seguente, hanno in senso preciso: questo vi aiuterá ad usare gran parte dell'informazione.

I simboli danno l'informazione necessaria prima di raggiungere un edificio o un posto, seguito dai particolari dell'entrata, e quindi dell'accesso all'interno dell'edificio. L'esistenza di un ascensore, scale e gabinetti accessibili e delle facilità di ristore e dato in simboli. Dove appropiato, sono notati alcune facilità speciali per la gente con problemi di vista o d'udito.

Nella gran parte delle situazioni le facilità per chi usa la sedia a rotelle saranno anche adatti per quelli con altre infermitá o problemi d'accesso.

L'informazione che un edificio ha una entrata senza gradini e che è accessibile al 60% per una sedia a rotelle è simbolizzato così:

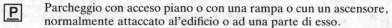 E2 N19 60%

L'informazione che il parcheggio è difficile e che l'area è collinosa, che ci sono due gradini all'entrata, che il pianterreno rappresentato 60% del tutto non ha livelli divisi ma che sono 19 gradini per andare nel sotterraneo è simbolizzato così:

Significato dei simboli:

P	Parcheggio con acceso piano o con una rampa o cun un ascensore, normalmente attaccato all'edificio o ad una parte di esso.
[P]	Parcheggio normalmente possibile entro 100 metri.
P / TC	Parcheggio probablemente difficile. Area di scalo esterna per Taxi/automobili: entro 20 metri dall'entrata.
H	Area collinosa.
F	Area piana.
D	Possibili lunghe distanze.
⌂	Superfici irregolari per accedere all'edificio.
U	Sedie a rotelle disponibili per l'uso.
🦽	Un amico o un accompagnatore per handicappeti è consigliato, per esempio a causa di possibili ostacoli.
⚠	Acceso particolarmente difficile.
Γ	Utili segnali indicatori.
⚠	Inesistenti/inadeguati segnali indicatori.
👁	Esposizioni/facilita` speciali per la gente con problemi visivi.
M	Entrata principale piana.
A	C'è un'entrata piana o un accesso piano. Normalmente aperto.
[A]	C'è un'entrata piana. Aperta su richiesta.
▰	Gradini/scale
E	Entrata E3 o E1+1 etc indicano i gradini all'entrata principale. Le alternative sono indicate così: E12/2

N   Dentro. Dove sommati, i numeri indicano i gradini del pianterreno. Se si può andare sù o giù, è indicato in questo modo: per esempio 25 gradini sù o 14 giù.

Corrimani su entrambi i lati.

Corrimani su entrambi i lati in alcune parti dell'edificio.

Accesso piano, con rampe o con ascensore dappertutto, dope alcuni gradini dall'entrata (se ci sono).

Accesso piano, con rampe o con ascensore in alcune parti dell'edificio, dopo alcuni gradini all'entrata (se ci sono).

Ascensore con porte più grandi di 70, profondità 90, larghezza 110. Piano dalla sala d'entrata o equivalente.

Ascensore (ma ci sono possibili problemi, per esempio: accesso con gradini o di piccola dimensione).

Porte strette o buchi, per esempio tra segni. Non c'è altro passagio <75cm.

Porte strette o buchi ma possono essere evitati o ci sono altri passaggi <75cm.

Toilet speciale per persone su sedia a rotelle, con trasferimento a fianco >80cm.

Toilets con accesso piano.

Telefono ad altezza adatta per persone su sedia a rotelle.

Facilità di bar/ristorante accessibili per persone su sedia a rotelle.

Posti a sedere disponibili.

Pochi o nessun posto a sedere disponibile.

Apparato speciale per sordi, per esempio amplificatore speciale o facilità auditive.

Albergo con accesso piano/ ascensore alle facilità principali (accettazione, camere da letto e ristorante) e con camere specialmente adatte per i clienti handicappati, e un gabinetto per gli handicappati con posto per trasferimento a fianco.

Albergo con camera adatta.

Albergo con almeno una camera da letto sul pianterreno.

Albergo con, al massimo, 5 gradini da salire per raggiungere le facilità principali (accettazione, camere da letto e ristorante). Il numero fra parentesi indica quanti gradini ci sono.

GERMAN

Obwohl der Reiseführer in englischer Sprache verfaßt ist, wird ein großer Teil der Informationen über Unterkünfte und die wichtigsten Sehenswürdigkeiten in Form von Symbolen zusammengefaßt und dargestellt. Da die Symbole klare Merkmale haben wird es Ihnen ermöglicht, größten Nutzen aus den Informationen zu ziehen. Ihre genaue Bedeutung wird in der nachstehenden Liste erläutert.

Die Symbole geben Informationen, die Sie wahrscheinlich benötigen, bevor Sie ein Gebäude bzw. Gebiet erreichen. Sie sind ergänzt durch Einzelheiten über den Zugang und den Gegebenheiten innerhalb des Gebäudes bzw. Areals. Etwaige Fahrstühle, Treppen sowie zugängliche Toiletten und Eßgelegenheiten werden aufgeführt. An gegebener Stelle wird auf besondere Einrichtungen für visuell Behinderte oder Schwerhörige hingewiesen.

In den häufigsten Situationen werden Einrichtungen, die für den Rollstuhlfahrer geeignet sind, auch für Besucher mit anderen Behinderungen zweckmäßig sein.

Die Information, daß ein Gebäude einen ebenen Eingang hat und zu 60% für Rollstuhlfahrer zugänglich ist, wird wie folgt dargestellt:

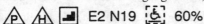 E2 N19 60%

Die Information, daß das Parken problematisch und das Gebiet hügelig ist; daß der Eingang zwei Stufen hat; daß das Erdgeschoß 60% des gesamt zugänglichen Bereiches ist; keine Zwischengeschoße vorhanden sind aber 19 Treppenstufen zum Untergeschoß führen sind, wird wie folgt dargestellt:

Schlüssel für die Symbole

[P]   Parken mit ebenem Zugang, Lift oder Rampe, normalerweise angrenzend an das Gebäude oder Teil des Gebäudes.

[P]   Parken normalweise innerhalb von 100m möglich.

/P\   Parken könnte schwierig sein.

T/C   Haltemöglichkeit für Taxi bzw. Auto nicht weiter als 20m vom Eingang.

/H\   Hügeliges Gebiet.

F   Flaches Gebiet.

Möglicherweise müssen größere Entfernungen zurückgelegt werden.

 Der Weg zum Gebäude führt über unebenes Gelände.

 Rollstühle stehen zur Verfügung.

 Es ist empfehlenswert, für (w) einen Bekannten bzw. Begleiter mitzubringen, z.B. aufgrund der Größe oder aufgrund von Unebenheiten.

 Der Zugang ist besonders schwierig.

 Gute Beschilderung.

 Beschilderung schlecht/fehlt.

 Besondere Ausstellungen/Einrichtungen für Sehbehinderte.

 Ebener Haupteingang.

 Es gibt einen ebenen Eingang oder Zugang. Normalerweise offen.

 Es gibt einen ebenen Eingang. Wird bei Bedarf geöffnet.

 Stufen.

E Eingang E3 oder E1+1 etc. weist auf Stufen am Haupteingang hin. Alternativen werden wie folgt angezeigt: E12/2.

N Innen. Etwaige Zahlen beziehen sich auf Stufen, die hinauf ins Erdgeschoß bzw. hinunter vom Erdgeschoß führen. Wo beide Richtungen benutzbar sind, ist dies wie folgt angegeben: N+25/−14, d.h. 25 Stufen hinauf oder 14 hinunter.

 Überall beidseitiges Geländer.

 Teilweise beidseitiges Geländer.

 Überall flacher Zugang/Rampe/Lift, nach etwaigen Stufen am Eingang.

 Teilweise flacher Zugang/Rampe/Lift, nach etwaigen Stufen am Eingang.

 Lift, größer als T70 B90 L110. Flach vom Foyer o.ä.

 Lift, aber mögliche Probleme wie z.B. Zugang mit Stufe oder kleine Abmessungen.

 Unumgehbare schmale Türen oder Zwischenräume z.B. zwischen Ausstellungsteilen <75cm.

Schmale Türen oder Zwischenräume, die jedoch umgangen werden können <75cm.

 Besondere Toiletteneinrichtung für Rollstuhlfahrer, die an sed Seite ausreichenden Platz für einen Rollstuhl bietet >80cm.

 Toiletten mit ebenem Zugang.

 Telefon in passender Höhe für Rollstuhlfahrer.

 Café/Restaurant für Rollstuhlfahrer zugänglich.

 Sitzmöglichkeiten.

 Kaum/keine Sitzmöglichkeiten.

 Einrichtungen für Schwerhörige, z.B. Induktionsschlaufe oder besondere Hörgeräte.

 Hotel mit ebenem Zugang bzw. Fahrstuhl zu den wichtigsten Einrichtungen (Rezeption, Schlafzimmern und Restaurant) und mit eigens für behinderte Gäste angelegten Zimmern sowie mit einer Behindertentoilette, die an der Seite ausreichenden Platz für einen Rollstuhl bietet.

 Hotel mit geeignetem Zimmer.

 Hotel mit mindestens einem Schlafzimmer im Erdgeschoß.

 Hotel mit höchstens 5 Stufen zwischen den wichtigsten Einrichtungen (Rezeption, Schlafzimmern und Restaurant). Die Zahl in Klammern bezieht sich auf die Zahl der Stufen.

Spanish

Aunque la guía está escrita en inglés, la mayoría de la información sobre el alojamiento y los lugares de interés está resumido en símbolos. Es nuestra intención que estos símbolos puedan permitirle a usar la información, porque están regidos por criterios muy claros. El significado preciso se describe en la lista siguiente.

Los símbolos determinan la información que Ud. pueda necesitar antes de llegar a un edificio o sitio particular, seguido por detalles de la entrada y de acceso dentro del edificio. Está definida también la existencia de ascensores, de escaleras, de lavabos accesibles y de facilidades donde se puede comer. A propósito, facilidades para los invidentes o para los que son duros de oído están anotadas.

En la immensa mayoría de los casos especiales, las facilidades adecuadas para usarios de sillas de ruedas serán adecuadas también para personas con otras invalideces o problemas de acceso.

La información indicando que un edificio tiene una entrada plana y que está accesible por 60% para usarios de sillas de ruedas está representada por:

$\widehat{P}$ $\widehat{A}$ ▣ E2 N19 ⟨&⟩ 60%

La información que el estacionamiento puede ser difícil y que el sitio está desigual; que hay dos escalinatas en la entrada; que la planta baja representando 60% del entero, no tiene dos niveles pero que hay −19 escaleras al sótano está representado por:

Símbolos:

P	Estacionamiento con acceso plano, por ascensor o por rampa, normalmente unido al edificio o formando parte de él.
⟨P⟩	Estacionamiento normalmente posible dentro de los 100 metros.
⟨P⟩	Estacionamiento puede ser difícil.
T/C	Parada de taxis/coches al exterior – dentro de los 20 metros de la entrada.
H	Zona desigual.
F	Zona plana.
D	Posibilidad de largas distancias.
△	Superficie desigual para llegar al edificio.
U	Sillas de ruedas disponibles.
⟨&⟩	Un amigo o acompañamiento sería aconsejable (a causa del tamaño o de la superficie).
△	Acceso difícil.
⎡	Buena señalización.
⚠	Mala señalización.
👁	Demostraciones/Facilidades especiales para los invidentes.
M	Entrada principal plana.
A	Hay una entrada/llegada plana. Normalmente abierta.
⟨A⟩	Hay una entrada plana. Abierto a solicitud.
▣	Escaleras.
E	Entrada E3 o E1+1 etc. indica el número de escaleras en la entrada principal. Las alternativas están indicadas así: E12/2.

N Al interior. Donde hay números añadidos, indican el número de escaleras hacia arriba o de la planta baja. Si se puede ir de cualquier lado, está indicada así: N+25/−14 (25 escaleras por arriba o 14 por abajo).

Pasamanos en los dos lados en todas partes del edificio.

Pasamanos en los dos lados en algunas partes del edificio.

Superficie plana/rampas/acceso por ascensor en todas partes del edificio, después de algunas escaleras en la entrada.

Superficie plana/rampas/acceso por ascensor a algunas partes del edificio, después de algunas escaleras en la entrada.

Ascensor más grande que grande que 70cm (puerta), anchura 90cm y longitud 110cm. Plano desde el vestíbulo o del equivalente.

Ascensor, pero problemas posibles, por ejemplo, acceso con escaleras o ascensor pequeño.

Puertas estrechas o con aberturas. No se puede evitarlos <75cm.

Puertas estrechas o con aberturas pero se puede evitarlos <75cm.

WC Facilidad especial en los lavabos para usario de silla de ruedas con posibilidad de trasladarse de un lado a otro >80cm.

WC Lavabos con acceso plano.

Teléfono a una altura conveniente para usario de silla de ruedas.

Facilidades especiales en el restaurante/cafe para usario de silla de ruedas.

Asientos disponibles.

Pocos asientos disponibles/ falta de asientos.

Facilidades disponibles para los duros de oído. (aparatos de oído)

Un hotel con acceso a todas las facilidades principales (recepción, habitaciones y restaurante) y con cuartos adaptados para huéspedes minusválidos y un lavabo para minusválidos con suficiente espacio para trasladarse.

Un hotel con cuarto adaptado.

Un hotel con un mínimo de una habitación en la planta baja.

Un hotel con un máximo de cinco escaleras entre las facilidades principales (recepción, habitaciones y el restaurante). El número entre el paréntesis indica el número de escaleras.

Index.